REGIONAL COOPERATION FOR SUSTAINABLE FOOD SECURITY IN SOUTH ASIA

T0265195

This volume foregrounds the importance of regional cooperation in the context of food security challenges in South Asia. South Asia holds the key to global achievement of SDG targets of ending hunger and malnutrition – it accounts for nearly one-third of food-insecure people on the planet, with every third child suffering from stunting due to malnutrition. Similar food preferences, production systems, and the transboundary nature of agrarian ecosystems call for coordinated action by South Asian countries, complementing national actions dealing with food security challenges.

In this volume, leading experts discuss the perspectives of key South Asian countries in leveraging regional cooperation for addressing food security challenges and reflect on the potential of cooperative actions in different areas. The book proposes a ten-point regional policy agenda covering cooperation for combatting climate change, regional trade liberalization, operationalization of regional food reserves, leveraging technology, sharing of good practices, regional institution building, coordinated positions in multilateral trade negotiations, addressing trans-boundary outbreak of livestock diseases, strengthening food safety standards, and the management of shared natural resources.

A key volume on accomplishing SDGs in the South Asian context, this book will be of immense interest to policy makers, researchers, and development practitioners. It is also essential reading for scholars and researchers in the areas of development studies, South Asia studies, food security, environment and sustainability.

Nagesh Kumar is Director and Head of the South and South-West Asia Office, New Delhi, of the United Nations Economic and Social Commission for Asia and the Pacific (UNESCAP). He has previously served as the UNESCAP Chief Economist and Director, Macroeconomic Policy and Development Division, and Director of Social Development Division at UNESCAP headquarters in Bangkok.

Joseph George is a trade and development analyst with ten years of experience in the field of regional economic integration in South Asia. Currently serving as a Research Associate at the South and South-West Asia Office of the United Nations Economic and Social Commission for Asia and the Pacific (UNESCAP), he provides research support for implementation of UNESCAP's programmes on regional cooperation for sustainable development in the South Asian region.

REGIONAL COOPERATION FOR SUSTAINABLE FOOD SECURITY IN SOUTH ASIA

Edited by Nagesh Kumar and Joseph George

Routledge
Taylor & Francis Group

LONDON AND NEW YORK

First published 2020
by Routledge
2 Park Square, Milton Park, Abingdon, Oxon OX14 4RN

and by Routledge
52 Vanderbilt Avenue, New York, NY 10017

Routledge is an imprint of the Taylor & Francis Group, an informa business

British Library Cataloguing-in-Publication Data
A catalogue record for this book is available from the British Library

Library of Congress Cataloging-in-Publication Data
A catalog record for this book has been requested

ISBN: 978-1-138-08272-4 (hbk)
ISBN: 978-0-367-36507-3 (pbk)
ISBN: 978-0-429-34650-7 (ebk)

Typeset in Bembo
by Apex CoVantage, LLC

MIX
Paper from
responsible sources
FSC
www.fsc.org   FSC™ C013985

Printed in the United Kingdom
by Henry Ling Limited

Dedicated to the memory of
Saman Kelegama (1959–2017)

CONTENTS

FIGURES

TABLES

CONTRIBUTORS

Estiaque Bari is Senior Research Associate, Centre for Policy Dialogue, Bangladesh.

Sachin Chaturvedi is Director General, Research and Information System for Developing Countries, India.

S. Mahendra Dev is Director, Indira Gandhi Institute of Development Research, India.

Sherajum Monira Farin is Research Associate, Centre for Policy Dialogue, Bangladesh.

Dilani Hirimuthugodage is Research Officer, Institute of Policy Studies, Sri Lanka.

Mehreen Iqbal is Research Assistant, Sustainable Development Policy Institute, Pakistan.

Late Saman Kelegama was Former Executive Director, Institute of Policy Studies, Sri Lanka.

Towfiqul Islam Khan is Senior Research Fellow, Centre for Policy Dialogue, Bangladesh.

Indra Nath Mukherji is Former Professor of South Asian Studies, School of International Studies, Jawaharlal Nehru University, India.

Posh Raj Pandey is Chairman, South Asia Watch on Trade Economics and Environment, Nepal.

Mustafizur Rahman is Distinguished Fellow, Centre for Policy Dialogue, Bangladesh.

Abid Qaiyum Suleri is Executive Director, Sustainable Development Policy Institute, Pakistan.

Upali Wickramasinghe is Senior Economist, Food and Agriculture Organization of the United Nations.

PREFACE

With nearly one-third of the people suffering from food insecurity on the planet and with every third child suffering from stunting due to malnutrition, South Asia holds the key to global achievement of the Sustainable Development Goal (SDG) targets of ending hunger and malnutrition (SDG targets 2.1 and 2.2). Denied chances of leading healthy lives and opportunities to partake in development, large sections of the society find themselves trapped in a reinforcing cycle of poverty and food deprivation, spreading the schisms of inequality in South Asia's economic and social foundations.

While ensuring food security through adequate food availability and equitable distribution system primarily remains preserve of the governments – national and subnational – collective and coordinated actions at the regional level could play an important complementary role to national actions. In particular, similar food preferences, production systems and other commonalities and the transboundary nature of agrarian ecosystems warrant a coordinated action by South Asian countries in dealing with the food security challenges. A coordinated approach would also be more effective in addressing the new risks to agricultural production from global warming and natural disasters and for harnessing the potential of sustainable agriculture. While intra-regional trade can help in addressing short-term demand and supply mismatches, coordinated regional responses can also prove more effective in correcting trade distortions in international agricultural markets. The relevance of regional cooperation is recognized and some initiatives have been taken, including establishment of the SAARC Food Bank. But such initiatives remain in early stages of their effective functioning and operationalization.

The impetus for this volume came from the South Asian Policy Dialogue on Regional Cooperation for Food Security organized by the South and South-West Asia Office of UNESCAP (UNESCAP SSWA) in August 2013. Facilitated by a United Nations Development Account (UNDA) Project on Knowledge Networks, the policy dialogue involved participation of senior policy makers and representatives of think-tanks from across the subregion. The resounding emphasis on the relevance of regional cooperation at the dialogue provided stimulus for further exploration through a series of studies commissioned to analyse the national perspectives of key South Asian countries as well as thematic issues of regional cooperation. These studies have been discussed at the dialogues organised by UNESCAP SSWA in different locations over the past four years, including at the South Asia Economic Summits held in Colombo, Islamabad, Kathmandu, New Delhi, Dhaka and the UNESCAP/RIS policy dialogue organised in New Delhi in October 2018, and they have benefitted from the feedback. This volume puts together the revised versions of the studies along with an overview of the key conclusions and policy lessons emerging from them.

The completion of the volume provides an opportunity to put on record our indebtedness to several organizations and individuals. The funding made available by the UNDESA, New York, under the UNDA project on Knowledge Networks supported organisation of most of the policy dialogues and studies. A specific request from the SAARC Secretariat for technical assistance provided the stimulus for undertaking the study on operationalisation of the SAARC Food Bank. I wish to thank the contributors of the chapters put together in the volume for their commitment and for responding to various deadlines. A number of policy makers and other experts contributed to this volume by serving as resource persons at the policy dialogues and providing their feedback. They include, among others, A. Ganesh Kumar, Alakh Sharma, Debapriya Bhattacharya, late G.K. Chadha, George Mavrotas, Jayantha D. Samarasinghe, Manoj Panda, Mohammad Azeem Khan, Mouhammad Javed Malik, Nimal Dissanayake, P.K. Joshi, Purvi Mehta-Bhatt, Ramesh Chand, Rukmani Ramani, S. Bhide, Sumiter Broca, T. Nanda Kumar and Tayan Raj Gurung.

At UNESCAP SSWA, Matthew Hammill helped in coordinating the project until his lateral move to the UN headquarters in New York in June 2018. Joseph George took over after Matt moved out, specifically supporting the process of substantively editing the volume and preparing it for publication. Uma Rao and Raju Rana have supported the project in many different ways all along.

I wish to thank Riccardo Dunn of UNESCAP, the UN Publications, New York, and the Routledge team for efficiently handling the publication of this book with great care.

Finally, a personal note: this volume is dedicated to the memory of Dr Saman Kelegama, who unfortunately passed away on 23 June 2017 in Bangkok. Executive Director of the Institute for Policy Studies of Sri Lanka, Saman was one of the most eminent economists of the country and of South Asia. Passionate about economic development and regional cooperation, Saman was a pioneer of many regional initiatives in South Asia, including the South Asia Economic Summits and the *South Asia Economic Journal*, which we co-founded. A close friend and collaborator for over two decades, Saman contributed to this volume with a chapter on Sri Lankan perspectives. It is sad that he is no longer here to receive this book!

Nagesh Kumar
New Delhi, May 2019

ABBREVIATIONS

AAY	Antyodaya Anna Yojana
ACCSQ	ASEAN Consultative Committee on Standards and Quality
ADARSA	Alliance for Democratising Agricultural Research in South Asia
ADER	average dietary energy requirement
ADESA	average dietary energy supply adequacy
ADMP	Agricultural Development Master Plan
ADP	antidumping measures
ADS	Agriculture Development Strategy
AERR	ASEAN Emergency Rice Reserve
AFSP	Agriculture and Food Security Country Investment Plan
AFSR	ASEAN Food Security Reserve
AIFS	ASEAN Integrated Food Security
ALOP	Appropriate level of Protection
AMAF	Additional Market Access Frontier
AoA	Agreement on Agriculture
APLAC	Asia Pacific Laboratory Accreditation Corporation
APSF	animal protein sourced food
APTERR	ASEAN Plus Three Emergency Rice Reserve
BAFRA	Bhutan Agriculture and Food Regulatory Authority
BCCSAP	Bangladesh Climatic Change Strategy and Adaptation Plan
BISA	Borlaug Institute for South Asia
BISP	Banazir Income Support program
BMI	Body Mass Index
CACP	Commission for Agricultural Costs and Prices
CARICOM	Caribbean Community
CBD	Convention on Biological Diversity

CCFICS	Codex Committee on Food Import and Export Certification and Inspection System
CFA	Climate Forecast Application
CGAL	Central Grain Analysis Laboratory
CILSS	Committee for Drought Control in the Sahel
CIMMYT	International Maize and Wheat Improvement Center (in Spanish)
CMP	Crop Maximization Program
COFAF	Committee on Food, Agriculture and Forestry
COP	cost of production
CSA	climate-smart agriculture
CSA	Civil Society Alliance
CWE	Cooperative Wholesale Establishment
DES	dietary energy supply
DFID	Department for International Development
EAERR	East Asia Emergency Rice Reserve
EIC	Export Inspection Council
FAO	Food and Agriculture Organization
FCB	Food Corporation of Bhutan
FFW	Food For Work
FGDs	focus group discussions
FHB	Family Health Bureau
FNSP	Food and Nutrition Security Policy
FPCCI	Federation of Pakistan Chambers of Commerce
FPMU	Food Planning and Monitoring Unit
FPS	fair price shops
FSB	Food Security Board
FSSAI	Food Safety and Standards Authority of India
GACP	Good Agriculture and Collective Practices
GAFSP	Global Agriculture and Food Security Program
GAP	Good Agricultural Practices
GCARD	Global Conference on Agricultural Research for Development
GCM	General Circulation Models
GCP	Good Collection Practices
GDP	gross domestic product
GHI	Global Hunger Index
GR	Gratuitous Relief
GSP	Generalized System of Preferences
HCR	head count ratio
HL NNFSSC	High Level National Nutrition and Food Security Steering Committee
HRID	Human Resources and Institution Development
ICAR	Indian Council for Agricultural Research
ICDS	Integrated Child Development Scheme

ICRISAT VLS	International Crops Research Institute for the Semi-Arid Tropics Village Level Studies
IFAD	International Fund for Agricultural Development
ILAC	International Laboratory Accreditation Corporation
ILRI	International Livestock Research Institute
IPC	Integrated Phase Classification
IPHT	Institute of Post – Harvest Technology
ISFNS	Information System for Food and Nutrition Security
ITEC	The Indian Technical and Economic Cooperation
ITI	Industrial Technology Institute
ITPGRFA	International Treaty on Plant Genetic Resources for Food and Agriculture
KIIs	key informant interviews
LANSA	Leveraging Agriculture and Nutrition in South Asia
LDC	least-developed country
LIC	low-income country
LMICs	lower-middle-income economies
MDGs	Millennium Development Goals
MDM	Midday Meal programme
MFDM	Ministry of Food and Disaster Management
MGNREGA	Mahatma Gandhi National Rural Employment Guarantee Act
MINFAL	Ministry of Food, Agriculture, and Livestock
MNFSR	Ministry of National Food Security and Research
MNSP	Multi-Sector Nutrition Plans
MoAD	Ministry of Agriculture Development
MoAF	Ministry of Agriculture and Forests
MOE	Ministry of Education
MOFA	Ministry of Federal Affairs and Local Development
MoH	Ministry of Health
MoHP	Ministry of Health and Population
MOLD	Ministry of Local Development
MPI	multidimensional poverty index
MRAs	Mutual Recognition Agreement
MRI	Medical Research Institute
MSAPN	Multi Sector Action Plan for Nutrition
MSP	minimum support prices
MTDF	Multi Donor Trust Fund
NABL	The National Accreditation Board for Testing and Calibration Laboratories
NAP	National Agriculture Policy
NAPA	National Adaptation Plan of Action
NDTF	National Development Trust Fund
NFC	Nepal Food Corporation

NFHS	National Family Health Survey
NFSA	National Food Security Act
NFSCC	Nutrition and Food Security Coordination Committee
NFSO	National food Security Ordinance
NGOs	non-governmental organizations
NNC	National Nutrition Council
NNP	National Nutrition Policy
NPC	National Planning Commission
NRHM	National Rural Health Mission
NSCN	National Steering Committee on Nutrition
ODF	Open Defecation Free
OECD	Organisation for Economic Co-operation and Development
OMS	Open Market Sales
PAL	physical activity levels
PASSCO	Pakistan Agricultural Storage and Supply Corporation
PDS	Public Distribution System
PFDSs	public food distribution systems
PMB	Paddy Marketing Board
PoFI	Prevalence of Food Inadequacy
PoU	Prevalence of Undernourishment
PQO	Plant Quarantine Order
PSDP	Public Sector Development Programme
QRs	Quantitative restrictions
RESOGEST	The West Africa Regional Food Security Reserve (in French)
RFNSP	Regional Food and Nutrition Security Policy
RIMES	Regional Integrated Multi-Hazard Early Warning System for Africa and Asia
ROO	Rules of Origin
RoSA	rest of South Asia
RoW	rest of the world
RRA	relative rate of assistance
SAARC	South Asian Association for Regional Cooperation
SAARC-DFS	SAARC Declaration on Food Security
SAC	SAARC Agricultural Centre
SAC	South Asia Countries
SAFANSI	South Asia Food and Nutrition Security Initiative
SAFTA	South Asia Free Trade Area
SAIC	SAARC Agricultural Information Centre
SAME	SAARC Market for Electricity
SARSO	South Asian Regional Standards Organization
SARS	SAARC Regional Standards
SDGs	Sustainable Development Goals
SEDMC	SAARC Environment and Disaster Management Centre
SEWA	Self Employed Women's Association

SFB	SAARC Food Bank
SFBIS	SAARC Food Bank Information System
SFSR	SAARC Food Security Reserve
SMC	SAARC Member Countries
SMRC	SAARC Meteorological Research Centre
SPANDAN	System of Promoting Appropriate National Dynamism for Agriculture and Nutrition
SPFS	Special Program for Food Security
SPS	sanitary and phytosanitary measures
SRETS	SAARC Regional Energy Trade Study
SRR	seed replacement rate
STC	State Trading Corporation
STCs	sectoral technical committees
STRASA	Stress Tolerant Rice for Africa and South Asia
SUN	Scaling up Nutrition
TAADs	Trans-boundary Aquatic Animal Diseases
TACN	Technical Advisory Committee on Nutrition
TADs	Trans-boundary Animal Diseases
TBT	technical barriers to trade
TCA	Technical Cooperation Agreement
TCARD	Technical Committee on Agriculture and Rural Development
TFP	total factor productivity
TLP	Tariff Liberalization Programme
TRIPS	Trade Related Aspects of Intellectual Property Rights
UNCTAD	United Nations Conference on Trade and Development
UNEP	United Nations Environment Programme
UNESCAP	United Nations Economic and Social Commission for Asia and the Pacific
VAM	Vulnerability Analysis and Mapping
VGD	Vulnerable Group Development
VGF	Vulnerable Group Feeding
WDI	World Development Indicators
WFP	World Food Programme
WHO	World Health Organization
WITS	World Integrated Trade System
WTO	World Trade Organization

1

REGIONAL COOPERATION FOR SUSTAINABLE FOOD SECURITY IN SOUTH ASIA

An overview and policy lessons

Nagesh Kumar and Joseph George

Introduction

South Asia has high stakes in the global fight against hunger under the framework of the Sustainable Development Goals (SDGs), with the unattained responsibility of uplifting the largest concentration of undernourished people in the world. About 277 million people were reported to have suffered from hunger in the subregion in 2017, accounting for one-third of the world's food deprived population.[1] One in every three children affected by stunted growth due to poor nutritional intake belongs to South Asia.[2] Adverse health conditions inflicted by malnourishment at early stages often last a lifetime, with serious implications for human resource development of the subregion. South Asia is also reported to have one of the highest incidences of what is referred to as hidden hunger or micronutrient deficiencies.[3] As the numbers stack up, they leave no doubt as to the severity of food insecurity prevalent in the subregion.

Food insecurity in South Asia continues to be unacceptably high despite notable progress made during last two decades. The subregion came close to achieving the MDG (Millennium Development Goals) target of halving the proportion of under-nourished people by 2015 from 1990 levels, by bringing the figure down to about 16% from its baseline of 24%.[4] In absolute terms, during the ten-year period from 2005–15, the headcount of undernourished in the subregion reduced by 55 million to reach 284 million, registering an overall decline by 16.2%. However, this decline had been much sharper in proportional terms, considering that the overall population grew by 15.1% during the same period.

Notwithstanding the progress made, the responsibilities ahead are far greater. As we move towards the SDGs, the target is of eradicating hunger. Goal 2 (Zero Hunger) of the SDGs calls to 'end all forms of malnutrition by 2030'. This would take a much higher rate of decline of food deprivation than the past decades. It is assessed that at the current rate, South Asia would have as many as 252 million undernourished people by 2030, adjusting for population growth, with hardly any improvement from the baseline of hunger headcount.[5] As South Asia's rate of reduction in undernourishment is observed to be slowing down in recent years, the subregion faces a daunting task ahead on its way to the SDG target of zero hunger.

Along with the responsibilities of reaching the new higher targets of food security, the policy challenges in the way of meeting them are also on the rise. Hunger in South Asia is observed to be the result of a complex mix of factors acting through one or more of all the four pillars of food security, viz. availability, access, utilization and stability. Sensitivities of the agriculture sector in the subregional countries illustrate this. Slowdown in agricultural productivity in South Asia has a direct adverse impact on food availability, while also exerting its influence on food access by way of declining farm income. Livelihood dependency on agriculture has not declined proportionate to the dip in share of agriculture in the subregional economies. The slow and steady tilt in the terms-of-trade against agriculture, in favour of manufacturing and services, has had its effect on access of the agriculture dependents to food. It is perhaps a cruel irony that often those who produce food are found insecure of access to it. Growing agrarian distress due to climate change in the recent times, casting shadows on not only availability and access but also on stability and utilization, poses new threats to food security.

It is clear from the observations made so far in the South Asian context that most of the food security challenges are common to subregional countries, especially as they share similar agrarian structures, development stages, climatic zones, market orientation and cultural practices that shape up how food is produced and consumed. Shared challenges call for shared solutions and, indeed, many of the policy strategies followed by subregional countries already have certain common features. Regional cooperation can help to raise the likelihood of success of nationally followed responses through exploiting the synergies. However, despite strong economic rationale, cooperative approach in the subregion remains suboptimal and suffers from institutional weaknesses. This Volume is produced in the spirit of fostering greater regional cooperation for food security in South Asia. It is the result of a series of studies commissioned by UNESCAP, taking stock of the food security situation, enquiring into the challenges to national food security policies and opportunities that South Asian Member States could pursue together.

South Asia's food security challenges

At 14.2% in 2017, the prevalence of undernourishment in South Asia is second only to sub-Saharan Africa (23.2%) and considerably higher than the world average of 10.9%.[6] On account of substantially higher population density compared to other subregions, South Asia has the highest hunger burden when the prevalence rate is translated into headcount of undernourished people, signifying that rate of reduction also has to be the highest for South Asia in order to achieve food security targets. It is therefore of alarming concern that the rate of reduction in number of food-insecure people has been slowing down in the subregion. While the incidence of undernourishment diminished by a compound annual rate of close to 3% between 2005–10 with an overall reduction by 13.7%, the rate since then (2010–17) has been as low as 0.8% with an overall reduction by only about 5%.[7]

Food insecurity is found primarily tangled with issues related to development of the agriculture sector, which has direct implications for both availability of and access to food in equal measures. This is especially so in developing regions such as South Asia, where higher population growth demands proportional growth in agricultural output to sustain per capita consumption and where the majority of the workforce is either partially or wholly dependent on agricultural income. The rise in agricultural productivity has been therefore critical for ensuring food security from the point of view of both availability and access. Following the Green Revolution, which began in the early 1960s in the subregion, agriculture productivity notably improved with the introduction of high-yielding seeds, chemical fertilizers and pesticides, and investments in irrigation and mechanisation, accompanied by public policies of input subsidies and price controls. Increase in both cultivated land area and yield-per-hectare contributed to rise in output, particularly in the case of cereals.[8]

The surge in productivity faltered by 1990s, primarily because the increase in input intensity on which it relied could not be sustained.[9] Input intensification pushed soil fertility to its limits, while also putting stress on water and other natural resources, exacerbated by overuse of chemical compounds and unsustainable farming practices. With severe constraints on further arable land expansion, and with even a reversal in conversion of non-agricultural land in many of the subregional countries,[10] the remaining source of productivity growth appears to be that of yield. The single most difficult challenge before South Asia is to effectuate another surge in agriculture productivity without harming the ecological sustainability of its farmlands. A second green revolution, as much as it is necessary, cannot afford to follow the pathways of the first and must integrate sustainability fully if it is to be successful.

While total factor productivity (TFP) in agriculture improved in the aftermath of the Green Revolution, labour's contribution to it was not impressive.[11] Disproportionately low agricultural wages compared to returns to land and capital meant limited opportunities for upward mobility through education and skilling. A large number of small-scale farming households also face similar constraints as food expenditures account for a high share of their total expenditure. Without social security coverage, exogenous shocks can pull marginal survivors back to the fold of food deprivation. Without measures to ensure that dividends of increased productivity do result in upliftment of living standards of marginal dependence, productivity gains may be negated by welfare spending drain. This aspect is not properly factored into the subregional policy frameworks.

Another challenge facing South Asia is that of bringing about a new wave of technological innovations in agriculture. Efforts to raise productivity and yield cannot ignore the environmental sensitivities of agriculture. An infusion of modern technological innovations is direly required in diverse areas of sustainable agriculture such as soil and water conservation, resource management, preservation of biodiversity, irrigation, mechanisation, fertilizers, seeds, pest management, post-harvest processing, storage and distribution etc.[12] Meeting the demands of research and development require more calibrated policy responses, and developing these remains a major challenge for the future management.

A grossly neglected aspect of food security discourse is that of dietary diversity and expansion of consumption basket. Often foodgrain security is equated with food security, ignoring micronutrient deficiency and its harmful health hazards. It is pointed out in the context of India that the share of consumer expenditure on cereals has reduced to account for a less than 40% of total food consumption spending. Consumption basket has expanded considerably to include items such as edible oils, sugar, milk, eggs, meat, fish, vegetables and fruits.[13] The demand for no-grain food items is slated to rise at a pace in tandem with that of per capita income. As productivity shortfalls also exist in the case of many non-grain food items, South Asia is inadequately prepared to meet the multidimensional challenges of issues of dietary diversity.

It will neither be feasible nor prudent to expect to fulfil South Asia's long-term food requirements with domestic production alone. With current trends and projections, meeting the future demand for food products, taking also into account the nutritional content and dietary fulfilment, the subregion would have to mainstream trade as a critical aspect of its strategies. Besides trade, the scope and reach of public support programmes need to be scaled up. The SDG framework places specific emphasis on public spending in agriculture, which is not currently found to be commensurate with the sector's growing requirements in the subregion. Public investments are critical not only in terms of direct investment in agricultural research and extension, but also towards linking markets, rural farm services such as irrigation systems as well as non-agricultural investment to enhance the rural institutional environment and improve human well-being, including investments in education, sanitation and clean water supply and healthcare.[14]

Inefficient targeting of public welfare programmes has been a persistent issue in South Asia. In the light of the growing resource burden, plugging leakages in delivery assumes special significance. About 80% of farm holdings in India belong to small-scale farmers.[15] With the exception of Pakistan, other South Asian countries share similar land holding patterns. Small-scale farmers are often found to have fewer access opportunities in terms of inputs, credit, technology and markets. More importantly, a large majority of them are left out of public welfare programmes with higher exposure to risks. Perhaps the most essential caveat in the subregion's efforts for zero hunger target is that they face the possibility of being weighed down by widening inequalities.

Climate change and the emerging new threats to food security

An exogenous hazard looming large over agricultural productivity is that of climate change. It threatens to thwart all aspects of agrarian planning, and the future of food security undeniably depends on how successful humanity becomes in surviving it through adaptation or mitigation. Though some of the effects of climate change are already manifested by way of extreme weather events, frequent droughts, flash floods and a number of irregularities observed in the natural habitat, its triggers, onset and possible impacts are not yet sufficiently understood. This makes planning for preparedness extremely difficult. South Asia is identified as one of the most vulnerable subregions. As a projection of climate scenarios for the year 2050 reveals, the likelihood of food insecurity due to climate change is found to be the largest in South Asian countries.[16]

Climate change is expected to exert its impact through all dimensions of food security in complex ways. Output, and consequently livelihoods, of agrarian sectors including livestock, fisheries and forestry are expected to be adversely affected. Shortage of food products and erosion of income would inflict a dual impact on millions of poor, especially those who are out of social security nets. A large number of the world's marginal agricultural dependents exposed to such risks live along the major transboundary river-basin systems in South Asia, particularly concentrated in the Indo-Gangetic plain.[17] Spread of communicable diseases, deterioration in sanitary conditions, polluted drinking water and risks of food contamination arising out of erratic climate can further worsen food utilisation and nutritional status. Furthermore, disruptions and damage caused by extreme climate events would compromise the stability of food availability, access and utilisation.[18]

Combating climate change requires significant departure from the conventional approaches to food security. To a large extent it hinges on the ability to develop and utilise new technological solutions. The current R&D priorities followed by subregional countries in their agricultural policy and planning need to be stretched beyond yield and productivity and factor in the demands of what is referred to as the 'climate-smart agriculture' (CSA) approach.[19] The CSA approach calls for raising agricultural productivity through sustainable means, enhancing adaptive capacity and resilience and reducing the carbon footprint of agriculture. The latter assumes special significance as agricultural activities are both sources and sinks of greenhouse gases. Agriculture, fisheries and forestry together account for about 21% of global GHG emissions. The aggregate contribution of the food system is even larger, accounting also for usage of agrochemicals as well as energy use in farming operations, post-harvest processes, storage and distribution. The extent of R&D resource commitments, both financial and non-financial, required of the South Asian countries to meet these requirements are enormous.

Substantial reconfigurations are also required in the case of conventional public policy strategies for food security. For instance, more than input subsidies, future farm support programmes need to incentivise shifts to sustainable farming practices. Adaptation strategies also imply large-scale training and capacity building exercises. Given that the scope for market-based interventions in this field is limited, public support programmes would be required for procurement and usage of resilient crop varieties, prudent water and energy usage and allied areas of support. Fund allocation for contingency food reserves, disaster relief and safety nets also need to be expanded. It is estimated that the population under poverty line could increase by up to 122 million with climate change, compared to the scenario without it.[20] Another challenge is that of ensuring delivery of public support programmes for adaptation to a large number of poor small-scale land holders. Substantial scaling-up of public support needed to battle climate impacts can be expected to inflict serious resource drain on the subregional countries.

Rationale for regional cooperation and key policy lessons

Slowdown in South Asia's yearly rate of improvement in the food security situation in recent times, at a time when nothing short of an unprecedented acceleration in progress would suffice, is an indication that the subregion now confronts what may be called its bottom territory of food deprivation, or that critical domain of extreme hunger that is the most difficult to tackle. It implies that conventionally followed policy responses are likely to be found wanting. In order to be effective, a future course of actions should be founded on innovative solutions capable of addressing the new challenges, and the chances of finding such solutions are much higher when they are collectively sought. While some of the targets of Goal 2 of the SDGs, such as correcting trade distortions in world agricultural markets, cannot be achieved without international cooperation, fulfilling others can be found to be often better through cooperation than otherwise.

Regional cooperation for food security is hardly a new concept in South Asia. In fact, sustainable agriculture and food security were among the most important priorities in the early years of SAARC. The Agreement Establishing South Asia Food Security Reserves was signed as early as 1987. The 15th SAARC Summit adopted what is referred to as the Colombo Statement on Food Security, identifying six thematic areas, including food production, investments in agro-industries, agricultural technologies, market interventions and management of risk. Successive rounds of SAARC Summits have provided a mandate for cooperation in a wide range of topics related to food security, including, among others, the call for establishing regional food and seed reserves. The directives promised cooperation in areas ranging from agricultural productivity to technology, trade, food safety, price control, biodiversity, climate change and natural resource management. However, regionally coordinated policy responses in each of these areas are yet to take definitive shape.

As discussions in the previous sections reveal, substantial increase in budgetary commitments are required to fulfil the new and reconfigured public policy targets of food security. Besides the obvious advantages of resource mobilisation, the single most important benefit of regional cooperation would be that of greater allocative efficiency. Some of the key areas of joint interventions for South Asia, valued against the subregions' challenges, are with respect to building resilience to climate change, trade liberalisation, operationalisation of the SAARC food and seed banks, technical capacity building and knowledge sharing, improving governance through regional institutions, management of natural resources etc. A ten-point regional action agenda on food security emerging from this volume is provided as follows:

Cooperation for combating the adverse effects of climate change

The rationale for collective efforts is clearly evident as far as combating risks and vulnerabilities exposed by climate change is concerned. While impacts of climate change generally have a cross-border spread, even localised incidents within national boundaries can indirectly affect other countries. Given transboundary interdependencies and disparities inability to cope with climate hazards among subregional countries, a collaborative approach is required to implement enabling technologies, mobilise finance and develop collective resilience to climate risks. South Asia is home to some of the most sensitive transboundary agro-ecological zones and maintaining their productivity will need collective actions to preserve the productive base of natural resources and ecosystems of such zones, while enhancing their capacity to withstand climate variability. The Ganges–Brahmaputra–Meghna basin, the largest delta in the world spread across southern Bangladesh and parts of eastern India, is a case in point. Livelihoods of about two-thirds of the population in Bangladesh are tied to agriculture and fisheries along the fertile floodplains of the delta, which is increasingly under threat of sea-level rise and subsidence, a decrease in sediment supply, an increase in groundwater salinity and deteriorating water quality, exacerbated by the loss of protection from mangrove forests and sand dunes.

Comprehensive regionally coordinated action plans are required to save such sensitive ecosystems from floods and soil erosion, storm surges and extreme cyclonic events. Maintaining the efficiency and productivity of climate sensitive agricultural systems will need to preserve the productive base of natural resources and ecosystem services while increasing the capacity to withstand risks, shocks and climate variability.[21] Regional approaches would help to harness greater resource mobilisation potential, multi-stakeholder partnerships and alliances to tackle complex issues of transboundary environmental risks that are long-term in nature, the solutions for which are hardly possible exclusively through unilateral measures at the national level. For example, if not contained properly, climate change is highly likely to lead to the regional spread of invasive pests and pathogenic crop infections, which will require collective preventive measures. Strengthened regional or subregional cooperation can help to close knowledge gaps based on better participatory evaluation of sensitivities of agrobiodiversity and sustainable farming. Accordingly, adjustments to national coping strategies can be made in terms of adaptive cropping patterns and livestock management.

One of the main areas in which regional cooperation can deliver over unilateral measures to a large extent is by way of integrating the use of climate forecasts into cropping decisions. While doing so can substantially improve the scalability and economic viability of sustainable farming practices, the capacity for the same is limited in most of the South Asian countries. The only viable solution to overcome this constraint in the short-run is to make existing national climate monitoring capacity regionally available so that seamless use of climate information is possible for all countries for guiding decisions. An encouraging development in this regard is the emerging leadership of certain regional institutions. For instance, RIMES (Regional Integrated Multi-Hazard Early Warning System for Africa and Asia), a project supported by UNESCAP, has adopted a Climate Forecast Application (CFA) model to put to use its climate forecast tools for sustainable agriculture.[22] The model aims to provide short-term weather forecasts with three to five days lead time for planning daily day farming work, medium-term seasonal forecasts with one month or more lead time to help guide seasonal crop planning, and long-term climate change projections are useful in long-term agricultural planning. In fact, this initiative even has the potential to influence or guide research on climate resilient crop varieties.

Cooperative approaches should reflect each country's individual priorities for improving its responsiveness to climate change, balancing tradeoffs between their respective short-term and long-term requirements. At the same time, South Asian countries also need to ensure that the depth of their collaboration is progressively enhanced, especially as countries will be required to pursue multiple objectives across the economic, social and environmental dimensions of sustainability. This can be systematically achieved by extending cooperation from one area of intervention to the next. For instance, transboundary water cooperation for flood control can form a basis for longer-term cooperation on a range of other issues such as technical cooperation for conservation of river basins, many of which are shared by two or more South Asian countries. Climate finance is an area which can also bind the South Asian countries together. Systemic capacity constraints currently hamper both access to and effective use of climate finance. If the subregional countries ramp up joint financing, and also weed out inefficiencies of absorption at the funding end and inefficiencies of delivery at the receiving end, then regional financing can facilitate better transition to sustainable agriculture in each participating country.

Regional trade liberalisation in agriculture

Perhaps the most obvious avenue for regional cooperation is that of regional trade in agriculture. Market distortions has been emphasised as a major cause of food insecurity in the South Asian context, acting through the pillar of accessibility. Recognising its importance, Goal 2 explicitly calls for 'preventing trade restrictions and distortions in world agricultural markets' as a means of implementation target. Trade as a correctional mechanism for market imperfections comes into play in the context of food security not only with respect to markets for food products but also in the cases of markets for agricultural capital goods and inputs, imparting greater region-wide allocative efficiency.[23]

The current levels of intraregional trade in food products in South Asia is found to be suboptimal due to undue regulatory restrictions as well as procedural and infrastructural barriers to trade. Trade in agriculture is observed to be afforded more protection compared to nonagriculture sectors. Intraregional food trade is also highly concentrated, as over 90% regional food exports is constituted by a few product categories such as cereals, dairy products, sugar, vegetable oils, tea and spices. Country participation is also skewed as India and Pakistan account for almost 77% of overall intraregional food exports in the subregion. The share of processed food in intraregional trade has been observed to be considerably lower compared to non-processed food. This may be a validation of fact that quality standards related issues dampen the subregions trade as imposition of quality standards is observed to have more severe effect on the processed food sector than the non-processed food sector.

Import of nearly all agricultural outputs, including livestock and processed food products are subjected to some kind of sanitary and phytosanitary (SPS) certification and import permit. Often the procedural inefficiencies with respect to testing, certification and inspection are found to be greater trade deterrents than the standards themselves. Trade in food commodities, especially non-processed food, is also dependent on timely delivery due to short shelf-lives and therefore relies heavily on facilitative trade infrastructure. Longer turnaround times due to transshipment and congestion at border points, and absence of testing and quarantine facilities and cold storage chains at the South Asian land customs stations, affect trade to a large extent.

With the exception of the land-locked countries of Afghanistan, Bhutan and Nepal, whose top exporters are South Asian partners, trade in agricultural products of the subregional countries are predominantly oriented towards external trading partners. For most of the South Asian countries their major import sources and export destinations of food and agricultural products are outside the region, with some accounts putting such external trade as constituting more than 90% of the subregion's overall agriculture trade.[24] There are substantial gains to be reaped by merely internalising costly external trade to the extent possible. Chapter 4 of this volume explores such possibilities of replacing external imports of important food items with imports from South Asian trading partners, where supply capacity for the same exists within the subregion. This exercise identifies a list of 397 food products with a combined internal trade potential of about US$ 10 billion per annum, amounting to about 40% of the current aggregate intraregional trade of the subregion. Realising this potential can result in huge benefits in terms of price and supply stability.

South Asian countries should cooperate on a host of regulatory and trade facilitation reforms for achievement the full potential of intra-regional food trade. On the infrastructure side, the priority is to ensure that the land customs stations are equipped to the adequacies of handling food products. Procedural reforms should focus on minimising the cost of compliance with standards through Mutual Recognition Agreements (MRAs). A host of existing policy instruments available under SAFTA and institutions set up under the SAARC framework can be used to expedite reforms in this regard, as observed in Chapter 5. Initiatives that are underway at SARSO (South Asian Regional Standards Organization) for efficient and transparent regional standards can exert a substantial impact on food trade in the subregion.

Operationalising regional food reserves: the SAARC food and seed banks

Food reserves have the primary objective of buffering against unexpected supply shocks, and they are followed as a key strategy in many parts of the world with notable success.[25] Regional reserves help to conduct stockpiling exercise among a group of countries, allowing greater efficiency, proportional sharing of responsibilities and better risk management. The scope and flexibility of food reserve system in Southeast Asia under the ASEAN Integrated Food Security (AIFS) Framework is noted to have been enhanced with entry of China, Japan and South Korea to form the ASEAN Plus Three Emergency Rice Reserve (APTERR).[26] Creating food reserves at the regional level is of critical importance for South Asia given the subregion's exposure to market failures aggravated by food emergencies. Particularly, the net food importing countries of the subregion face high risks of ensuring timely delivery from import sources, which require a month or more of turnaround time of pulling through the supply channels in the absence of reliable reserves.

The decision to establish the SAARC Food Bank (SFB), improving upon its predecessor the SAARC Food Security Reserve (SFSR) set up in 1987, adopted by the 14th SAARC Summit in 2007, is therefore an important step taken in the right direction. Along with providing a centrally coordinated and quicker delivery system, SFB can help member countries to deal with disruptions in the commercial food distribution networks, illegal speculative hoarding and possible escalation of procurement costs during crisis times and price volatilities. However, as exposed in Chapter 5 of this volume, SFB suffers shortcomings such as inadequate volumes of reserves, stringent eligibility rules, absence of an agreed pricing modality and insufficient funding. By strengthening its operational provisions, particularly with respect to procurement, pricing, distribution and institutional arrangements, SFB can serve as an effective regional food security system.

In 2011, the SAARC Leaders had endorsed a SAARC Seed Bank Agreement and a Framework for Materials Transfer Agreement. The objective of the proposed seed bank was to foster 'seed security' in the region, increase seed replacement ratio, address seed shortage via collective action and act as a Regional Seed Security Reserve for member states of SAARC. However, the SAARC Seed Bank has failed to become operational because of inability of three Member States of SAARC viz. Pakistan, Afghanistan and Maldives to ratify the agreement as yet. The importance of regional seed banks has been recognised by the Agenda 2030 in SDG target 2.5. Given its criticality for regional cooperation in preservation of genetic resources for safeguarding long-term food security, not only should the South Asian countries move ahead to implement the agreement but they should also consider its scope to cover even the genetic resources of commercial crops and livestock.

Leveraging technology and knowledge sharing

While the criticality of innovations and technological advancements has been highlighted with respect to all aspects of food security, it is also disturbingly a weak area of intervention in South Asia. The predominant issue is that of resource shortages and capacity constraints. Resource limitations faced by smaller countries, replicability of agricultural innovations and scale and scope economies in utilising expertise and capacity of institutions in relatively resource rich countries justify regional R&D programmes. Collaborative knowledge initiatives led by national institutions such as the Indian Council for Agricultural Research (ICAR) covering education, research, training and allied service and commercial linkages, provide useful platforms. A notable venture with an intended regional reach is the Borlaug Institute for South Asia (BISA), a non-profit international research institute dedicated to food, nutrition and livelihood security as well as environmental rehabilitation in South Asia, resulting out of collaboration between ICAR and the International Maize and Wheat Improvement Center (CIMMYT).

In order to inspire more collaborative research, fortifying the capacity and outreach of national institutions, R&D should be conceptualised and endorsed as a regional public good in the subregion. The rationale for this is quite evident in cases such as sharing of early warning systems for transboundary hazards by a group of countries. Organisation of agricultural research is mostly located in the public sector across all South Asian countries. Given that many areas of agricultural research are found increasingly of interest to private investments, regional policies on R&D collaboration should take into account possibilities of synergies with research capacities established by private corporations.

Under cooperative arrangements countries with low capacity can make use of technologies through partnerships. One of the main concerns is the responsiveness of R&D to local needs. As called for by the first Global Conference on Agricultural Research for Development (GCARD 1), there is need to develop bottom-up decentralised research processes to engage effectively with communities and end-users. Initiatives such as the Alliance for Democratising Agricultural Research in South Asia (ADARSA), a group of organisations of farming communities from subregional countries, calls attention to the importance of ensuring outreach of research to small-scale farmers and disadvantaged agrarian participants through farmer-scientist dialogues.[27]

Sharing of development experiences and good practices in food security policies

An evaluation of the ongoing set of national policy frameworks for food and nutrition security in South Asian countries shows that they broadly fall into four categories; (a) improving agricultural productivity and production systems; (b) enhancing agricultural R&D, dissemination and sharing; (c) managing food security risks and vulnerabilities; and (d) safety nets.[28] As was exposed earlier in this chapter, as in the case of agricultural productivity measures, plenty of avenues for international cooperation exist in each of these categories to improve the effectiveness of national initiatives. While safety nets are in operation in almost all of the subregional countries by way of public policies for enhancing stability of consumption, they have been noted to have produced suboptimal results, indicating opportunities of learning from each other. Local information and delivery is also essential. Sharing experiences could provide valuable lessons for improving beneficiary targeting, outreach and depth and efficiency of coverage of public welfare programmes.

South Asia countries have a variety of different social protection programmes aimed at food security.[29] India's PDS is perhaps the largest direct foodgrain distribution system in the world. Coupons and direct cash transfers, employment guarantee programmes and mid-day meals are among the most commonly used tools across subregional countries. A key determinant for the success of such programmes, besides efficient delivery, is the choice of the policy mix. For instance, the relative merits of PDS and cash transfers as optional substitute strategies is often debated in the context of India.[30] Experimental evidence shows the cost-benefit calculus varies across programmers and countries varies with size and scope and also on variables such as literacy gaps, level of financial inclusion, coverage of civil registration etc. Efficiency and accountability in programme delivery are necessary conditions for successful projects. Cross-learning can have a substantial impact on future design and efficiency in implementation.

Modalities of stakeholder participation is another key area of synergy between South Asian countries. In Bangladesh, food security progress is often attributed to the contribution of nongovernmental organizations (NGOs) in terms of establishing upward and downward accountability. A participatory approach is often helpful in ensuring effective delivery, especially when government institutional gaps are large. Seemingly small measures such as proper information dissemination about entitlements can have notable impacts by way of empowering recipients to demand full entitlements, reducing leakages and increasing efficiency.[31]

Building regional institutions

Implementation, monitoring and administration of regional policies and programmes also requires regional institutions empowered with governance responsibilities and authority. The potential portfolio of governance of integrated food systems is vast in its scope, as it ought to take as its reference points the dynamics of agricultural research production, distribution, markets, trade, reserves and a host of allied aspects of management. Institutions, infrastructure support, R&D etc. are capital-intensive efforts that need secretarial support. Setting up of the SAARC Agricultural Centre (SAC) provides headway for South Asia in this direction. Growing up from its predecessor, the SAARC Agricultural Information Centre (SAIC), established as early as 1988, the SAC was constituted with a broader mandate of addressing the food and agricultural needs of the subregion in a comprehensive manner.

The SAC is predominantly engaged in information sharing and capacity-building, with a number of need-based programmes such as training on farm mechanization for sustainable intensification of agriculture in SAARC region, integrated past management, development of small-scale fisheries, water management etc. There is potential for the organization to act as a coordinator and interlocutor between national technical institutions; standard setting bodies must be harnessed for effective administration of regional food security programmes. Deeper integration warrants a centrally coordinated executive body. Even regional groupings with weak institutional and budgetary capacities, regional secretariats, could play an executive role in relatively low-cost activities, such as regional market information dissemination and supporting training and networking functions.[32] The opportunity for South Asia is to elevate existing institutions with greater catalytic and executory responsibilities.

Coordinated positions in international forums and multilateral negotiations

Given their shared and overlapping interests, South Asia could benefit from a coordinated position in WTO and other global forums. South Asia has both offensive as well as defensive interests in the WTO Agreement on Agriculture. The offensive interests relate to addressing the huge amount of agricultural subsidies, tariffs and non-tariff barriers and other forms of protectionism practiced by the industrialized countries that render many agricultural exports of developing countries including the South Asian countries uncompetitive. The defensive interests include protection of the livelihood security concerns of the small and marginal farmers from cheaper imports of agricultural products through special safeguard mechanisms. Developing countries have formed coalitions for addressing the offensive and defensive interest (namely G-20 and G-33) and a number of South Asia countries have been active players in these coalitions. The public stockholding of food for public distribution programmes by developing countries such as India emerged as an important contentious issue in recent years on which a 'peace clause' was proposed at the Bali Ministerial Conference of WTO in 2013 as an interim measure, which was later on reaffirmed at the Nairobi Ministerial Conference in 2015. Although the Doha Round negotiations have been virtually stalled for the past decade, the point about the need and effectiveness of a coordinated position in multilateral negotiations remains valid in view of their common concerns.

Addressing the transboundary outbreak of livestock diseases

Addressing transboundary issues requires South Asian countries to achieve a greater level of regulatory coordination to the extent of implementing harmonised rules. The need for this is evident in many areas such as livestock and fisheries management. With rapidly growing intraregional trade and dietary dependence on poultry and bovine livestock and their products as well as on the vast shared marine fisheries wealth, South Asia is highly prone to the risks of high impact transboundary animal diseases (TADs). Given that livestock contributes more than 25% of agricultural GDP and provides livelihoods for roughly about 150 million of the subregional population, particularly women, transmissible zoonotic diseases or contagious deceases affecting aquatic life can wreak havoc on fragile livestock-based food systems and economies. The adverse effects could be potentially of massive proportions as there are synergies between crops and livestock. Stronger regional measures are required to monitor, prevent and control disease outbreaks. One of the main aspects of regional cooperation in this regard is harmonisation of national animal health regulations and disease control strategies.

Certain initiatives are underway within the SAARC framework. Training workshops on international animal health regulations, SPS standards and the development of a SAARC Animal Disease Information System are among them.[33] The primary objective of the ongoing initiatives is to improve regional capacities to manage and control TADs and enhance biosecurity among SAARC countries. Further work is required for a harmonised and well-coordinated regulatory regime enabling regional surveillance, reporting and investigation, establishment of regional epidemiology centres with modern laboratory facilities and setting up of regional preventive and rapid response mechanisms. The work of International Livestock Research Institute (ILRI), which has a presence in India and Pakistan, can be leveraged for strengthening these efforts.[34]

Strengthening food safety and nutritional standards

Safety is a critical, but often neglected, aspect of food security. The importance of safety is entrenched in all the internationally followed definitions, incorporating it as an integral part of food utilization. Access to safe foods remains a major issue, manifested primarily through food borne ailments and micronutrient deficiencies, which are widely prevalent in South Asia. Policy challenges in this regard are predominantly related to weaknesses in regulatory capacity for design, implementation, surveillance and control of national level legislations on safety standards. Limited technical capacities and financial resources, lack of alignment with international standards and alert systems, rapid changes in food technologies, multiplicity of regulatory domains and the impact of climate change on food production, distribution and consumption add to the constraints of existing food safety regulatory environments in South Asian countries.

Notwithstanding the challenges, awareness of the importance of food safety is observed to be gradually on the rise in South Asia. For instance, the Food Safety and Standards Act of 2006 has facilitated a shift from a multi-level and multi-department control to a singular apex authority in India, enabling better enforcement of food safety regulations. The Food Safety and Standards Authority of India (FSSAI), established under the Act to function as a single reference point for all matters relating to food safety, strives to achieve a high degree of consumer confidence in quality and safety of food through an effective, transparent and accountable regulatory framework. Similar reforms are underway in Bangladesh, Nepal, Pakistan and Sri Lanka. However, severe capacity constraints in this area are prevalent in all South Asian countries.

There are several ways regional cooperation can contribute to the improvement of food safety regulatory regimes in South Asia. Besides more awareness about health hazards and a regional alert system on contamination, cooperative arrangements can help to adopt a multisectoral approach to identify and prioritize food safety actions. A 'Regional Food Safety Strategy' developed for South-East Asia under the aegis of WHO is an example of the merits of regional approaches.[35] The Strategy for South-East Asia functions through partnerships and networks, which strengthen national level food safety frameworks. Another dimension is that of integrating food safety standards under regional trade rules, ensuring consistency between domestic and mutually agreed regional food standards with due regard to internationally agreed safeguards to public health and consumer protection.

Collectively managing shared natural resources, including water and energy resources

The importance of natural resource management for sustainable food systems cannot be understated. The criticality of resource management is accentuated by the complex ways of interaction between various resource bases, demanding an integrated and wholistic approach to resource management that permeates national borders. The FAO had developed and promoted what is referred to as the 'water-energy-food-nexus', recognising that any action relevant for one of the triad – water security, energy security and food security – would essentially have implications for the other two. In line with this realisation, the FAO has led development of an approach "to assess and manage the water-energy-food nexus to inform decision-making processes and to guide the development of 'Nexus-sensitive' policies, supporting countries in designing and implementing them in a participatory manner".[36]

Manifestations of the water-energy-food-nexus in various forms are clearly visible in South Asia. Rising demand had commensurate increase in competition for water and energy resources between agriculture, fisheries, livestock, forestry and numerous other primary, and even secondary and tertiary, sectors of the subregion, with unpredictable impacts on livelihoods and the environment. While hydropower trade is pitched as a gamechanger and is aggressively pursued in South Asia, with investments from India and multilateral donors flowing into projects in Bhutan an Nepal, there are rising concerns of possible displacement of agrarian dwellers in the catchment areas of such projects as well as in the downstream agroecological systems across borders.[37] However, such areas of potential competition and conflict can be turned into opportunities under regional cooperation frameworks. Bilateral accords such as the Indus Water Treaty (1960) signed between India and Pakistan for sharing the Indus River system and the treaty (1996) signed between Bangladesh and India for sharing the waters of the Ganges can be building blocks in this regard.

A number of proposals addressing various aspects of the water-energy-food-nexus are under consideration at SAARC. On energy, the SAARC Framework Agreement for Energy Cooperation (Electricity) signed in 2014, can be seen as a millstone on the way to the SAARC Energy Ring and SAARC Market for Electricity (SAME) concepts. However, regional level initiatives on water have not been equally prominent as food or energy.[38] Absence of a 'Nexus-approach' in the regional development framework can turn out to be costly in terms of escalation in resource-based conflicts. Frequent droughts and floods and other manifestations of water crises, and their direct effects on food systems, have been raising alarm bells in South Asia. As a result, topics such as confluence of the blue economy and the mountain economy, together constituting the core of the natural resource base of South Asia along with its riverine systems, has been gaining traction in the subregion in recent years. The South Asian community must contextualise these discussions against long-term sustainability and food security and take firm steps towards an integrated regional framework on natural resources.

Organisation of the book

This book is divided into two parts. Part I deals with regional outlook towards food security, appraising the challenges and opportunities of regional cooperation based on an exploratory analysis of various aspects of food deprivation in South Asia and their triggers. Chapters in this part place specific emphasis on agricultural trade liberalisation as a market correctional strategy and on regional food reserve as a supply stabilisation mechanism, given their significance as two of the most potent policy responses immediately available at the disposal of South Asian countries. Chapters in Part II respectively subject national food security policy portfolios of five of the largest South Asian countries to closer examination to find how national initiatives can be leveraged at the regional level.

Part I: regional perspectives on food security

In Chapter 2, Upali Wickramasinghe reviews South Asia's progress, challenges and opportunities for realising sustainable food security in the post-2015 development agenda. Following an assessment of the magnitude of food deprivation and what is expected of the subregion in terms of achieving Goal 2, the chapter finds the origins of the problem in a mix of interlinked factors. These include failure of native food production systems, stock management and distribution policies, food trade liberalisation, agricultural support measures and targeting of national food security programmes, along with the failure of containing food wastage. South Asia's average dietary energy supply is inadequate to reduce the Prevalence of Undernourishment (PoU) to the 5% level. The author presents a strong case for much greater effort at the regional level for coordinating policy responses given the transboundary implications of food production systems, distribution and trade with huge implications for food security. The region can do much more to improve agricultural productivity and production, enhance agricultural R&D, disseminate and share knowledge, manage agro-ecological zones including large river-basin systems, manage food security risks and vulnerability and share knowledge on implementing safety nets. Achieving the post-2015 development agenda also requires covering food security beyond PoU to all forms of malnutrition, to meet different physical activity levels and transitory food insecurity, all within a framework of sustainable development and structural transformation in agriculture.

In Chapter 3, I. N. Mukherji identifies freer intraregional trade in food products as a partial but effective solution that can contribute to substantially enhance food security. A detailed product-by-product analysis of the composition of food exports and imports of South Asian countries is conducted, with the objective of identifying agricultural and primary products – that have both high regional trade potential and high sensitivity from a food security point of view. The concept of Additional Market Access Frontier (AMAF) is employed to assess the potential for imports of important food items by each South Asian country from regional trading partners, possibly at a cheaper price than current imports from the rest of the world. In aggregate, the analysis has shown trade complementarity in a wide range of food products within South Asia. The study offers a set of policy recommendations for selection of food products for trade liberalisation measures under SAFTA.

Chapter 4 by Sachin Chaturvedi subjects the agricultural trade landscape of South Asia to examination, with a view to find opportunities that trade offers to alleviate food insecurity in the subregion. Empirically evidence validate the role of agricultural trade in enhancing food security. Though the SAARC Declaration on Food Security warrants a joint commitment to ease movement of agricultural goods across boundaries, and despite a regional trade liberalisation mechanism, trade remains suboptimal. The most important of trade challenges emanates from restrictive measures and inconsistent application of product standards that affect free flow of agricultural produce, leading to high food prices. Similarly, various tariff and nontariff measures affect trade in agricultural inputs. The dynamics of intraregional food trade is analysed in terms of nontariff measures applied on it by way of SPS and TBT, followed by some key recommendations for utilising available trade channels.

In Chapter 5, Mustafizur Rahman, Estiaque Bari and Sherajum Monira Farin assess the key provisions informing the SAARC Food Bank (SFB) initiative, identify the weaknesses that undermine effective operationalisation of the SFB and come up with an evidence-informed institutional architecture to raise operational efficacy of the SFB. The authors conduct a comparative analysis of similar initiatives in other regions and find that regional food reserves could play an important role in alleviating food insecurity in emergency situations. Historically, the stockpiling of agricultural commodities – particularly staple grains – has successfully acted as a buffer to natural disasters, seasonal discrepancies and market turbulences. Though the economic rationale of reserves as a safeguard mechanism and as a mechanism for price control is recognised in South Asia, adequate steps have not been taken to strengthen the SFB. The Authors highlight the need for demonstrated and strong political support towards raising the efficacy of the SFB. Even with respect to obligatory information sharing, Member States have not fulfilled their commitments, as the quantum of food reserves have not been disclosed along with locations of warehouses designated for SFB reserves. Initiatives such as the launching of the SAARC Food Bank Information System (SFBIS) by the SFB Board may help to address these issues. Following an objective assessment of the shortcoming in the conceptualisation of SFB, the Chapter provides key recommendations for its implementation including pricing, distribution and institutional reforms.

Part II: national food security strategies – leveraging regional cooperation

In Chapter 6, Mustafizur Rahman and Towfiqul Islam Khan assesses the state of food security in the context of Bangladesh. While the country has made notable progress, especially in terms of meeting the MDG target of halving the proportion of undernourished people from 1990 levels, it remains challenged by high poverty rates, severe climate change impacts, land utilisation constraints and price volatilities. Bangladesh is highly vulnerable to international food price shocks as a net food importing country. The authors stress on the need to diversify production and import sources to improve the robustness of domestic markets against price shocks. Bangladesh has the potential to improve agricultural productivity and close yield gaps in a variety of crops and improve efficiency in the usage of inputs. The chapter calls for expanding the scope and coverage of national plans for climate change adaptation, for enhancing Bangladesh's participation in food security initiatives under the SAARC framework including agricultural trade liberalization under SAFTA and for engaging with neighbouring countries for share concerns of conserving and managing river water basins and other natural resources.

In Chapter 7, S. Mahendra Dev analyzes the case of India and observes that despite impressive achievements, including self-sufficiency in foodgrains, high imbalances in food consumption continues. Growth of aggregate food production remains below potential with notable yield gaps in many crops. Diversification of consumption baskets to include more nongrain food items has contributed to nutritional improvements, but it has also led to price inflation in certain cases. Micronutrient deficiencies and higher undernutrition among women and children is a serious concern. Reviewing various national policies such as those related to rural reforms to benefit small land holders and the public distribution system (PDS), in the light of the government's priority of doubling farm income by 2022, the author notes the inadequacies of implementation, particularly in terms of targeting and stopping leakages. With a larger portfolio of public food security policies and programmes such as the Mahatma Gandhi National Rural Employment Act (MGNREGA), Integrated Child Development Scheme (ICDS), National Rural Livelihoods Mission etc., India is well positioned to lead knowledge and experience sharing with South Asian countries for mutual benefits. As a larger partner, India also wields greater responsibilities in addressing the subregional concerns of sustainable natural resource management with a food security dimension.

In Chapter 8, Posh Raj Pande undertakes a review of trends and determinants of food security challenges in Nepal. The newly adopted Constitution of the country recognises food security as fundamental human right, stating that 'every citizen has the right to be safe from the state of being in danger of life from the scarcity of food'. Despite significant improvement in production of cereals and of several vegetables crops, a majority of the rural poor in Nepal faces availability and access constraints. Import dependency, particularly in the case of cereals, has been growing at an annual average rate of 14% since 2000. Per capita food production is observed to be highly fluctuating and volatile and worsening in terms of stability in the recent past. The chapter evaluates the prospects for Nepal against the national policy framework and actions to address food security and analyzes the extent to which drivers of food security in Nepal can be supported by regional cooperation with its South Asian neighbours. The Rights to Food Security and Food Sovereignty Related Act of 2018, enacted to implement the constitutional rights of the citizens to food, food security and food sovereignty, is one of the major steps in this regard. As a host of mountainous terrains and its plains, which are highly climate sensitive, partnerships for climate resilient agriculture systems is among the areas that Nepal would benefit the most from in terms of regional cooperation.

In Chapter 9, Abid Qaiyum Suleri and Mehreen Iqbal review the food security situation in Pakistan and note that it is among the greatest challenges for the country. High prevalence of undernutrition, particularly severe among women and children, has led to Pakistan being poorly ranked in the Global Hunger Index (GHI). The situation is worsened by increasing exposure to climate hazards and natural disasters. Pakistan has achieved significant progress in productivity of certain crops, particularly cereals, and has transformed into a net exporter of these crops. However, high yield gaps exist in other crops, leading to low diversification of food baskets. Issues of food utilization are of concerns in Pakistan due to inadequacies of access to safe drinking water and sanitation facilities. The authors discuss the key features of food security strategies and policies led by the Ministry of National Food Security and Research (MNFSR) of Pakistan, observing that the national food security policy has been drafted with the objective of meeting the zero hunger targets under the SDGs. The authors also highlight the potential of regional cooperation under the SAARC framework on a number of priorities, such as combating climate change, sharing research capacities and integrating agricultural markets, in which Pakistan could participate and make highly useful contributions.

In Chapter 10, the late Saman Kelegama and Dilani Hirimuthugodage examine food security concerns of Sri Lanka. Stagnant rates of reduction of undernutrition in the country, where prevalence of stunting of children under 5 has increased since 2009, has been in contrast with its higher per capita income growth and development. The Chapter considers the evolution of agricultural and food security policies in a historical perspective and reveals the political economy considerations behind national reforms. The agricultural and food policy regime in Sri Lanka has struggled to meet conflicting objectives of self-sustenance in the food sector through protectionist approaches and import liberalisation to stabilise food market prices. The efforts for self-sufficiency were largely focused on rice production with notable success, while later efforts to diversify production into other staple food items is yet to result in significant achievements. Failure of market and trade reforms to enable access to critical inputs has been a major obstacle in the way of diversification. Frequent changes and inconsistencies in the agricultural trade liberalisation positions of successive governments also stood in the way of a focused long-term national food market stabilisation strategy. Sri Lanka currently has a wide suite of government led food security programmes ranging from welfare schemes based on direct targeting through various distribution channels to support subsidies and incentives catering to the needs of food production and post-harvest processes. Initiatives cover enhancement of nutritional intake to setting up of agro-processing enterprises at the rural level. However, there are avenues for improvement in the design and implementation of the public programmes. The authors note that Sri Lanka stands to gain through efforts to enhance intraregional agricultural trade, including trade of agricultural inputs, and by offering technical cooperation in the field of agricultural research and technology transfer with other South Asian countries.

Notes

1 FAO Food Security Indicators, accessed in October 2018.
2 UNICEF (2018). South Asia currently has a higher percentage (35%) and number (59.4 million out of 151 million) of stunted children than any other region in the world.
3 Ibid. Some of the subregional countries exhibit alarmingly high levels of nutritional deficiencies, while others have pockets of unusual severity.
4 United Nations (2015).
5 See Chapter 2 of this volume.
6 FAO Food Security Indicators, accessed in October 2018.
7 FAO (2017) reports that the number of people suffering from hunger may be on the rise in Asia, worsening the slowdown in progress towards food security targets.
8 Anik et al. (2017). Also see Hazell (2009). Rice and wheat yields more than doubled in Asia from the 1960s to 1990s.
9 Piya et al. (2011).
10 See IFPRI (2002) for an exposition on the Green Revolution's negative environmental impacts that have still to be adequately redressed.
11 See Kumara (2008) and Bashir (2000).
12 Chand (2010).
13 Rising incomes and growing urbanization are rapidly changing the composition of the food basket – away from cereals to high-value food products including fish and meat. See Gupta (2018).
14 FAO (2016b).
15 Agricultural Census data shows that about 99 million out of 121 million agricultural holdings in India in 2000–01 were small and marginal farmers. See Dev (2015).
16 UNESCAP (2017).
17 See UNESCAP (2017)
18 FAO (2016a).
19 CSA is one of the 11 Corporate Areas for Resource Mobilization under the FAO's Strategic Objectives. See FAO (2016b). See Lipper et al. (2018).
20 FAO (2016a).
21 UNESCAP (2017).
22 For an exposition on application of CFA, see Srinivasan et al. (2011).
23 See Martin (2017). For an exposition of linkages between agricultural trade and food security, see FAO (2016b).
24 See Chapter 3 of this volume.
25 FAO food bank regional network.

26 Briones (2011), ADB.
27 See Bhutani (2013).
28 See Chapter 2 of this volume.
29 See UNESCAP SSWA (2013).
30 See OECD/ICRIER (2018),
31 See Banerjee et al. (2015).
32 See Matthews (2003).
33 See ADB and FAO (2017).
34 ILRI, which leads the Consultative Group on International Agricultural Research (CGIAR) research programmes on the prevention and control of agriculture-associated diseases and sustainable management of the crop-livestock system, works with partners worldwide to enhance the roles that livestock play in food security, principally in Africa and Asia. ILRI's new Delhi office currently serves as a regional hub in South Asia.
35 See WHO (2014).
36 See FAO (2014).
37 FAO (2011) points out that large-scale water infrastructure projects can have multiple impacts, producing hydropower and water storage for irrigation etc., but it may also have large-scale socio-economic implications by way of resettlements. Similarly, bioenergy crops may help improve energy supply but at the cost of increased competition for land and water resources with impacts on local food security.
38 Pratap (2018) makes a case for SAARC countries' accession to the International Watercourses Convention and establishment of a SAARC cooperation mechanism for water sharing.

References

ADB and FAO (2017), 'SAARC Food Security Through Control of Transboundary Animal Diseases', Technical Assistance Consultant's Report, Project Number: 47019-001, Asian Development Bank and the Food and Agriculture Organization.

Anik, A. R., S. Rahman and J. R. Sarker (2017), 'Agricultural Productivity Growth and the Role of Capital in South Asia (1980–2013)', *Sustainability*, Vol. 9(3), p. 470.

Banerjee, A., R. Hanna, J. C. Kyle, B. A. Olken and S. Sumarto (2015), 'The Power of Transparency: Information, Identification Cards and Food Subsidy Programs in Indonesia', NBER Working Paper, No. 20923.

Bashir, Z. (2000), 'The Role of Agricultural Growth in South Asian Countries and the Affordability of Food: An Inter-Country Analysis', *The Pakistan Development Review*, Vol. 39(4), Part II, pp. 751–767.

Bhutani, S. (2013), 'Re-Searching Agriculture in South Asia: The Law and Policy Context for Agricultural Research and Development and Its Impact on Smallholder Farmers', International Institute for Environment and Development (IIED), London.

Briones, R. M. (2011), 'Regional Cooperation for Food Security: The Case of Emergency Rice Reserves in the ASEAN Plus Three', ADB Sustainable Development Working Paper Series, No. 18, Asian Development Bank, Manila.

Chand, R. (2010), 'SAARC Agricultural Vision 2020', *Agricultural Economics Research Review*, Agricultural Economics Research Association, Vol. 23, pp. 197–208.

Dev, S. M. (2015), 'Challenges and Opportunities of Small Farmers in India', *International Journal of Academic Research*, Vol. 2(1) pp. 94–101.

FAO (2011), 'Climate Change, Water and Food Security', FAO Water Reports, No. 36, Rome, Food and Agriculture Organization of the United Nations.

FAO (2014), 'The Water-Energy-Food Nexus: A New Approach in Support of Food Security and Sustainable Agriculture', Food and Agriculture Organization, Rome.

FAO (2016a), 'The State of Food and Agriculture: Climate Change, Agriculture and Food Security', Food and Agriculture Organization, Rome.

FAO (2016b), 'Asia and the Pacific Regional Overview of Food Insecurity: Investing in a Zero Hunger Generation', Food and Agriculture Organization Regional Office, Bangkok.

FAO (2016c), 'How Does Agricultural Trade Impact Food Security?', Trade and Food Security Policy Briefs, No. 17, Food and Agriculture Organization, Rome.

FAO (2017), 'Asia and the Pacific Regional Overview of Food Insecurity: Investing in Food Systems for Better Nutrition', Food and Agriculture Organization Regional Office, Bangkok.

Gupta, S. (2018), 'Changing pattern of food consumption and the emerging relevance of livestock products in India', *International Journal of Research in Economics and Social Sciences*, Vol 8(2), pp. 451-460.

Hazell, P. B. R. (2009), 'Transforming Agriculture: The Green Revolution in Asia', in *Millions Fed: Proven Successes in Agricultural Development*, David J. Spielman and Rajul Pandya-Lorch (Eds.), Chapter 3, pp. 25–32. International Food Policy Research Institute (IFPRI), Washington, DC.

IFPRI (2002), 'Green Revolution. Curse or Blessing?', International Food Policy Research Institute, Washington, DC.

Kumara, P., S. Mittal and M. Hossain (2008), 'Agricultural Growth Accounting and Total Factor Productivity in South Asia: A Review and Policy Implications', *Agricultural Economics Research Review*, Vol. 21(2), pp. 145–172.

Lipper, L., N. McCarthy, D. Zilberman, S. Asfaw and G. Branca (Eds.) (2018), *Climate Smart Agriculture: Building Resilience to Climate Change*, Natural Resource Management and Policy Series, Springer, Singapore.

Martin, W. (2017), 'Agricultural Trade and Food Security', ADBI Working Paper Series, No. 664, Asian Development Bank Institute, Tokyo.

Matthews, A. (2003), 'Regional Integration and Food Security in Developing Countries', Training Materials for Agricultural Planning 45, Food and Agriculture Organization, Rome.

OECD/ICRIER (2018), 'Agricultural Policies in India', OECD Food and Agricultural Reviews, OECD Publishing, Paris.

Piya, S., A. Kiminami and H. Yagi (2011), 'Sources of Agricultural Productivity Growth in South and Southeast Asia', *Trends in Agricultural Economics*, Vol. 4(1), pp. 18–29.

Pratap, R. (2018), 'Building Peace Over Water in South Asia: The Watercourses Convention and SAARC', *Athens Journal of Law*, Vol. 4(1), pp. 7–26.

Srinivasan, G., K. M. Rafisura and A. R. Subbiah (2011), 'Climate Information Requirements for Community-Level Risk Management and Adaptation', *Climate Research*, Vol. 47, pp. 5–12.

UNESCAP (2017), 'Disaster Resilience for Sustainable Development: Asia-Pacific Disaster Report 2017', United Nations Publication, Sales No.: E.17.II.F.16.

UNESCAP SSWA (2013), 'Regional Cooperation for Inclusive and Sustainable Development: South and South-West Asia Development Report (2012–13)', United Nations Economic and Social Commission for Asia and the Pacific South and South-West Asia Office and Routledge, New Delhi.

UNICEF (2018), 'Child Stunting, Hidden Hunger and Human Capital in South Asia: Implications for Sustainable Development Post 2015', UNICEF Regional Office for South Asia, Kathmandu, Nepal.

United Nations (2015), 'The Millennium Development Goals Report', UN Secretariat, New York.

WHO (2014), 'Regional Food Safety Strategy, 2013–2017', World Health Organization Regional Office for South-East Asia.

World Bank (2008), 'The World Development Report: Agriculture for Development', The World Bank Group, Washington, DC.

PART I

Regional perspectives on food security

2

REALIZING SUSTAINABLE FOOD SECURITY IN SOUTH ASIA

Progress, challenges and opportunities

Upali Wickramasinghe[1]

Introduction

The world adopted the Sustainable Development Goals agenda on 25 September 2015, which aims at realising a set of goals to *end poverty, protect the planet and ensure prosperity to all.* Ending hunger, achieving food security and improving nutrition are enshrined in SDG-2, and it has eight specific targets to be realised by 2030. More specifically, it aims to realize two food security and hunger reduction targets: (a) end hunger and ensure access to safe, nutritious and sufficient food to all people, (b) end all forms of malnutrition, including achieving the internationally agreed targets on stunting and wasting in children under 5 years of age, and address the nutritional needs of adolescent girls, pregnant and lactating women and older persons. While the SDG targets in general are to be realised by 2030, the target on malnutrition is to be realized by 2025, which has, effectively indicated the urgency of realising the targets on malnutrition because of its fundamental nature and impact on all other development targets.

Nearly two and half years have passed since the signing the SDG framework. The time is right to ask: Where does South Asia[2] stand in the process of realising food security targets? This chapter provides the current state of South Asia's progress towards the realisation of food and nutrition security targets and reviews the extent to which the region has addressed the fundamental constraints to realising these targets.

This chapter is organised as follows. The second section reviews the progress South Asia has made in realising food security since holding the 1992 World Food Summit, which provides an anchor to monitor progress. The third section reviews critical factors that appear to have a stronger bearing on food and nutrition insecurity in South Asia and policy measures taken by selected countries in the region. The fourth section provides a review of opportunities for realising food security within the current economic, social and political context in South Asia, with some references to a possible regional agenda.

South Asia's progress towards realizing food security

By the turn of the 21st century, the world is estimated to have 906 million under-nourished people,[3] of which nearly 30%, or about 260 million undernourished people, live in South Asia (FAO, 2017). By the end of the Millennium Development Goals (MDG) period, the number of undernourished people in the world had declined to about 776 million, reducing the number of undernourished people by 130 million. Considering the fact that the world population increased from 6.1 billion to 7.4 billion, the actual number of people who escaped food insecurity is over 300 million.

Although the number of undernourished people has not declined in absolute terms from 2000 to 2015, the number of people who would have potentially been affected by undernourishment is much larger because population during the same period grew from 260 million to 1.8 billion. To get a sense of the potential number of undernourished people in absence of a reduction of food insecurity, consider the extreme case where PoU did not decline but remained at the same level as in 1999–2001. This would imply that South Asia would have 327 million undernourished people in 2015 instead of 148 million. Thus, South Asia has effectively brought down the number of chronically undernourished people by nearly 180 million.

By any measure this is an achievement, although not as impressive as the progress that Eastern Asia has made during the same period. The South Asian region continues to hold the largest number of undernourished people in the world; in terms of the prevalence undernourishment, the region is just above that of Sub-Saharan Africa. Yet South Asia continued to hold the largest undernourished people on earth by the end of the MDG period (Figure 2.1).

Even within South Asia the progress towards realising food security has been quite uneven. By the end of the MDG period, prevalence of undernourishment (PoU) in Nepal and the Maldives had dropped to 8%, whereas it was still as high as 23% in Afghanistan and Sri Lanka (Figure 2.2). During the 15-year period, Nepal's PoU declined by 6% per annum, while it was declined by only 1% in Pakistan. In India, the population increased by nearly 260 million during the MDG period, while PoU came down to 14.5% with an annual rate of decline of 1%, whereas in Sri Lanka, the population grew by 2 million and PoU declined from 29% to 22%, with a rate of decline of 1.8%.

Information on child malnutrition not only provides invaluable information on the nutritional status of a community or a population but also a valuable guide to what is to be expected in the future because children who suffer from growth retardation due to poor diets or recurrent infections tend to have a greater risk of developing chronic health problems, impaired cognition capacities in extreme cases and impeded labour productivity, and hence the possibility for less than optimal economic growth performance. It has been well established that poor nutrition

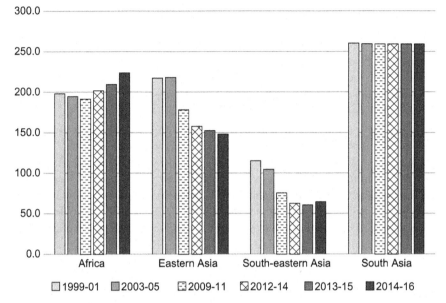

FIGURE 2.1 Number of undernourished people in selected regions and years (in millions)

Source: FAO (2018) and World Bank (2018)

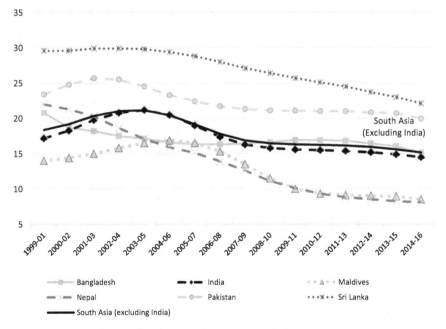

FIGURE 2.2 Prevalence of undernourishment in South Asia

Source: FAO (2018) and World Bank (2018)

among children weakens the immune system, increasing disease incidence and severity (Tomkins and Watson, 1989), thus contributing to growth retardation. Moreover, malnutrition is transferred from the present to the future generation through mothers to children in pregnancy.

According to two of the most commonly used indicators on malnutrition among children aged 5 years or lower – wasting, underweight and stunting,[4] South Asian countries have high child malnutrition (Figure 2.3). South Asia[5] as a group had the highest prevalence of underweight children in 2012, with 30% of children moderately or severely underweight, but it also experienced the largest, absolute decline since 1990 (United Nations, 2014b). For the latest year in which data are available, stunting is above 40% in Bangladesh, India and Pakistan. Underweight among children is above 40% in India and Bangladesh; it is close to 30% in Nepal and Pakistan and around 20% in the Maldives and Sri Lanka. In Bhutan, indicators suggest a mixed picture. The measures on underweight and wasting indicate a lower level of child malnutrition, but stunting is relatively high. Malnutrition is highly correlated with the level of household income. In South Asia, 60% of children in the poorest quintile are underweight, compared with 26% of those in the richest quintile (United Nations, 2011). Notwithstanding the nuances that should be taken into account in interpreting the data, it is evident that a significant proportion of children in South Asia continue to suffer from severe forms of malnutrition.

Malnutrition in pregnancy is also relatively high in South Asia. The prevalence of anaemia during pregnancy, for example, varies from 29.3% in 2005 in Sri Lanka

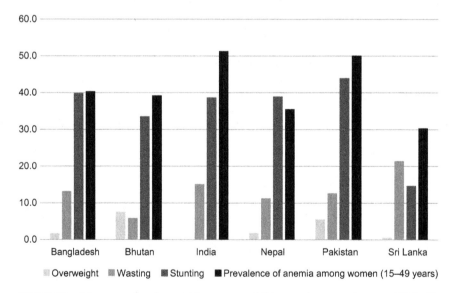

FIGURE 2.3 Measures of undernutrition among children and women (average 2010–15, in %)

Source: FAO (2018) and World Bank (2018)

to 61% in Afghanistan in 2001. Improving maternal nutrition before, during and immediately after pregnancy is a proven intervention to reduce child malnutrition (United Nations, 2014a).

Overweight – the other side of malnutrition, but a serious impediment to health – is still not a major issue in South Asia, except for urban, more affluent communities. In 2011, overweight affected 7% of preschool children (43 million) worldwide (WHO, 2013), and the rate of increase over the past 20 years has been similar in developed and developing countries, whereas some regions have experienced drastic increases (WHO, 2013). Although South Asia has not yet caught up with other regions on overweight and obesity, as can be observed from the global data available from the WHO report mentioned earlier, people, especially women, in high socio-economic status in South Asia are likely to be affected by overweight and obesity (Griffiths and Bentley, 2005).

Causes of food insecurity in South Asia

Why is food insecurity persistent in South Asia? Indeed, food insecurity is a multi-dimensional issue involving agricultural production systems and its vulnerability to weather conditions and climatic change, the socio-economic dimension of development, especially income distribution and access to resources and services, which are often summarised by four dimensions: food availability, food accessibility, vulnerability and utilization. The first three aspects are discussed briefly in the section that follows.

Food availability

Food availability is determined by food production, the amount of food stored and withdrawn from previous stocks, food imports and exports, food waste and the amount of food used as seeds, and is indicated by several measures. Average dietary energy supply adequacy[6] (ADESA) is one such generally accepted measure of food availability. A scatterplot between ADESA and PoU across the world (Figure 2.4) shows that there is a threshold that a country must reach before it can expect to bring down its PoU to the natural rate of undernourishment of 5%, beyond which no country can guarantee further reduction as it is natural for some people to experience food insecurity for reasons other than the four food security dimensions – for example some idiosyncratic factors such as diseases or of their own choices. It was noted that ADESA and PoU have a correlation of −0.8 and that as a rule of thumb ADESA needs to reach a minimum level of 115%, but on average 120%, in order for a country to be able to bring down PoU to a 5% level.

ADESA and PoU in combination indicate whether food insecurity is primarily due to inadequate food supply or other factors such as weaknesses in the food distribution systems. If, for example, ADESA is high but there is high PoU, it can be due to high-income inequality, weak food distribution system or difficulties in accessibility.[7] Low ADESA with low PoU may indicate the existence of high public

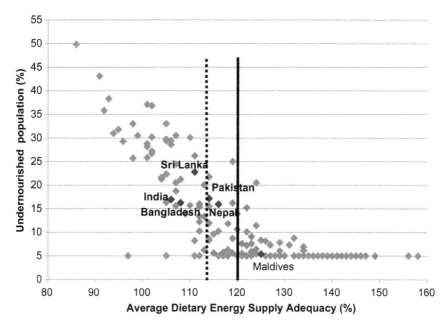

FIGURE 2.4 Average dietary energy supply adequacy and prevalence of undernourishment

Source: FAO (2018) and World Bank (2018)

safety net programmes or extremely low food losses, low-income inequality and efficient distribution systems.

In South Asia, the Maldives has reached ADESA of above 120 (Figure 2.5), with PoU of 5%. Pakistan and Sri Lanka are located in the neighbourhood of 115% of ADESA but with high PoU; and India has slightly lower ADESA with PoU lower than Sri Lanka and Pakistan. These factors indicate that the current levels of dietary energy supply will need to be further strengthened to ensure food security for the region. Nepal and the Maldives have managed to increase their ADESA rates over time much faster than other countries in South Asia, indicating the possibility for a country to realise food security, and as in Nepal, even without a high per capita GDP.

Food accessibility

Literature on food security identifies that food insecurity is often caused not by lack of food but rather due to a lack of or inadequate access to food, caused by many other fundamental factors including income poverty, inadequate access to productive resources for households, or members within a given household (limited access to land for women), social customs and taboos, food preferences, cooking methods, efficiency of food distribution systems and population dynamics. Failure to access resources often lead to failures to food access, which prolongs

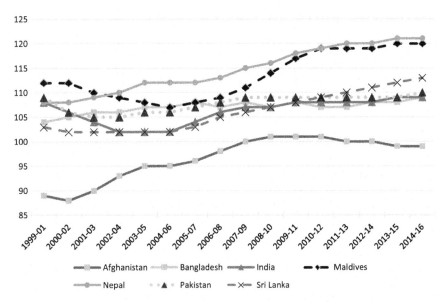

FIGURE 2.5   Average dietary energy supply adequacy (%)

Source: FAO (2018) and World Bank (2018)

social hierarchies, thus transmitting food insecurity and malnutrition through generations.

In South Asia, per capita GDP has been rising in all the countries during the last 16 years, and it can be observed that per capita GDP has been rising faster in the Maldives, Sri Lanka and Bhutan compared to others (Figure 2.6). While the Maldives has also realised a high degree of food security, Sri Lanka's food insecurity measured by PoU continues to be high, indicating that there is no direct association between food insecurity and per capita GDP, and indicating income growth per se does not lead to better food security outcomes.

Vulnerability

Vulnerability refers to variation in food availability, accessibility or utilization due to external forces such as food production variation arising from weather, civil wars that disrupt food distribution systems or variation in income distribution that result in a segment of population not having access to adequate food. Per capita food supply variability is found to have a high degree of variability in South Asia, with multi-year cycles in India and Sri Lanka but with a tendency to make some improvements in Nepal and Pakistan (Figure 2.7). A part of the high variability of per capita food supply can be explained by food production variability across countries. By comparing per capita food supply variability with food production variability, one can easily see that the two variables are highly correlated. While

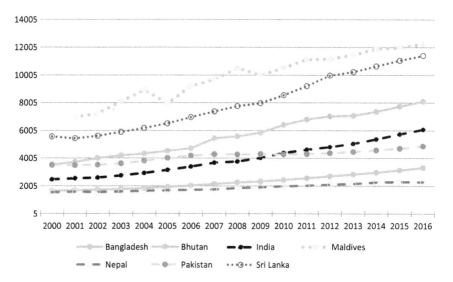

FIGURE 2.6 Gross domestic product per capita (Purchasing Power Parity Equivalent, constant 2011 International Dollar)

Source: World Bank (2018)

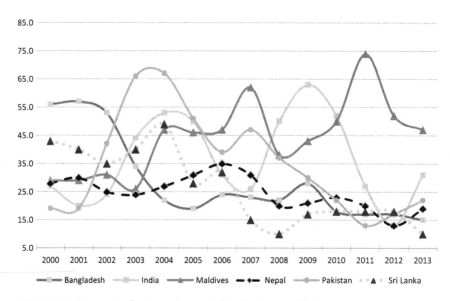

FIGURE 2.7 Per capita food supply variability (kcal/caput/day)

Source: FAO (2018) and World Bank (2018)

reducing food production variability could technically improve food availability for households, alternatives can also be considered, for example, providing access to better insurance mechanisms, such as through weather-indexed crop insurance.

Empirical evidence suggests that food consumption in rural areas has a high seasonal variation. Rural farm households have little savings and disposable assets, making them more vulnerable to food insecurity with even smaller variations of their incomes, triggering households to reduce their food intake, starting with food items that are relatively expensive such as meat, eggs, milk and vegetables (Jodha, 1978) as a first step in their coping strategy. Income shocks arising from a crop failure due to a prolong drought or a pest attack can significantly reduce food consumption. Income shocks over two or more periods (e.g., an additional month in the case of daily wage earners or into second crop season in the case of farmers) can devastate farm households and push them into deeper crisis of food insecurity (Jodha, 1978; Deaton, 1993; Wickramasinghe, 1995). Safety nets, if well designed, can help households to minimise transitory food insecurity episodes.

Binding constraints for realising food security

To identify probable causes for food insecurity in South Asia, this chapter reviewed food balance sheets from five countries in South Asia. Food supply within the country consists of local production adjusted for imports, exports and stock changes. Domestic food is used in several ways including for human consumption, as seeds, as inputs in industrial processing, as food waste and as animal feed.

In Bangladesh, the share of local production in total supply is close to or above 100% in several food commodities including cereal, sugar, meat, offal, eggs and fish. Imports do not figure high in major commodity groups, and food exports are limited to a handful of commodities (Annex Tables 2A.1 and 2A.2). On food utilization, over 80% of domestic food supply is used for human consumption, usage for industrial processing is limited to sugar and oil crops and wastage of food is relatively high in cereals (6%), but wastage in commodities such as starchy roots, fruits and vegetables stands at 10%.

In India, local food production exceeds 100% of domestic supply in almost all commodity groups by a significant margin, with the exceptions of tree-nuts and vegetable oils. Correspondingly, the share of imports in total domestic supply is close to zero in many commodity groups, with the exceptions of tree-nuts, vegetable oils and stimulants. A very high share of food is used for human consumption. Food wastage is significantly high in starchy roots and fruits. The high food production and high PoU in India implies that food production is not the main issue hampering the realisation of food security for all; there are probably additional issues such as greater income inequality.

In Nepal, the share of local food production in total food supply is high in cereals, starchy roots, sugar, meat, offal and eggs and milk, which are staple food commodities for a large majority. It was noted that about 72% of food is used for human consumption, one of the lowest in South Asia. Of the balance, 15% is used as feed, while 11% is estimated to go to waste, especially in starchy roots (14%), sugar (10%) and vegetables (10%). Nepal also imports a significant proportion of its food, giving rise to high variability, which was especially observed to have occurred in recent years. For Nepal, reducing food waste, especially in starchy foods, is likely to give an immediate boost to domestic food supplies, further enhancing food security.

In Pakistan, local production as a share of food supply is high (import share is low), especially in starchy roots, vegetables, fruits, meat and fish, giving the country a much higher possibility for enhancing food security. Imports are limited to those with inadequate local production, namely pulses, tree-nuts, oil-crops, vegetable oils and spices. Food waste is low, except for starchy roots, eggs and milk, each with 10% wastage. Two issues that appear to have a strong bearing on food security are weak food accessibility and food distribution.

In Sri Lanka, local food production as a share of domestic supply is low across all major food commodity groups, and especially in cereals with a share of 78%, the lowest share among the five countries considered. This has resulted in high import dependency on cereals (42%), starchy roots (42%), pulses (96%), vegetable oils (75%), vegetables (22%), spices (61%), milk (76%) and fish (31%). Wastage in vegetables and fruits is 10%. It appears that food insecurity in Sri Lanka is more than supply-demand balances but related to a more complex set of structural factors.

In summary, the current level of dietary energy supply at the household level in South Asia is inadequate to meet food requirements for all to have adequate access to food. This is a result of many underlying factors, including food production systems, stock management policies, food waste, food industry and trade. Identifying the binding constraints at each country's level should receive a priority in policy analysis, which would require more specific country level analysis linking macro and micro levels (household level).

Food security strategies, approaches and programs

Ensuring food security has been a key focus of South Asian countries in development planning and strategies. This section reviews food and nutrition security policies, strategies and programmes that are currently in operation across South Asia, with a view to identifying policy priorities for regional interventions.

National policies

Bangladesh

The National Food Policy Plan of Action 2008–2015 (PoA-2008) developed by the Food Planning and Monitoring Unit (FPMU) of the Ministry of Food and Disaster Management (MFDM) has three objectives: (a) adequate and stable supply of safe and nutritious food, (b) increased purchasing power and access to food and (c) adequate nutrition for all individuals, especially women and children.

Objective (a) is supported by four interventions: increasing production, managing food stocks, strengthening market linkages and managing vulnerability. Each intervention is supported by several actions. Proposed actions for increasing food production include increasing development and dissemination of crop and non-crop technologies, developing irrigation and increasing the supply of quality seed, high value crops, fish and livestock products. Managing food stocks is attempted through private- and public-sector programming. For managing vulnerability, increasing farmer access to credit, establishing a domestic early-warning system and stabilising farmers' income through producer price support have been proposed.

Interventions for realizing objective (b) include managing vulnerability to disasters, improving access to food during lean periods, enhancing market participation of women and disabled people and supporting expansion of agro-based processing and quality of technical and vocational education. Objective (c) is supported through increasing the availability of balanced and nutritious food for vulnerable people and food fortification; enhanced long-term nutritional planning; nutrition education; food safety and quality; access to safe water and sanitation; and promoting breastfeeding and better service provision (e.g., maternity leave).

Bangladesh has implemented a variety of social safety net programmes with the objective of enhancing access to food among vulnerable people and communities offered through government ministries or departments such as the Department of Social Services, Department of Women's Affairs and government projects. These safety nets include allowances and unconditional transfers, food security and disaster assistance, employment/workforce-related human development/social empowerment and subsidies (Rahman et al., 2011). Safety net programmes targeting food security include Vulnerable Group Feeding (VGF), Test Relief (TR) Food, Vulnerable Group Development (VGD), Open Market Sales (OMS), Gratuitous Relief (GR)–Food, Food Assistance in Chittagong Hill Tracts Area and Food for Work (FFW). As estimated by Rahman et al. (ibid.), the outlay for social safety nets stands at over US\$ 1.6 billion. They have contributed to consumption in poor households in the face of risks and shocks, supplement household incomes and enhanced human capital and access to basic services, but Bangladesh has followed "an experimental approach to building its safety net portfolio with significant trial and error in programmes driven by many actors" (Rahman, ibid., p. 51).

Food policy Working group consisting of 13 ministries or divisions were identified for implementing the PoA-2008.

Bhutan

The Government of Bhutan adopted the Food and Nutrition Security Policy of the Kingdom of Bhutan 2014 (FNSP-2014) as its official policy governing food and nutrition security in 2014, and the Ministry of Agriculture and Forests (MoAF) will lead the implementation with support from the Ministry of Health (MoH) (GoBH, 2014).

FNSP-2014 aimed to realize four goals: (a) ensure availability of safe and adequate varieties of food to meet food requirements; (b) enhance physical, economic and social access to safe, affordable and adequate food; (c) promote appropriate consumption practices and enable optimum utilisation of food by all; and (d) sustain a conducive and stable environment for availability, accessibility and utilisation of food.

The framework covers all key dimensions of food security. Key policies include measures to increase domestic production; enhancing the distribution of imported food through markets; maintaining a national food security reserve under the Food Corporation of Bhutan (FCB) comprising of rice, oil and sugar; and promoting the commercial market and FCB distribution system. For enhancing accessibility, it proposed the promotion of income generating activities and programme support for fruit crops, vegetables and livestock production. FNSP-2014 recognized the non-availability of a national safety net programme but recognized the role played by traditional social safety networks in ensuring food security. The need to manage rising food prices and significant regional variation of calorie intake, low consumption of protein, vitamins and minerals and managing natural disasters (frequent and intense extreme weather events), which affect farm incomes, were among other policies proposed for enhancing nutritional security.

India

The National Food Security Ordinance 2013 (NFSO-2013) provides the legal foundation for ensuring food security (GoI, 2013). Key provisions of the NFSO-2013 include: (a) entitlement to receive five kilograms of food-grains per person per month on subsidized prices; (b) school feeding programme; and (c) a food security allowance to persons in the case of non-supply of food-grains or meals to entitled persons. As for the system of administration, the NFSO-2014 proposed (a) mechanisms to develop a system to identify eligible households; (b) reforms in the targeted public distribution system; (c) female empowerment through the distribution of ration cards to the eldest woman above 18 years of age of the household; (d) grievance redressal system; and (e) obligations of state government. Additional schedules of the ordinance identified further provisions, including subsidised prices under the targeted distribution system; nutrition standards; provisions for advancing food security through such activities as revitalization of agriculture, procurement and storage; and access to safe and adequate water, sanitation, healthcare and nutritional education.

Joshi (2013)[8] identified three key challenges in implementing the bill: (a) identification of the poor and ensure that subsidised food reaches the real needy, poor and undernourished; (b) huge subsidy burden at the cost of investment for generating employment through other developmental activities; and (c) sustainability of the scheme in a scenario of a changing food basket and climate change.

In India, public safety net programmes have been in existence since 1951, offered by both the central government and state governments. Desai et al. (2010) identified six types of public safety net programmes that existed in 2005. They included: Public Distribution System (started in the 1960s and modified and supplemented by *Antyodaya* in 2001); school assistance (free books and uniforms); Midday Meal (MDM) programme; Integrated Child Development Services (ICDS) (since the mid-1970s); Food for Work Programme (started in 2000); and Programmes for elderly (NOAP) and Widow Pension and Annapurna. The review of Desai et al. (ibid.) concluded that: (a) programmes that have existed for a long time have extended outreach; (b) while programmes have attempted to introduce targeting, the complexity of Indian inequality across class, caste, community and regional lines has made it difficult for implementation, and hence programmes with self-targeting or neutrality have become politically attractive.

Maldives

Agricultural Development Master Plan 2006–2020 (ADMP-2006) continues to provide the policy framework for food policy and agricultural development in the Maldives (Government of Maldives, 2006). ADMP-2006 aimed at improving food security, nutrition and income among others through gradual commercialisation of agriculture, raising productivity of land, labour, water and human resources. ADMP-2006 proposed six elements: (a) promotion of garden farming for household consumption; (b) commercialisation of agriculture by linking farmers with resorts; (c) leasing out selected islands for farming on commercial basis; (d) promotion of value addition for generating higher employment and income; (e) adoption of sustainable technological options; and (f) ensuring a regional balance of agricultural development and gender equity.

An FAO-led review of agriculture in the Maldives identified that the development of the sector is constrained by a host of factors, including high cost and low return to agricultural investment as a key constraint in attracting the private sector to invest in agriculture. This is primarily due to the small amount of land available, poor soil quality and lack of access to sufficient water. Difficulties in navigating the waters during the monsoon seasons, especially during January to March and July to October, and with the currently available relatively smaller boats, exacerbate food insecurity in outer islands. The government-owned food corporation maintains food storages in strategic locations to ensure food is available for inhabitants of remote locations.

Nepal

In Nepal, food policy is governed under the Nepal Agriculture and Food Security Country Investment Plan (AFSP-2010) (GoN, 2010). This plan is aligned with the country's needs and government priorities, and it addresses key constraints and development challenges facing Nepal in the area of agriculture and food security. The areas covered include agricultural productivity, limited livelihoods opportunities, inefficient food distribution system, weak market linkages, poor infrastructure and lack of awareness of the general public on good food habits. Enhancing food security of vulnerable populations and livelihood opportunities; reducing food and health risks among vulnerable populations and improving income earning employment opportunities for targeted communities; and contributing to enhance nutrition security through the promotion of diversified diets, increased nutrient intake, improved feeding habits and caring of pregnant and nursing women are the main objectives.

The plan envisaged using multiple tools for achieving these objectives. They include development and adoption of technology for livestock and crops sectors; making available high quality seeds to farmers on continuous basis; enhancing agricultural productivity; and direct and targeted interventions to enhance food and nutrient intake by vulnerable populations. The Global Agriculture and Food Security Program (GAFSP) awarded a grant of US$46.5 million in 2011 to implement activities to enhance food security.

Pakistan

Pakistan never had a national food policy except some regional level programs launched by the government (Mittal and Sethi, 2009). One such programme is the Special Program for Food Security (SPFS), implemented with the support from FAO (Ahmad and Farooq, 2010). This was subsequently scaled up and covered 100 villages under the Crop Maximisation Program (CMP-I), which was further expanded to cover over 1,000 villages under CMP-II. Professionals and stakeholders, however, questioned its success on grounds of its outreach and depth of coverage (Ahmad and Farooq, 2010).

Successive governments have given high priority to self-sufficiency in wheat. Several instruments have been implemented for this purpose. One such mechanism is stock management through the Pakistan Agricultural Storage and Supply Corporation (PASSCO). In addition, successive governments have given support prices to wheat growers, maintained wheat stocks, established agro-industrial units for processing and preserving food items and expanded storage capacity (FAO, 2008). A formal price support system was first introduced in the 1960s by fixing wheat prices, which later extended to rice, sugarcane, maize, potato, onion, gram and oilseed. Keeping domestic prices of agricultural commodities lower than world prices has been a long-term policy, and a tool often used for this purpose was the scheme for compulsory procurement, which later was replaced by a system of voluntary procurements.

Pakistan too has implemented a number of safety net programmes, including cash transfers, school-feeding, safe motherhood and child nutrition programs. These safety nets covered over 2 million people (Ahmad and Farooq, ibid.). The Banazir Income Support Program (BISP) was a large-scale programme that offered support services to low-income people, but its outreach and depth of coverage has been limited. The Ministry of Health has implemented programs to improve nutritional status of selected communities with support of the World Food Program and NGOs (FAO, 2009).

In a speech on 23 April 2013, the President of Pakistan indicated that a national food and nutrition security policy was in the process of being finalized. Key elements identified in the President's speech include: commitment to develop the agricultural sector, the need to sustain production of wheat as the staple food of more than 180 million people and the need for greater investment and coordination within and across countries in agricultural research.

Sri Lanka

Sri Lanka's food security policy is covered under the Sri Lanka National Agricultural Policy (NAP-SL) (GoSL, 2014) and the National Nutrition Policy of Sri Lanka 2010 (NNP-2010) (GoSL, 2010). NAP-SL recognises the importance of the agricultural sector for the economy: it states that more than 70% of the population living in rural areas depend on agriculture for their livelihoods and contributes to 18% of national GDP and 30% of employment. It identified sluggish growth; regulatory constraints; fragmented land use; and insufficient availability of water, credit, seed, technical know-how, marketing facilities, storage, transportation and poor farming practices as main reasons for sluggish agricultural growth.

Goals and objectives identified in the NAP-SL include increasing agricultural production and productivity; maximizing benefits and minimizing adverse effects of globalisation on domestic and export agriculture; adoption of sustainable, productive farming systems and improved agro-technologies; promotion of agro-based industries; and enhanced income and living standards for farming communities.

GoSL has implemented several programs in recent years for enhancing food security: national campaign for encouraging the production of indigenous food crops under *Api Wawamu – Rata Nagamu* (Let's grow – develop the country) programme;[9] special programmes targeting identified priority sectors (water, soil); northern agricultural development; crop forecasting; dry zone livelihood support; and national agricultural research.

A national safety net programme titled the *Samurdhi* (prosperity) programme is in operation for many years, which provides a monthly allowance for low-income households along with a scheme for encouraging savings in the formal banking sector that allows households the possibility to use it as collateral for securing microcredit.

Common themes emerging from national policies

The national policy frameworks for food and nutrition security currently in operation in South Asian countries can be classified into the following broad themes: (a) improving agricultural productivity and production systems; (b) enhancing agricultural R&D, dissemination and sharing; (c) managing food security risks and vulnerabilities; and (d) safety nets.

Improving agricultural productivity and production

The need to enhance agricultural productivity and production is a common theme of food policy frameworks in South Asia, which also have significant implications for regional cooperation. South Asian countries share many agro-ecological zones, natural resources, river-basin systems, common topographies, climatic conditions and weather. Agro-ecological zones often extend beyond national political boundaries. Mruthyunjaya et al. (2003) classified South Asian agro-ecological regions into seven: hot arid, semi-arid, sub-humid to cold arid mountain, irrigated sub-humid, high rainfall humid and sub-humid to humid coastal. The contiguous regions of Indian Punjab and Pakistani Punjab, Indian Bengal and Bangladesh, and *terai* regions of India and Nepal are some examples. These zones provide a basis for regional policy planning. Regional planning on an agro-ecological basis becomes stronger when it is noted that agricultural production in most of the productive and favourable agricultural regions with better soil and irrigation systems that fuelled the Green Revolution in the 1960s and 1970s has reached a plateau because of over-exploitation.

Identifying sustainable management practices covering soil, water and biodiversity in these areas is an imperative and can offer greater economies of scope, particularly for implementing joint agricultural development programmes in managing water, soil, biodiversity, pest management, vulnerability mapping and planning. Agro-processing and regional marketing mechanisms involving farmers and the private sector, facilitated by government entities, is another area of greater potential. Joint research efforts based on these agro-ecological regions can be a vehicle for greater regional cooperation. Such programmes may lead to identifying practical and more sustainable solutions. Regional marketing mechanisms may also allow for greater benefits to societies through the efficient use of common infrastructure (road networks and irrigation systems) and expansion of trading opportunities for agricultural inputs, outputs, technology and machinery.

Agricultural R&D, dissemination and knowledge sharing

National food and nutrition frameworks in South Asia have emphasised the need to develop appropriate technology for favourable and unfavourable areas, develop drought and flood resistant seed varieties, disseminate new technologies to farmers and share knowledge among research institutes and expertise across countries. In addition, R&D in seed production, germplasm, livestock rearing and animal production, post-harvest losses management, ago-processing and value addition, soil conservation and biodiversity management have also been identified as key areas for intervention.

The inability of smaller countries to secure adequate investment in R&D programmes as a key constraint has been recognized. This is particularly a compelling reason because of the long gestation period between investing in R&D and yielding tangible results. R&D requires persistent effort and investment commitments over many years. Long gestation periods often lead governments to give low priority to investment in R&D, owing to competing and urgent demands on government budgets but also due to lack of a long-term view of development requirements. Investment is only one part of the problem. Inadequate human resources and laboratory facilities as well as supplies on a regular basis are known to hinder progress in agricultural R&D.

Regionally coordinated agricultural R&D efforts would allow sharing of agricultural R&D across South Asia and are likely to yield better results due to greater economies of scale and scope. The SAARC process already has several such mechanisms, but their effectiveness in developing agricultural R&D is yet to be assessed and remedied, if required. Identifying and implementing a sustainable financing mechanism will require deeper probing and planning for it to become an effective instrument for sustainable food security.

Managing food security risks and vulnerability

Vulnerability is a key dimension of food insecurity (United Nations, 2012a). Risks pose threats to availability, accessibility and food absorption. Availability is affected through shortfalls in food production due to floods, droughts and inability to import or transport food. Accessibility is affected by income shortfalls, changes in prices, loss of employment and shocks emerging from international commodity markets. Weaknesses in absorption arise due to biological factors (disease prevalence), but they are often a result of environmental factors such as inadequate access to clean water, sanitation, lack of clean energy and lack of knowledge of food preparation.

These risks may affect food security temporarily, but often with long-term consequences. Transitory food insecurity caused by natural disasters requires rapid responses; but long-term and persistent food security risks, often caused by structural weaknesses, need change in economic policy and reforms. These structural weaknesses may include but are not limited to weak rural infrastructure, imperfect and fragmented markets, lack of inadequate agricultural credit, insurance schemes and periodic non-availability of agricultural inputs (seeds, pesticides and fertilizer). They often exacerbate food insecurity risks.

Some risks need to be managed nationally, but a regional approach is required when issues involve transboundary implications such as climate change, pest and disease spreads, natural disasters and policy spillovers.

The SAARC has a long list of programmes that cover such regional issues. In 2003, SAARC established a Trans-boundary Animal Diseases Coordination Unit, along with a Regional Support Unit, equipped with an epidemiology unit for the surveillance of different diseases. Although on plan, the progress in identifying regional reference laboratories for control of foot & mouth disease, *Peste des petits ruminants* and avian influenza is limited. There is unmet demand for controlling trans-boundary animal diseases through the establishment of surveillance, early warning system, regulatory policies, public awareness programs, epidemiology studies, diagnosis and control strategies. Similarly, there is potential for controlling, adapting to and mitigating climate change. Monitoring climate change at the regional level is likely to be cost-effective and will offer greater economies of scale and scope.

Ensuring food safety and quality is another area for potential cooperation, particularly in view of freer agricultural trading environment being pursued through regional trading arrangements. In such an eventuality, consumers will need reassurance that food they import and consume is safe and free from pesticide residues and other undesirable elements. For this, cultivation methods, processing, storage and transportation methods need to be monitored, and consumers ought to be informed of their quality and safety. Harmonization of policies on Sanitary and Phytosanitary (SPS) measures across countries is another area with greater potential for regional cooperation.

South Asia launched the new SAARC Food Bank (SFB) during the 14th SAARC Summit held in New Delhi. New guidelines on withdrawals and negotiations, and definitions on food shortages and quality standards of grains, have now been established. Whether the new guidelines will allow countries in the region to effectively use the SFB reserves to receive grain supplies through the system is yet to be seen. A recent review, however, suggested that even the new guidelines do not contain a clear mechanism to release stocks when disasters occur; neither does it identify storage facilities or border points where food stocks can be delivered (Robinson, 2011).

Safety nets

Safety nets programmes can directly or indirectly enhance food security, primarily through their impact on enhancing stability of consumption. All the South Asian countries, with the exception of Afghanistan and Bhutan, have implemented safety net programmes. A considerable amount of financial, human and other resources are spent on safety nets. While some programmes have contributed to enhancing food security, their true impacts are not well understood. Some countries have implemented them on experimental bases. Beneficiary targeting, outreach and depth of coverage are often difficult, but some countries such as India have a vast experience in implementing safety net programmes that could provide valuable lessons to other countries in the region. The regional forum may perhaps be the best instrument for sharing such knowledge.

Towards realising food security within the Sustainable Development Goals framework

As noted earlier, two and half years have passed since the signing of the new global development framework – the Sustainable Development Goals framework – which aims to realise food security and nutrition security goals by 2030 and 2025, respectively.

Is it a feasible target? The answer is very clearly no for the vast majority of people in South Asia, if food insecurity declines at the rates of decline each country experienced during the MDG period. Consider the case of PoU. If the PoU declines at the current rate of its decline, how many people in South Asia would still be food insecure? At the rate of decline of 1.2 per annum, South Asia's PoU will decline only to 12%, and the region will still have as many as 252 million undernourished people by the end of the SDG period. At a country level, the rates will be as high as 17% for Pakistan and Sri Lanka. Only Nepal and the Maldives will realise the 5% threshold level, which could be considered the natural rate of food insecurity for all practical purposes.

What would be the required level of decline per annum of PoU to reach the 5% food insecurity level? Purely considering the compound rate of decline per year of PoU during the 15 years from 2000 to 2015, it should decline by 7% per annum to reach the 5% level by 2030 in South Asia; 9% for Pakistan and Sri Lanka; 7% for Bangladesh and India; and 3% for the Maldives and Nepal (the current rates). There is no single, fit-for-all solutions, however, for any country to realise food security targets. Each country must devise its own policy and strategy, depending on the binding constraint(s), and the policies will vary from increased food production to improving access to food through better policies for improving income distribution, improving efficiency of food distribution systems and reducing vulnerability to various food dimensions. Given the complexity of issues, efforts are required at global, regional, national, subregional, local and household levels.

The Zero Hunger Challenge

The Zero Hunger Challenge called for stakeholders to act to ensure everyone has access to enough nutritious food all year round, no more malnutrition in pregnancy and early childhood, and no more childhood stunting[10] (United Nations, 2012b). Realizing these goals will require countries to act on some critical facets: ensuring everyone has access to food and ensuring everyone has access to food all year round. Not only will this require a broad effort at all levels, but the adoption of more rigorous measurement of food insecurity, as the PoU itself is a highly restricted definition.[11]

The Zero Hunger Challenge also called for ensuring food security all year round. Variation of food consumption within a year has been well recognized as a critical issue, especially among those who rely on daily wage earnings or seasonal agriculture. Aggregate data on food production and consumption often obscure seasonal variation of food production and consumption in any given year (Sahn, 1989).

In India, while seasonal variation of rainfall, production and consumption over different regions is large, the enormity of the Indian economy greatly dampens the incidence of covariate risk of production and consumption (Walker and Ryan, 1990). Based on the ICRISAT VLS (International Crops Research Institute for the Semi-Arid Tropics Village Level Studies) data set, Behrman and Deolalikar (1989) showed that there is a seasonal shift in food, especially proteins, consumed by households in semi-arid tropical regions in Southern India. The study further points out that paying attention to the lean season is important for nutritional security because vulnerable children are likely to be particularly exposed to malnutrition risk when food is scarcest. Seasonal variation of food consumption is further confirmed by village level studies including Pintrup-Anderson and Jaramillo (1989) on North Arcot, India.

Covariation of production and consumption can also be observed among farming communities in North-Central parts of Sri Lanka; and households employ a myriad of coping mechanisms to smoothing out consumption with limited success in the presence of high transaction costs (Wickramasinghe, 1995, 1997). In Bangladesh, this is known as *monga*, which refers to seasonal deprivation of food during the pre-harvest season of *Aman* rice; it affects mostly the farmers and labourers in the northwest region due to lack of employment opportunities during the months of September to November. This significantly increases household vulnerability to food shortages (Khandker, 2009; Salahuddin et al., 2009). Based on household income and consumption data, Khandker (ibid.) shows that average household income and consumption are much lower during *monga* season than in other seasons, and that seasonal income greatly influences seasonal consumption. It also finds that lack of income and consumption smoothing is more acute in greater Rangpur, the North West region, than in other regions, causing widespread seasonal food deprivation.

These studies show that intra-household food distribution; the nature of household preferences; the ability of the household to obtain food seasonally, as conditioned by the patterns of earnings, prices, and savings; the timing of production, trade and food stock withdrawals; and food storage and processing are all important in addressing food insecurity and its root causes.

Sustainable development goals agenda: targets and challenges

The SDG agenda for food security in South Asia is both comprehensive and challenging. First, it needs to ensure food security to an estimated 2 billion people the region will have by 2030. Doing so without damaging the environment further will determine the extent to which sustainable food security can be achieved.

SDG Goal 2 (End Hunger, achieve food security and improved nutrition and promote sustainable agriculture) has identified eight sub goals. Goals 2.1 and 2.2 indicate the need to work towards ending hunger and ensuring access to safe, nutritious and sufficient food all year round and end all forms of malnutrition by 2030. The subsequent six goals relate more to mechanisms for ending hunger and malnutrition. They include: (a) doubling agricultural productivity of small-scale food producers; (b) ensuring sustainable food production systems and implementing resilient agricultural practices; (c) maintaining genetic diversity; (d) increasing agricultural investment; (e) correcting and preventing trade restrictions and distortions in world agricultural markets; and (f) adopting measures to ensure the proper functioning of food commodity markets and their derivatives.

If *ending hunger and achieving food security for all* is not to become a mere slogan, many things should happen at the ground level. With reference to the first goal, which calls for ending hunger and ensuring access to safe, nutritious and suffi-cient food all year round by all the people, in many instances countries need to explore much more beyond some measurements to identify the true nature of food insecurity.

Doubling agricultural productivity and incomes of small-scale food producers

The call for doubling agricultural productivity and incomes of *small-scale food producers* can go a long way in addressing some of the fundamental, structural issues related to food insecurity, particularly given that this group is highly susceptible to food insecurity shocks. The question is whether doubling food production among smallholders will increase food production to meet the needs of 2 billion people estimated to live in South Asia by 2030. FAO estimated that food production will need to be increased by 100% in developing countries by 2050 to meet the rising population.

The available evidence suggests that smallholders' contribution to food production is close to or slightly above 50% of total farm output (Thapa and Guiha, 2011). Attaining even this target is becoming difficult for a number of reasons. Whether the smallholder agriculture can be revitalized so as to generate adequate surplus and achieve food security targets is an open-ended question without clear-cut answers. It appears that it is a difficult target for several reasons. First, smallholders generally occupy relatively less productive or marginal lands, often without irrigation facili-ties; hence increasing productivity of smallholder agriculture will require significant technological advances in seed varieties and new forms of agricultural practices. Second, agricultural productivity even in farmlands with irrigation has reached a plateau, or even declined in some areas including in major irrigated areas of Asia such as the Indo-Gangetic plain. This is primarily due to displacement of cereals by more profitable crops, diminishing returns to modern varieties when irrigation and fertilizer use are already at high levels and the low price of cereals that farm-ers receive relative to input costs, making additional intensification less profitable (Hazel, 2009). Third, smallholders in South Asia are characterized by small land parcels, rudimentary production technologies, weak or non-existent access to agri-cultural extension services, unorganised labour institutions and small capital/labour ratios. In countries where agricultural capital stock has grown, it has grown slowly, often at a slower rate than growth in rural populations. Thus they are unable to produce a surplus large enough to generate adequate income for the family, keeping them in perpetual poverty and food insecurity.

Ensuring sustainable food production systems

The SDG framework also calls for ensuring sustainable food production systems and implementing resilient agricultural practices for increasing agricultural productiv-ity and strengthening capacity for adaptation to climate change, extreme weather, drought, flooding and other disasters. It further calls for maintaining genetic diversity of seeds, plants and animals by managing genetic materials, establishing genetic banks at national, regional and international levels and ensure access to and fair sharing of benefits from the use of genetic resources and traditional knowledge. These mechanisms provide some critical aspects required for realizing agricultural sustainability. However, sufficient flexibility needs to be built into the framework to allow for community acceptance of sustainability goals and to accommodate community aspirations and constraints, depending on their stage of development. This is particularly noteworthy when sustainability is viewed as a process rather than a particular state, requiring each community, society or country to identify specific goals and objectives of sustainability relevant for that society. A society is unlikely to agree to and adhere to goals and objectives imposed on them from the outside. Thus, post-2015 development agendas need to include mechanisms to identify societal goals and objectives on food security that are identified based on local knowledge and available resources within the system.

Agricultural systems are likely to face stresses arising from physiological conditions (soil, temperature and rainfall), changing market conditions (commodity and inputs price changes), social aspects (labour availability and aspirations) and capacity of self-organisation (learning and social institutions and networks). Identifying factors that enhance resilience of an agricultural system and devising mechanisms to strengthen those factors will be required to ensure system sustainability. The post-2015 development agenda will need to initiate a dialogue with national authorities and regional organizations for identifying sustainable goals and objectives together with factors of system sustainability.

Managing climate change will require managing the landscape effectively. It requires natural ecosystems and agricultural production systems within each countries' political boundary to be managed effectively. However, ecological systems often spread beyond national boundaries. For example, the Ganges-Brahmaputra River Basin system in continental South Asia spreads across Bangladesh, Bhutan, India, Nepal and Myanmar. Sustainability of food production systems will demand effective management of these macro ecological systems optimally. If managed well, these systems can be a powerful force of resilience because these macro regions and ecological systems have the capacity to absorb regional climatic variations far better than their constituent subregions acting alone. Even when weather can have an impact, a large region is likely to be able to withstand food production to meet the requirements of the entire region. In this context, the post-MDG agenda should also devise mechanisms for effectively managing large ecosystems.

Climate change and its impacts have made it even more difficult for the region to eliminate food insecurity. Extreme weather events push millions into transient food insecurity, but they also create a discernible influence on the long-term viability of food production systems. This is partly owing to the geographical and topographical features of the region that opens up possibilities for high vulnerabilities to disasters such as extreme temperatures, irregular rainfall, melting of glaciers, forest fires, rising sea levels, mountain and coastal soil erosion and saline water intrusion (UNEP,

2003; UNESCAP, 2013). Water basins are overused, polluted and salinized, leading to water shortages and decreased crop production. First, variations in temperature and precipitation is likely to have a big impact on agricultural production, as 70% of food production in South Asia is linked to monsoon rains. Second, it is due to the nature of agricultural production practices being used. Agriculture is the main user of water resources, and over the years per capita water availability is estimated to have declined by 70% in the region since 1950 (Langton and Prasai, 2012). The demand for water is growing faster due to population growth, increased industrial and agricultural activities. Thus, current water-intensive agricultural practices are unlikely to be sustainable in the long run. With these effects, it is possible for 15–30% decline in productivity of most rice and cereal varieties across South Asia (IFAD, 2008) and a 4–10% decline in cereal production by the end of the 21st century (Khatun and Hossain, 2012).

A common obstacle to managing ecological systems is what was termed as the 'tragedy of the commons' (Hardin, 1968). According to Hardin, two fundamental reasons lead to the tragedy of the commons: everyone owns them, and no one does at the same time; and they are 'open to all' for using. Hardin believed that open use of common resources cannot be sustainable and are likely to end up in ecological disasters, and thus recommended private property rights as a solution. However, the tragedy of the commons is not inevitable, and there are many successful cases where common properties are used effectively without undermining their regenerative capacity (Ostrom, 2008). Design principles suggested by Ostrom (ibid.) for the sustainability of common property systems include: (a) effective monitoring by the society, rather than imposed from above; (b) graduated sanctions for those who break rules; and (c) access to cheap conflict resolution mechanisms. It is high time for individual nations, as well as South Asia as a region at large, to identify such mechanisms for managing South Asia's ecological resources for ensuring sustainability of ecosystems and food security.

Investing in agriculture and proper functioning of agricultural markets

The last three proposals – investing in agriculture, correcting and preventing trade distortions and adopting measures to ensure proper function of food markets – are undoubtedly useful for revitalizing agriculture in developing countries. The proposal refers to the Doha Development Round as the reference for taking action to correcting and preventing trade distortions. Given the failure of the Doha Round negotiations to identify a mechanism acceptable to both developing and developed countries to correct agricultural trade distortions, it is unclear at this stage how the process can be taken forward. The proposal on investment calls for investing in rural infrastructure, agricultural research and extension services, technology development and plant and livestock gene banks to enhance agricultural productive capacity in developing countries, in particular in least developed countries. While investment in enhancing agricultural productivity is undoubtedly necessary, investments are also required in enhancing market participation of smallholders in developing countries, generating and disseminating knowledge on nutritional value of nationally and locally available food varieties so as to create better food habits.

The call to adopt measures to ensure the proper functioning of food commodity markets appears to be limited to containing extreme food price volatility. Other critical functions of the market mechanisms, more specially, for attracting investment into agriculture by farmers and the corporate sector and for reducing producer transaction costs in participating in markets, which in many ways are fundamental to competitiveness of the agricultural sector, are missing from this discourse. It is difficult to attract investment into agriculture both from farmers themselves and the private corporate sector without having effective and competitive agricultural markets for inputs, outputs and services. The current systems are distorted by many factors: cartels of input suppliers, millers, transporters and wholesale traders; agricultural policies including imports and exports that are determined by political economy considerations than economic efficiency; agricultural price distortions emanating from agricultural subsidies; and anti-agricultural bias created by incentives to industrial and services sectors. As Gulati and Pursell (2008) showed, that the relative rate of assistance (RRA) provided to agriculture has been negative in Bangladesh, India, Pakistan and Sri Lanka with the exception of four years in India since 2004. This indicates that incentives for rural sectors have been less than incentives provided for their non-agricultural tradable sectors.[12] Recent research also indicate the need to link agriculture with industrial and services sectors for enhancing productivity, raising farmer incomes and allowing for broad-based structural transformation to take root in developing countries (Losch et al., 2012). All these factors have contributed to create a large wedge between farm gate and consumer prices. This became clearly evident during the 2007/08 food price crisis, where high international food prices transmitted to national consumer prices almost at the same level, but with limited or no gain to producers (Dawe, 2009).

Structural transformation in agriculture – a missing link

Ensuring the proper functioning of food commodity markets and their derivatives will require a broad-based approach to agricultural development encompassing structural transformation in agriculture and removing anti-agricultural bias in agricultural policy. This is because agriculture's role in economic development has changed from the traditional role it expected to play. As noted by Byerlee et al. (2009), globalization, integrated value chains, rapid technological and institutional innovations and environmental constraints have changed the context for agriculture's role. Thus a new paradigm where agriculture's multiple functions, including its role in triggering growth, reducing poverty, narrowing income disparities, providing food security and delivering environmental services need to be recognized.

Fulfilling multiple roles will require agriculture to go through radical structural transformation. The current structure of agriculture consisting of a very low share of agricultural value added in GDP with a high share of agricultural employment as a share of total employment cannot be sustainable because the current gap implies a widening poverty gap between those in agriculture and other sectors. In other words, those in agriculture are becoming poorer compared to those in other sectors. The current structure encourages agricultural labour to move out of it, usually to urban areas, than into productive agricultural activities (Mazumdar, 1987); discourages young and talented people from entering into agriculture; and discourages the farmers and the private sector in investing in agriculture. As a result, agriculture continues to rely on old production and processing technologies, trapping a large population in agriculture without being able to move out of poverty. The combined effect is felt through the inability of the agricultural sector to become a modern, market-oriented sector (Lewis, 1954; Kuznets, 1973; Chenery et al., 1986) and thus not being able to allocate resources according to their competitive advantages (Timmer, 2005). The first step for triggering a structural transformation is to remove anti-agricultural discrimination created by trade and other policies that support industrial and services sectors.

Notes

1 The opinions expressed in this chapter are those of the author and do not necessarily reflect official views or policies of the Food and Agriculture Organisation of the United Nations or its affiliated institutions.
2 South Asia includes Afghanistan, Bangladesh, Bhutan, India, the Maldives, Nepal, Pakistan and Sri Lanka. Data limitations prevented Afghanistan from considering in the analysis.
3 Prevalence of Undernourishment (PoU) expresses the probability that a randomly selected individual from a reference population consumes insufficient number of calories to cover his or her energy requirement for an *active and healthy life*. The indicator is computed by comparing the probability of *habitual daily Dietary Energy Consumption* with a threshold of Minimum Dietary Energy Requirement. This is adopted under the SDG framework (SDG Target 2.1/indicator 2.1.1).
4 Percentage of children between 0–5 years of age as a percentage of children in the same age group is measured under each of the three measures taking into account those less than –2 standard deviation of the WHO child growth standards median): wasting (weight-for-height); stunting (weight-for-age); underweight (weight-for-age).
5 Following the FAO geographic grouping system, this value includes Iran (Islamic Republic of) as part of South Asia.
6 The FAO methodology of estimating the measure known as the Average Dietary Energy Supply Adequacy by combined food demand and supply side factors. Rather than relying on actual food demand, FAO relies on estimating physical food requirement of a country by estimating calorie requirements of the population to meet biological food energy requirements, which is conditioned by age, sex and level of physical activity. This is known as the average dietary energy requirement (ADER). Domestic food supply on the other hand is estimated by adding local production, imports and changes in food stocks and subtracting exports. This is equivalent to Dietary Energy Supply (DES). The ratio between DES and ADER gives the Average Dietary Energy Supply Adequacy (ADESA) ratio. This provides an estimate the adequacy of food supply to meet a nation's biological food requirements.
7 It can be observed that countries that have reached 5% PoU invariably have ADESA rates above 115 at minimum, but the average value is 120%. There are exceptions, however. Five countries, namely Moldova, Cyprus, Bulgaria, Japan and Slovakia, have reached 5% PoU

without reaching ADESA of 115%. On the other hand, there are four countries (Guinea, Guinea-Bissau, Cote d'Ivoire and China) that have exceeded ADESA of 120%, but PoU has not declined.

8 Joshi (2013) provides an excellent review, analysis and constraints to implementing the bill.

9 The annual report of the Ministry of Agriculture has identified 23 projects implemented under this programme prior to 2012 and additional 15 programmes proposed to be implemented in subsequent years (Government of Sri Lanka, 2014).

10 The Zero Hunger Challenge also requests countries to ensure that the food systems everywhere are sustainable, that greater opportunities for smallholder farmers to raise their productivity and income exist, and that they can cut losses throughout the food value chain.

11 Even if a country could realise 5% of PoU, it does not cover everyone because, by definition, PoU is a measure of chronic undernourishment, limited to measuring food security among people with a relatively moderate coefficient of 155 of physical activity level, which may not cover calorie requirements of daily labourers as in the measure known as the Prevalence of Food Inadequacy (PoFI). The methodology for estimating the commonly used PoU is designed to estimate food insecurity with the most commonly available data, and to avoid overestimation, based on the dietary energy requirement (MDER) coefficient, which depends on the physical activity levels (PAL). FAO calculations use the MDER coefficient of 155, which corresponds to a sedentary lifestyle. While this avoids the possibility for the undernourished group to include well-nourished people, it opens up for the possibility to ignore people who may be at risk of not having adequate access to food to meet their level of physical activity. To provide a measure that may also include this group, FAO estimates the Prevalence of Food Inadequacy (POFI) by setting the Physical Activity Level (PAL) coefficient to 175 rather than 155. By definition they cannot be considered chronically undernourished, but they are likely to have been affected by insufficient food. The new measure estimates the percentage of the population at risk of not covering the food requirements associated with normal physical activity and the chronically undernourished people. This measure would indicate that 30% of people in Sri Lanka; a quarter of the population in Bangladesh, India, Nepal and Pakistan; and 20% in the Maldives suffer from food inadequacy (see FAO, 2013).

12 This study covered the period up to 1955–2004. The policy environment has changed significantly in the recent past, hence the results may not necessarily be applicable for all the countries. Continued lacklustre performance of the agricultural sector compared to industrial and services sectors, especially the agricultural sector's inability to attract investment, may mean that anti-agricultural bias of policy may not have changed much in recent years; they may have worsened.

References

Ahmad, M. and U. Farooq (Winter 2010), 'The State of Food Security in Pakistan: Future Challenges and Coping Strategies', *Pakistan Development Review*, Vol. 49(4), Part II, pp. 903–923.

Behrman, J. R. and A. B. Deolalikar (1989), 'Seasonal Demands for Nutrient Intakes and Health Status in Rural South India', in *Seasonal Variability in Third World Agriculture: The Consequences for Food Security*, David E. Sahn (Ed.), Johns Hopkins University Press, Baltimore.

Business Recorder (2014), 'National Food and Nutrition Security Policy on the Cards', 23 April 2014.

Byerlee, D., A. D. Janvry and E. Sadoulet (2009), 'Agriculture for Development: Toward a New Paradigm', *Annual Review of Resource Economics*, Vol. 1(1), pp. 15–35.

Chenery, H. B., R. Sherman and S. Moises (1986), *Industrialization and Growth: A Comparative Study*, Oxford University Press, Oxford.

Dawe, D. (2009), 'Cereal Price Transmission in Several Large Asian Countries During the Global Food Crisis', *Asian Journal of Agriculture and Development*, Vol. 6, pp. 1–12.

Deaton, A. (1993), *Understanding Consumption*, Clarendon Press, Oxford.

Desai, S. B., A. Dubey, B. L. Joshi, M. Sen, A. Shariff and E. Vanneman (Eds.) (2010), *Human Development in India: Challenges for a Society in Transition*, Oxford University Press, New Delhi.

FAO (2008), 'Regional Strategies and Programme for Food Security in the SAARC Member States', Food and Agriculture Organisation and SAARC Secretariat.

FAO (2017), 'The State of Food Insecurity in the World', Food and Agriculture Organization of the United Nations, Rome.

FAO (2018), 'FAOSTAT', Food and Agriculture Organization of the United Nations. Database available at: http://www.fao.org/faostat/en/#home (accessed on 17 March 2018).

Government of Bangladesh (2008), 'National Food Policy Plan of Action (2008–2015)', Food Planning and Monitoring Unit (FPMU), Ministry of Food and Disaster Management, Dhaka, Bangladesh.

Government of Bhutan (2014), 'Food and Nutrition Security Policy of the Kingdom of Bhutan', Gross National Happiness Commission, Royal Government of Bhutan, Thimphu. Available at: www.gnhc.gov.bt/wp-content/uploads/2014/07/FNS_Policy_Bhutan_Changed.pdf

Government of India (2013), 'The National Food Security Ordinance', Ministry of Law and Justice, Government of India, New Delhi. Available at: www.prsindia.org/uploads/media/Ordinances/Food per cent20Security per cent20Ordinance per cent202013.pdf

Government of Maldives (2006), 'Agricultural Development Master Plan (2006–2020)', Ministry of Fisheries and Agriculture.

Government of Nepal (2010), 'Nepal Agriculture and Food Security Investment Plan', Government of Nepal, Kathmandu.

Government of Sri Lanka (2010), 'National Nutrition Policy', Ministry of Healthcare and Nutrition, Colombo.

Government of Sri Lanka (2014), 'Sri Lanka National Agricultural Policy', Ministry of Agriculture, Colombo.

Griffiths, P. and M. Bentley (2005), 'Women in Higher Socio-Economic Status Are More Likely to Be Overweight in Karnataka, India', *European Journal of Clinical Nutrition*, Vol. 59(10), pp. 1217–1220.

Gulati, A. and G. Pursell (2008), 'Distortions to Agricultural Incentives in India and Other South Asia', World Bank Agricultural Distortions Working Paper, No. 63, The World Bank.

Hardin, G. (1968), 'The Tragedy of the Commons', *Science*, Vol. 162(3859), pp. 1243–1248.

Hazel, P. B. R. (2009), 'The Asian Green Revolution', IFPRI Discussion Paper, No. 00911, International Food Policy Research Institute.

Huang, H., M. V. Lampe and F. V. Tongeren (2011), 'Climate Change and Trade in Agriculture', *Food Policy*, Vol. 36(S1), pp. S9–S13.

International Fund for Agricultural Development (2008), 'Climate Change Impacts – South Asia', Note Prepared Under The Global Mechanism: United Nations Convention to Combat Desertification.

Jodha, N. S. (1978), 'Effectiveness of Farmers' Adjustment to Risk', *Economic and Political Weekly*, Special Issue on Agriculture, A38–A48.

Joshi, P. K. (2013), 'National Food Security Bill and Need for a Stronger Implementation Strategy', Governance Knowledge Centre. Available at: http://indiagovernance.gov.in/thinkpiece/?thinkpiece=5

Khandker, S. R. (2009), 'Poverty and Income Seasonality in Bangladesh', Policy Research Working Paper, No. 4923. The World Bank, Washington, DC.

Khatun, F. and S. Hossain (2012), 'Adapting to Climate Change: Issues for South Asia', South Asia Watch on Trade, Economics and Environment (SAWTEE), Kathmandu.

Kuznets, S. (1973), 'Modern Economic Growth: Findings and Reflections', *American Economic Review*, Vol. 63(3), pp. 247–258.

Langton, N. and S. Prasai (2012), 'Will Conflicts Over Water Scarcity Shape South Asia's Future?', *CSIS Issue Perspective*, Vol. 2(1), Centre for Strategic and International Studies.

Lewis, A. (1954), 'Economic Development With Unlimited Supplies of Labour', *The Manchester School*, Vol. 22(2), pp. 139–191.

Losch, B., S. Freguin-Gresh and E. T. White (2012), 'Structural Transformation Revisited: Challenges for Late Developing Countries in a Globalizing World', World Bank.

Mazumdar, D. (1987), 'Rural – Urban Migration in Developing Countries', in *Handbook on Population and Family Economics*, M. R. Rozensweig and O. Stark (Eds.), Vol. 1A, Elsevier, Washington, DC.

Mittal, S. and D. Sethi (2009), 'Food Security in South Asia: Issues and Opportunities', ICRIER Working Paper Series, No. 240, Indian Council for Research on International Economic Relations, New Delhi.

Mruthyunjaya, S. Pal and R. Saxena (2003), 'Agricultural Research Priorities for South Asia', NCAER Policy Paper, No. 20, National Centre for Agricultural Economics and Policy, New Delhi.

Olson, R. O. (1960), 'Impact and Implications of Foreign Surplus Disposal on Underdeveloped Countries', *Journal of Farm Economics*, Vol. 42, pp. 1042–1051.

Ostrom, E. (2008), 'Design Principles of Robust Property-Rights Institutions: What Have We Learned?', Working Paper 08–19, Workshop in Political Theory and Policy Analysis, Indiana University.

Pintrup-Anderson, P. and M. Jaramillo (1989), 'The Impact of Drought and Technological Change in Rice Production on Intra-Year Fluctuations in Food Consumption: The Case of North Arcot', in *Seasonal Variability in Third World Agriculture: The Consequences for Food Security*, D. Sahn (Ed.), Chapter 16, pp. 264–284, Johns Hopkins University Press, Baltimore.

Rahman, Z. H., L. A. Choudhury and K. S. Ali (2011), 'Social Safety Nets in Bangladesh: Review of Issues and Analytical Inventory', Volume 1, Power and Participation Research Centre and UNDP.

Robinson, M. J. D. (2011), 'Regional Grain Banking for Food Security: Past and Present Realities From SAARC Initiatives', Policy Paper, CUTS International, Jaipur.

Sahn, D. (Ed.) (1989), *Seasonal Variability in Third World Agriculture: The Consequences for Food Security*, Johns Hopkins University Press, Baltimore.

Salahuddin, A., M. G. Neogi and N. P. Magor (2009), 'Addressing *Monga* Through a Collective Regional Forum Response in the Northwest of Bangladesh', Paper presented in the International Conference Entitled 'Seasonality Revisited: Perspectives on Seasonal Poverty', Institute of Development Studies, United Kingdom, 8–10 July 2009.

SAWTEE (2012), 'Managing Climate Change, Water Resources, and Food Security in South Asia', Paper presented at the 6th South Asia Economic Summit, Colombo, Sri Lanka, 2–4 September 2013.

Thapa, G. and R. Guiha (2011), 'Smallholder Farming in Asia and the Pacific: Challenges and Opportunities', Paper presented at the IFAD Conference on New Directions for Smallholder Agriculture, Rome, Italy, 24–25 January 2011.

Timmer, P. (2005), 'Agriculture and Pro-Poor Growth: An Asian Perspective', Working Paper, No. 63, Centre for Global Development.

Tomkins, A. and F. Watson (1989), 'Malnutrition and Infection: A Review', Policy Discussion Paper, No. 5, United Nations.

UNEP (2003), 'GEO Yearbook 2003', UNEP United Nations Environmental Programme.

UNESCAP (2013), 'Statistical Yearbook for Asia and the Pacific 2013', United Nations Economic and Social Commission for Asia and the Pacific, Bangkok.

United Nations (2011), 'The Millennium Development Goals Report 2011', United Nations, New York.

United Nations (2012a), 'Rio+20 Outcome Document: The Future We Want', United Nations, New York. Available at: www.uncsd2012.org/rio20inthenews.html

United Nations (2012b), 'The Zero Hunger Challenge'. Available at: www.un.org/zerohunger/

United Nations (2014a), 'Outcome Document – Open Working Group on Sustainable Development Goals', Introduction to the proposals of the Open Working Group for Sustainable Development Goals. Available at: http://sustainabledevelopment.un.org/owg.html

United Nations (2014b), 'The Millennium Development Goals Report 2014', United Nations, New York.

Walker, T. S. and J. G. Ryan (1990), *Village and Household Economies in India's Semi-Arid Tropics*, The Johns Hopkins University, Baltimore.

WHO (2013), 'Global Nutrition Policy Overview: What Does It Take to Scale Up Nutrition Action?' World Health Organization.

Wickramasinghe, U. (1995), 'Nature and Causes of Coping Strategies Among Low-Income Rural Households', Unpublished PhD Thesis, Department of Economics, University of Hawaii at Manoa.

Wickramasinghe, U. (1997), 'Choice of Coping Strategies Among Low-Income Rural Households Under Transaction Costs', *Vidyodaya Journal of Social Science*, Sri Lanka, Vol. 8(1 & 2).

Wickramasinghe, U. (2000), 'Services Trade as a "New Frontier" in South Asia: Is the Optimism Warranted?', *South Asia Economic Journal*, Vol. 1(2), SAGE Publications India.

World Bank (2018), 'World Development Indicators', The World Bank Group. Database available at: https://datacatalog.worldbank.org/dataset/world-development-indicators (accessed on 17 March 2018).

TABLE 2A.1 Domestic supply of food in selected countries of South Asia, 2011

Item	Bangladesh					India					Nepal					Pakistan					Sri Lanka				
	Total Supply (mt)	Local Prod (%)	Imp (%)	Stocks (%)	Exp (%)	Total Supply (mt)	Local Prod (%)	Imp (%)	Stocks (%)	Exp (%)	Total Supply (mt)	Local Prod (%)	Imp (%)	Stocks (%)	Exp (%)	Total Supply (mt)	Local Prod (%)	Imp (%)	Stocks (%)	Exp (%)	Total Supply (mt)	Local Prod (%)	Imp (%)	Stocks (%)	Exp (%)
Cereals – Excluding Beer	34855	102.6	14	-17	0	215538	109	0	-4	5	7067	100.8	6.1	-7	0	31231	116	0	7	23	3519	78	42	-7	12
Starchy Roots	8695	99.2	0	0	1	51179	101	0	0	1	2798	95.28	4.7	0	0	3577	111	1	0	12	538	74	29	0	3
Sugar Crops	4671	100	0	0	0	342382	100	0	0	0	2718	100	0	0	0	55330	100	0	0	0	729	100	0	0	0
Sugar & Sweeteners	2031	36.4	76	-10	3	29353	108	1	2	10	118	113.6	24	-36	0	4593	102	3	-3	1	604	6	103	-9	0
Pulses	621	37.8	62	0	0	20677	85	16	0	1	315	89.52	18	0	7	1415	57	43	0	0	237	9	96	0	4
Treenuts	142	74.6	67	0	41	1690	70	58	0	29	53	26.42	102	0	28	126	29.4	72	0	1	38	100	8	0	8
Oil crops	840	58.2	44	0	2	49911	104	0	-1	3	512	75.78	33	-9	0	6370	87.3	16	-3	0	1820	115	0	0	15
Vegetable Oils	1580	10.1	91	0	1	16414	57	49	-2	4	352	46.31	56	0	1	3063	34.4	73	-3	4	251	25	75	1	2
Vegetables	4332	91.6	9	0	0	105174	102	0	0	2	3366	97.45	2.8	0	0	5150	104	6	0	10	950	80	22	0	2
Fruits – Excluding Wine	4039	91.3	9	0	0	73712	100	1	0	1	1500	99.67	6.1	0	6	5684	110	4	0	14	865	95	8	0	4
Stimulants	65	93.8	9	0	2	733	175	17	6	98	11	154.5	18	-56	82	125	0	101	0	1	29	1155	83	0	1134
Spices	470	83	18	0	0	3733	115	3	0	17	169	155	15	0	14	281	69	36	0	6	109	63	61	0	24
Alcoholic Beverages	4	0	100	0	0	5933	102	1	0	3	53	88.68	13	0	0	20	2035	0	-200	1735	133	74	28	0	2
Meat	625	100	0	0	0	5163	121	0	0	21	327	100.6	0	0	1	2733	102	0	0	2	132	101	2	0	3
Offals	91	100	0	0	0	537	102	0	0	2	51	100	0	0	0	332	103	0	0	3	14	100	0	0	0
Animal fats	52	88.5	12	0	0	3670	101	0	0	1	40	82.5	18	0	3	893	92.4	8	0	0	18	11	106	0	11
Eggs	284	100	0	0	0	3425	102	0	0	2	36	100	0	0	0	592	100	0	0	1	68	99	1	0	0
Milk – Excluding Butter	4035	86.7	13	0	0	123619	100	0	0	0	1671	98.44	1.6	0	0	36897	99.3	1	0	0	908	25	76	0	0
Fish, Seafood	3063	102	2	0	3	7882	113	1	0	13	57	87.82	1.2	0	0	394	151	1	0	52	607	73	31	0	4

Source: FAOSTAT

TABLE 2A.2 Domestic utilization of food in selected countries of South Asia, 2011

Item	Bangladesh				India				Nepal				Pakistan				Sri Lanka			
	Total Supply (mt)	Food (%)	Manuf (%)	Waste (%)	Total Supply (mt)	Food (%)	Manuf (%)	Waste (%)	Total Supply (mt)	Food (%)	Manuf (%)	Waste (%)	Total Supply (mt)	Food (%)	Manuf (%)	Waste (%)	Total Supply (mt)	Food (%)	Manuf (%)	Waste (%)
Cereals – Excluding Beer	34855	83	0	6	215538	86	0	5	7067	72	0	11	31231	80	0	3	3519	89	1	5
Starchy Roots	8695	83	0	10	51179	77	0	17	2798	78	0	14	3577	85	0	10	538	74	0	7
Sugar Crops	4671	6	94	0	342382	3	88	2	2718	35	50	10	55330	10	80	0	729	54	46	0
Sugar & Sweeteners	2031	62	11	0	29353	92	0	0	118	100	0	0	4593	100	0	0	604	96	0	0
Pulses	621	95	0	3	20677	84	0	3	315	91	0	4	1415	80	0	2	237	88	0	3
Treenuts	142	95	0	6	1690	99	0	1	53	100	0	0	126	101	0	0	38	61	0	0
Oil crops	840	24	72	3	49911	16	68	4	512	4	93	2	6370	5	66	2	1820	77	23	0
Vegetable Oils	1580	60	0	0	16414	65	0	0	352	78	0	0	3063	69	0	0	251	24	0	0
Vegetables	4332	92	0	8	105174	94	0	6	3366	91	0	10	5150	96	0	4	950	89	0	10
Fruits – Excluding Wine	4039	91	0	9	73712	85	0	14	1500	97	0	5	5684	97	0	4	865	89	0	11
Stimulants	65	98	0	2	733	98	0	2	11	100	0	0	125	98	0	2	29	107	0	0
Spices	470	99	0	1	3733	97	0	3	169	99	0	2	281	99	0	1	109	100	0	2
Alcoholic Beverages	4	100	0	0	5933	42	0	0	53	91	0	0	20	70	0	0	133	82	0	0
Meat	625	100	0	0	5163	100	0	0	327	101	0	0	2733	100	0	0	132	100	0	0
Offals	91	100	0	0	537	100	0	0	51	100	0	0	332	100	0	0	14	100	0	0
Animal fats	52	96	0	0	3670	95	0	0	40	98	0	0	893	100	0	0	18	17	0	0
Eggs	284	82	0	10	3425	85	0	0	36	86	0	3	592	83	0	10	68	84	0	4
Milk – Excluding Butter	4035	79	0	8	123619	79	0	4	1671	81	0	5	36897	85	0	10	908	94	0	1
Fish, Seafood	3063	98	0	0	7882	91	0	0	57	95	0	0	394	89	0	0	607	90	0	0

Source: FAOSTAT

3

POTENTIAL FOR INTRAREGIONAL TRADE IN FOOD PRODUCTS IN SOUTH ASIA

Indra Nath Mukherji

Introduction: case for intra-regional trade in food products

Food deficit may arise due to a multitude of reasons. A number of supply side or demand side factors, or a combination of both, can trigger shortage of food availability (Iqbal and Amjad, 2010). While short-term fluctuations or long-term structural shifts in production may cause supply side shocks, changing patterns of consumption and rising real income can cause sudden and unexpected demand surges. It is difficult for countries with limited access to international markets for food products to insulate themselves from risks of unexpected shortages arising out of variations in domestic production or disruptions in the food supply chains due to exogenous input price shocks, oil price hikes or rising cost of post-harvest processing and marketing. Being a sensitive disaster-prone subregion, South Asia faces high risks of short-term supply shocks of this nature. Also, high rates of population growth and natural resource degradation make South Asia one of the most vulnerable regions to the impacts of climate change characterized by increased intensity and frequency of extreme climate events.

Given the multi-faceted factors affecting food availability in the subregion, open international trade in food products can help to minimize both short-term and long-term supply side risks. Though trade can only partially address the problem, certain favourable factors exist in the region that point to the possibility of expansion of trade in food products. First, it may be noted that the major cereal exporting and importing countries are within the region. Second, notwithstanding the restrictiveness in intra-regional agricultural trade, the share of such trade in the region's global trade is considerably higher.[1] However, during the peak of global food crisis in 2007–08, intra-agricultural trade among the South Asian countries declined drastically as food surplus countries such as India and Pakistan imposed export bans on their cereal exports. Even during the most serious phase of the crisis, institutional arrangement such as the SAARC Food Bank could not be made operational. Hence there remains considerable scope for further cooperation for expansion of intraregional food products trade through trade liberalization and well-designed regional stockholding policies.

This chapter examines the possibilities of expanding intraregional trade in food products by comparing the patterns of export and import of food products by South Asian countries. The second section provides the methodology for this study using UN Comtrade data. The third section examines the changing structure of intraregional food products trade of South Asian countries in terms of both commodity composition and in terms of geographical diversification. The fourth section identifies food categories and their products with high export potential. The fifth section examines tariff restrictions to trade on identified products, particularly on sensitive lists with high export potential. The last section provides a summary and highlights some major recommendations of the study.

Methodology

Various data sources have been used to undertake the present study. For the detailed analysis, UN Comtrade data has been used extensively to see the trade pattern of South Asia Countries (SACs) in the identified food products both at intra- and extra regional trade. For analysis of tariff barriers in SACs, relevant customs notifications issued by the national governments have been used. Declarations and notifications on sensitive lists available at SAARC Secretariat are also utilized.

Creation of database for food products trade

Trade data is generated accessing UN Comtrade database available under World Integrated Trade Solution (WITS). A database for all food products traded covering the period 2003–2012 has been created containing all food products traded under 6-digit 2002 HS classification (exported/imported) between Member States of SAR as also with the rest of the world (RoW). The trading partners beyond the region have also been identified. In all 0.4 million records have been generated.

The data so generated has helped us to map how each food category and products contained therein are traded with other countries in the region and with the rest of world. In order to obviate the effects of seasonal/yearly variations, the trade flows are generated for the years 2008–12 and the averages for two sub periods, viz. (2008–10) and (2010–12) are analyzed.

Period of analysis/selection of data classification

The food trade in South Asia comprises various types of heterogeneous products. Hence to study the nature of trade, food products are classified into various types.

For this purpose, the 2002 Harmonised System of Trade Classification has been used as available in 2014.

The period of analysis is based on the data availability for HS 2002 classification as obtained from UN Comtrade Database as accessed from World Bank World Integrated Trade Solution (WITS) website.[2]

HS 2002 classification provided data for the period 2003–12 for India, Pakistan, Maldives and Sri Lanka. Reported data for Afghanistan was for the period 2008–12. Mirror data accessed from all countries trade with Afghanistan revealed highly inflated data compared to the reported one. Reported data for Bangladesh was available from 2003–07. Mirror data for Bangladesh was obtained for the period 2008–12. The mirror data appeared to be in alignment with the reported one. Bhutan's reported data was available from 2005–11. Mirror data for Bhutan was obtained for 2003, 2004, and 2012. There appeared to be considerable under reporting of data. Nepal's reported data was available for 2003 and from 2008–11. Mirror data for Nepal obtained for 2004–08 and for 2012 reflected considerable under reporting. Given the nature of data availability, it was decided to cover the period 2008–12 for intensive analysis.

Apart for the period where this study uses mirror data, the participating countries' reporting data is used. But this is not to state that the reporting countries data will be free of errors. It is possible that the fob export figures of the one country may differ more than the cif-fob price difference of its importing partner country. For instance, discrepancies may result due to time lag if exports are registered in one year and the corresponding imports in the following year. It may arise due to misallocation of a partner country or a product for a reporting country. This only affects bilateral trade or respectively detailed product levels, not the overall trade. Besides re-exports or transit trade may be taken into account by some countries. Illegal trade can also contribute in a substantial manner when the importing/exporting country fails to record the imports/exports.

Classifying traded food products for product coverage

Since the study focusses on the role of trade in food security, it was decided to cover only food products and not agricultural products as is often studied in food security analyzes. The WTO classification of agriculture was considered for initial analysis. Under this list those products falling under the heading non-food were excluded. Tobacco and alcohol-based products were considered non-essential, non-merit food products and hence eliminated. Similarly, beverages such as tea and coffee were considered non-essential for food security and hence eliminated from the analysis.

Further, the objective was to classify food products in terms of their nutrient value. Hence the classification was made under the heads (broadly ranked in order of their importance and classified in terms of nutrient values) (Table 3.1).

The classification exhausts all food products excluding the non-merit products mentioned earlier and constitutes the universe for this study containing record of

TABLE 3.1 Selected food categories and their nutrient values

Sl. no	Food type	Nutrient value
1	Fruits and vegetables	Vitamin C, fibre, thiamine, riboflavin, B-6, niacin, foliate A and C, phytochemical fibre
2	Cereals	Carbohydrates
3	Sugar and related products	carbohydrate, vitamin C, potassium
4	Spices	antioxidants, minerals and vitamins
5	Processed foods	convenience food fortified with beneficial vitamins and minerals
6	Meat and fish	protein, fat, minerals
7	Fats and oils	essential fatty acids
8	Oilseeds	fats, proteins, carbohydrates
9	Fodder	livestock food
10	Milk products	calcium, vitamin D
11	Honey and non-alcoholic beverages	carbohydrates, low calorie vitamins and minerals

Source: Author's compilation from various sources

trade flows of 0.4 million food products, including quantity traded and SACs trade with individual countries in the rest of the world.

To understand the nature of trade flows among South Asian Countries (SACs), the following exercises were undertaken.

1 Food trade balance among countries in SAR and with the RoW, both in terms of total bilateral trade flows and trade flows in specific product categories and all identified products within each category.
2 The composition of trade (both exports and imports) of the region as a whole and of individual countries in the region is examined over two equal time periods: (a) 2008–10 and (b) 2010–12 in terms of identified product categories. The commodity composition is examined both in terms of composition of product categories and their geographic source and destination within the SAR.

Identifying products for trade liberalization

At the first stage a set of all identified food products at 6-digit (HS 2002) level of classification under each classified food category is prepared;

1 From the data so generated, the reporting countries' trade balance for each product with RoW and RoSA is highlighted giving an idea of the export capability in the identified products.

2 The country level and regional demand for each product category in the region with RoW is indicated to reflect the size of partner countries' market.

3 The reporting country's existing exports of all identified products to the RoSA are highlighted to indicate the existing size of regional market.

4 The Additional Market Access Frontier (AMAF) for each product is estimated as being the minimum of the products supply to RoW and regional demand from RoW. This brings out the trade frontier which could be exploited to deepen market within the region under static conditions. Once the AMAF is calculated at 6-digit level, and then it is aggregated at different product categories mentioned earlier (see Technical Appendix).[3]

5 The products are ranked in descending order of AMAF under each product category and the top ones having AMAF over US$ 1 million are identified for more detailed analysis (such as existing trade barriers on them by its partner countries in the region).

6 By aggregating values of products at 6-digit level, under each category, the AMAF of each product category is finally estimated and presented in descending value of AMAF for each reporting country. This brings out a macro perceptive of potential in food products trade deriving from micro analysis (bottom up approach).

7 Since Nepal has free trade with India in primary commodities, trade between India and Bhutan is free, and since these two countries have very minimal trade with countries other than India in the region, detailed analysis of food products trade for these two countries has not been undertaken.

Structure of intraregional trade of South Asia countries

Commodity composition

In this section we examine the changing structure and composition of identified food products trade among SACs. The first part of this section examines the commodity composition of each country's exports and imports to and from the region both in value and percentage terms. Table 3.2 presents the trends. The changing commodity composition of each SAARC Member States trade discussed draws from this table.

It will be observed that during the periods of reference, Afghanistan's major exports were food and vegetables, even though this share was seen to be declining. Bangladesh's major exports during these reference periods were meat and fish (notably fish) and this share was noticed to be increasing. India's major exports over the two reference periods were fruit and vegetables, sugar and related products, cereals and spices. The share of sugar and related products was seen to be increasing. Maldives predominant and only major export product group was fish and meat (notably fish).

Pakistan's most important food product group exported was cereals, whose share increased over the two reference periods. Fruits and vegetables were the next most

TABLE 3.2 Commodity composition of intra-regional trade of South Asian countries food products categories (average 2008–10 and 2010–12)

Countries	Food categories	Exports				Imports			
		Period 2008–10		Period 2010–12		Period 2008–10		Period 2010–12	
		Value (US$ mn)	Per cent	Value (US$ mn)	Per cent	Value (US$ mn)	Per cent	Value (US$ mn)	Per cent
Afghanistan	Fruits and vegetables	479	96	205	75	8	6	7	2
	Spices	13	2	57	21	1	1	–	–
	Fodder	8	2	8	3	–	–	–	–
	Meat & fish	–	–	2	1	23	17	21	8
	Honey and non-alcoholic beverages	–	–	–	–	25	18	40	15
	Milk products	–	–	–	–	23	17	33	12
	Sugar and related products	–	–	–	–	31	23	44	16
	Cereals	–	–	–	–	25	18	128	47
Bangladesh	Fruits and vegetables	28	17	14	4	829	36	635	23
	Honey and non-alcoholic beverages	7	4	14	4	829	36	635	23
	Meat and fish	106	65	163	47	31	1	45	2
	Sugar and related products	4	3	2	1	285	12	449	16
	Oil and fats	2	1	25	7	11	1	–	–
	Processed foods	12	7	14	4	41	2	86	3

(Continued)

TABLE 3.2 (Continued)

Countries	Food categories	Exports				Imports			
		Period 2008–10 Value (US$ mn)	Per cent	Period 2010–12 Value (US$ mn)	Per cent	Period 2008–10 Value (US$ mn)	Per cent	Period 2010–12 Value (US$ mn)	Per cent
	Milk products	–	–	1	1	56	2	42	2
	Cereals	–	–	–	–	891	39	1,263	45
	Fodder	–	–	–	–	–	1	32	1
India	Sugar and related products	1,149	25	1,724	30	6	1	–	–
	Cereals	1,022	23	1,228	22	–	–	–	–
	Fodder	26	1	65	1	115	9	116	9
	Fruits and vegetables	1,249	28	1,262	22	512	42	570	43
	Spices	417	9	558	10	242	20	270	20
	Processed foods	181	4	266	5	52	4	41	3
	Oilseeds	176	4	237	4	7	1	–	–
	Milk products	102	2	86	2	6	1	5	1
	Meat and fish	190	4	216	4	109	9	167	13
	Oils and fats	–	–	–	–	81	6	37	3
Maldives	Meat and fish	37	99	23	99	32	15	45	18
	Processed meat	–	–	–	1	2	1	3	1
	Sugar and related products	–	–	–	–	18	9	24	9
	Cereals	–	–	–	–	54	26	55	30
	Fruits and vegetables	–	–	–	–	68	32	77	30

						2	1	10	4
Pakistan	Honey and non–alcoholic beverages	—	—	—	—	8	4	6	3
	Milk products	—	—	—	—	22	10	28	11
	Processed foods	—	—	—	—	4	2	5	2
	Spices	—	—	—	—	57	7	26	2
	Cereals	733	37	1,511	43	157	19	210	20
	Sugar and related products	142	7	128	4	72	9	67	6
	Spices	18	1	19	1	—	—	—	—
	Processed foods	91	5	166	5	—	—	—	—
	Oils and fats	340	17	491	14	3	1	6	1
	Milk products	108	6	178	5	11	1	12	1
	Meat and fish	55	3	89	2	453	54	610	58
	Fruits and vegetables	426	22	855	24	—	—	—	—
	Honey and non–alcoholic beverages	24	1	49	1	—	—	—	—
	Fodder	10	1	30	1	—	—	—	=
	Oilseeds	—	—	—	—	73	9	112	11
Sri Lanka	Spices	163	37	210	45	164	16	210	14
	Fodder	110	25	127	27	12	1	17	1
	Cereals	3	1	8	2	150	15	218	15
	Fruits and vegetables	53	12	60	13	303	29	324	21
	Meat and fish	11	2	14	3	95	9	89	6
	Oilseeds	—	—	—	—	73	9	112	11
	Oils and fats	53	12	7	1	8	1	—	—
	Processed foods	26	6	32	7	61	6	65	4
	Processed meat and fish	5	1	5	1	—	—	—	—

(Continued)

TABLE 3.2 (Continued)

Countries	Food categories	Exports				Imports			
		Period 2008–10		Period 2010–12		Period 2008–10		Period 2010–12	
		Value (US$ mn)	Per cent	Value (US$ mn)	Per cent	Value (US$ mn)	Per cent	Value (US$ mn)	Per cent
	Sugar and related products	–	–	–	–	211	21	577	38
South Asia	Cereals	1,248	23	2,060	23	1,361	21	2,011	24
	Fruits and vegetables	1,543	29	2,765	30	2,315	35	2,390	29
	Sugar and related products	595	11	1,341	15	782	12	1,380	17
	Spices	656	12	812	9	636	10	753	9
	Oils and fats	352	7	?	?	144	2	89	1
	Meat and fish	251	5	487	5	361	6	441	5
	Milk products	142	3	225	2	163	2	150	2
	Processed foods	258	5	502	6	311	5	390	5
	Fodder	101	2	199	2	150	2	191	2
	Oilseeds	137	2	233	3	228	3	343	4
	Honey and non–alcoholic beverages	50	1	89	1	108	2	160	2

Source: Author's estimate using United Nations Commodity Trade Statistics (COMTRADE) and World Integrated Trade Solution (WITS) database

Notes: Normally the export of food products to the region (South Asia) should match the import of the same products into the region. However, there could be aggregation errors as brought out in the last paragraph of the section titled 'Period of Analysis/selection of data classification' of this chapter.

(–) *Implies nil or negligible trade.*

important product group whose share was also seen to be increasing over the two reference periods. Oils and fats came next in importance in Pakistan's exports. Spices and fodder were the two most important groups of food products in Sri Lanka's exports to the region, whose shares were seen to be increasing over the two reference periods.

With reference to the structure of imports, data in Table 3.2 reveals that the importers of cereals from the region were Bangladesh, Sri Lanka, Afghanistan and Maldives. Similarly, the most important importers of fruits and vegetables in the region were Bangladesh, Sri Lanka and Maldives. The major importers of sugar and related products were Bangladesh, Afghanistan, Pakistan, Sri Lanka and Maldives.

Generally, it will be seen that major exporters of any product group did not import products in the same group. The exception to this was in the case of fruits and vegetables in which case India and Pakistan both exported and imported products in this group in substantial quantities of substantial value.

From the perspective of the SAR, Figure 3.1 presents the export structure. We observe that the most important product group traded within the region was fruits and vegetables, followed by cereals, sugar and related products, spices, processed foods, meat and fish.

Geographical distribution

After having examined the product composition by countries, we now examine the geographical direction of trade of the 11 identified product categories.

The data and figures generated from them are based on author's estimate from UN Comtrade data as accessed from World Bank's World Integrated Trade System (WITS).

Table 3.3 presents the geographical distribution of intraregional trade by product categories and the trends. The changing geographic distribution of each SAARC Member States trade discussed draws from this table.

It can be observed in Table 3.3 that India and Pakistan were the two major cereal exporting countries in the region. The major importing countries in the region were Bangladesh and Sri Lanka. Sri Lanka was the largest exporter of fodder in the region, while India came next in importance.

India was also a major importer of fodder over the reference periods. Bangladesh was the next important importer, whose share increased over the two reference periods. India was the largest exporter of fruits and vegetables. The next important supplier was Pakistan. The share of Afghanistan declined over the same reference periods.

Imports of fruits and vegetables were fairly diversified in the region. Bangladesh, India and Pakistan were the major importers, followed by Sri Lanka. The trade flow data reveals considerable intra-agro trade taking place in fruits and vegetables across the region.

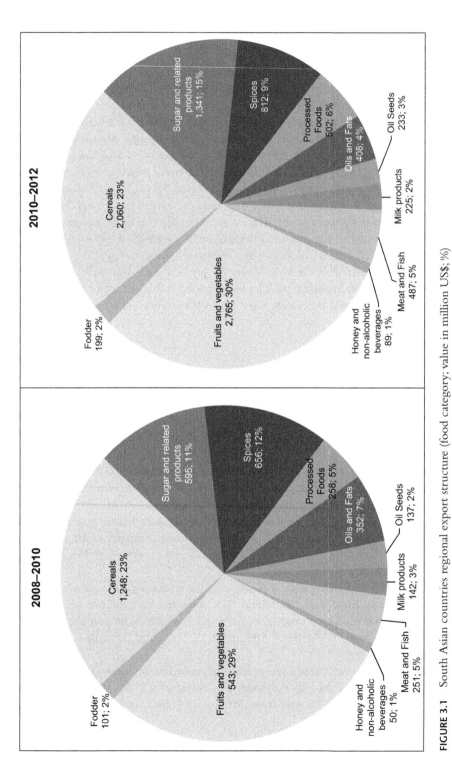

FIGURE 3.1 South Asian countries regional export structure (food category; value in million US$; %)

Source: United Nations Commodity Trade Statistics (COMTRADE)

TABLE 3.3 Structure of intraregional trade of South Asian countries by geographical distribution of product categories (average 2008–10 and 2010–12)

Food categories	Countries	Exports				Imports			
		2008–10		2010–12		2008–10		2010–12	
		Value (US$ mn)	Per cent	Value (US$ mn)	Per cent	Value (US$ mn)	Per cent	Value (US$ mn)	Per cent
Cereals	India	1,022	58	1,228	45	–	–	–	–
	Pakistan	733	42	1,511	55	–	–	–	–
	Bangladesh	–	–	–	–	891	75	1,263	74
	Sri Lanka	–	–	–	–	150	13	218	13
	Afghanistan	–	–	–	–	25	2	128	8
	Maldives	–	–	–	–	54	5	55	3
Fodder	Sri Lanka	110	71	127	55	12	9	17	10
	India	26	17	65	28	115	85	116	70
	Pakistan	10	7	30	13	–	–	–	–
	Afghanistan	8	5	8	4	–	–	–	–
Fruits and vegetables	India	1,249	56	1,262	50	512	24	579	26
	Pakistan	426	19	885	34	453	21	610	27
	Afghanistan	479	22	205	8	–	–	–	–
	Bangladesh	28	1	126	5	829	38	635	29
	Sri Lanka	53	2	60	3	303	14	324	15
Honey and non-alcoholic beverages	Pakistan	24	68	49	71	–	–	–	–
	Bangladesh	7	19	14	20	–	–	–	–
	India	4	12	6	8	78	74	105	67
	Sri Lanka	–	1	1	1	–	–	–	–

(Continued)

TABLE 3.3 (Continued)

Food categories	Countries	Exports				Imports			
		2008–10		2010–12		2008–10		2010–12	
		Value (US$ mn)	Per cent	Value (US$ mn)	Per cent	Value (US$ mn)	Per cent	Value (US$ mn)	Per cent
Meat and fish	India	190	47	216	43	109	36	167	44
	Bangladesh	106	27	163	32	31	10	45	12
	Pakistan	55	14	89	18	11	4	12	3
	Maldives	37	9	23	4	32	11	45	12
	Sri Lank	11	3	14	3	95	31	89	24
Milk products	India	102	48	86	32	6	6	5	6
	Pakistan	108	51	178	66	3	3	6	6
	Sri Lanka	2	1	2	1	7	7	2	2
	Bangladesh	–	–	1	1	56	55	42	45
	Maldives	–	–	–	–	8	7	6	7
	Afghanistan	–	–	–	–	23	22	33	34
Oilseeds	India	176	86	237	95	7	4	5	2
	Sri Lanka	18	9	3	1	16	11	19	9
	Pakistan	9	5	9	4	73	50	112	54
	Bangladesh	–	–	–	–	51	35	73	35
Oils and fats	Pakistan	340	82	491	91	3	3	7	13
	Sri Lanka	53	13	7	1	8	8	3	6
	India	20	5	14	3	81	78	37	72
	Bangladesh	–	–	25	5	11	10	4	7

Processed food	India	181	58	266	56	52	29	41	18
	Pakistan	91	30	166	35	3	2	6	2
	Sri Lanka	26	8	32	6	61	43	65	29
	Bangladesh	12	4	14	3	41	23	86	38
	Maldives	–	–	–	–	22	12	28	13
Processed meat And fish	Sri Lanka	5	59	5	45	5	45	1	5
	Pakistan	1	13	3	26	3	26	5	45
	Maldives	–	4	–	3	–	3	2	22
Spices	India	417	68	558	66	242	40	270	39
	Sri Lanka	163	26	210	25	164	28	210	30
	Pakistan	18	3	19	2	72	12	67	9
	Bangladesh	4	1	–	–	111	19	144	21
	Afghanistan	13	2	57	7	–	–	–	–
Sugar and related products	India	1,149	89	1,724	93	6	1	–	–
	Pakistan	142	11	128	7	157	22	210	16
	Bangladesh	–	–	–	–	285	40	449	35
	Afghanistan	–	–	–	–	31	4	44	3
	Sri Lanka	–	–	–	–	31	4	44	3
	Maldives	–	–	–	–	18	3	24	2

Source: Author's estimate using United Nations Commodity Trade Statistics (Comtrade) based on World Bank, World Integrated Trade Solution (WITS) database

Note: – Implies nil or negligible trade.

Pakistan was by far the largest exporter of honey and non-alcoholic beverages during both the periods. Bangladesh followed in importance. These two countries improved their shares marginally over the two reference periods. India, Afghanistan and Maldives were the largest importers of this product from the region. Over the two reference periods while the share of India declined marginally, those of Afghanistan showed a marginal increase.

India was the most important supplier of meat and fish products to the region, followed by Bangladesh and Pakistan. India and Sri Lanka were the largest importers of fish and meat products from the SAR. The other importers included Bangladesh, Maldives and Pakistan. Bangladesh and Maldives were mainly meat importers. Thus we observe, as in the case of meat and fish (notably fish products) there was considerable two-way trade flows within the region.

Pakistan and India were the two major exporters of milk products to the region. The major importers of milk products were Bangladesh and Afghanistan. India was the dominant exporter of oilseeds to the SAR. Afghanistan was the major importer of oilseeds in the SAR followed by Bangladesh and Sri Lanka.

Pakistan was by far the most dominant exporter of oils and fats in the SAR. Other far less important exporters were Bangladesh and India. India was by far the most dominant importer of oils and fats from the region. India was by far the largest exporter of processed foods to the SAR. Sri Lanka and Bangladesh were the other exporting countries from this region. Imports for processed foods are well distributed across the region. The main importing countries were Sri Lanka, Bangladesh, India and Maldives in order of their importance.

The main importing countries of processed meat and fish were India, Sri Lanka, Pakistan and Maldives. India was the major exporter of this product, followed by Bangladesh and Maldives India was the principal supplier of spices to the SAR followed by Sri Lanka. The import markets were more diversified among the countries in the region. The geographical destination of spices imports The major market was India, followed by Sri Lanka, Bangladesh and Afghanistan. India was the predominant supplier of sugar and related products to the region, followed by Pakistan. The major markets for sugar and related products were Sri Lanka, Bangladesh and Pakistan.

In summary, India was the dominant supplier of sugar and related products, spices and processed food, while Pakistan was the dominant supplier of fats and oils and honey and non-alcoholic beverages. Together, India and Pakistan were the dominant suppliers of cereals, fruits and vegetables and milk products. India and Bangladesh together were dominant suppliers of meat and fish, while India and Sri Lanka together dominated as suppliers of spices. Sri Lanka was the dominant supplier of fodder.

Bangladesh and Sri Lanka together accounted for the bulk of cereal, fruits and vegetables, processed food and sugar products markets in the region. India was the dominant market for oils and fats. The import market was generally more diversified indicating considerable intra-agro trade particularly in fruits and vegetables, meat and fish and in spices.

Thus in terms of major findings in the structure of trade in the SAR, Tables 3.2 and 3.3 seem to complement each other.

Identifying food products/categories with high AMAF

AMAF for products/food categories

The exports of Member States are classified in terms of their food types. The food products under each food category are classified at the HS 6-digit level. At the first instance each product under their respective food categories are listed. The details provided at this stage are generated covering trade flows over the period 2010 to 2012 to average out seasonal variations during the years.

The details provided at this stage include the reporting Member States' supply capability for each food product to RoW and to RoSA. For these products we ascertain each partner country's demand and the regional demand. Next we examine how much the reporting country is supplying to each partner country in the region. Finally we arrive at AMAF for each food product as being the minimum of supplying country's export to RoW and regional demand from RoW for the same. The AMAF so obtained at the product level are summed up to obtain AMAF at the product category level[4](see section on methodology).

Annex tables linked to the main tables in the text brings out the details of trade flows of all products contained in each food product category at 6-digit HS. All the details of trade flows are now available for each product for deeper understanding. The AMAF for each product is then sorted and ranked in terms of value. The products having AMAF above US$ 1 million are then identified for further detailed analysis.

Regional summary of AMAF

We summarize the AMAF for all food categories country-wise in Table 3.4. India has the highest AMAF across all products (US$ 6.85 billion), followed by Pakistan (US$ 1.71 billion) and Sri Lanka (US$ 0.98 billion).

Important food products for standardization

For freer flow of food products trade, steps could be taken to initiate standardization already initiated by SAARC Standards Organisation (SARCO). Action already initiated by SARSO includes some eight products.[5] This study also finds these products relevant. However, some notable food products that could be added to this list are indicated in Table 3.5.

TABLE 3.4 Additional Market Access Frontier (AMAF) by product categories and countries (US$ million)

	Afghanistan	Bangladesh	India	Maldives	Pakistan	Sri Lanka
Cereals	0	10	1,740	0	1,006	362
Sugar and related products	0	0	2,597	0	191	3
Processed foods	0	52	626	0	143	201
Fruits and vegetables	30	48	629	0	157	72
Spices	16	9	299	0	25	179
Meat and fish	0	78	175	12	127	80
Oils and fats	0	4	266	0	7	32
Oil seeds	19	19	161	0	28	12
Fodder	0	0	162	0	3	0
Milk products	0	0	157	0	4	1
Honey and non-alcoholic beverages	0	3	21	0	13	7
Processed meat and fish	0	3	15	8	8	3
Grand total	**66**	**226**	**6,848**	**20**	**1,712**	**951**

Source: Author's calculations

Note: In order to avoid double counting we assume each supplier's market access frontier when similar access by competing suppliers is absent.

TABLE 3.5 Major food products for standardization

Suppliers	Products	HS Code	AMAF ($million)
Afghanistan	Seeds of cumin	090930	57.14
Bangladesh	Meat and fish-other	030559	146
	Meat and fish-boneless	030379	22
	Meat and fish-other	030490	21
India	Sugar and related-other	170199	1,241
	Onions and shallots	070310	493
	Capsicum	090420	346
	Chickpeas	071320	207
Maldives	Tunas, skipjack	160414	0.34
Pakistan	Sugar and related-other	100190	50.72
	Sugar and related-other	170199	44.97
Sri Lanka	Cinnamon neither crushed nor ground	090610	92.5
	Pepper neither crushed nor ground	090411	47.9
	Cloves extracted	090700	12.5

Source: Author's calculations

Tariff barriers on identified products[6]

We next examine the tariff restrictions/barriers on the 397 products identified under this study for trade liberalization. This section examines the nature of tariff barriers being faced by the SAARC Member States (SMC) on their identified food products from their supplying partner countries in the region. The products face preferential tariffs under SAFTA and also from their bilateral free trade agreements with their partner countries in the region. Both these arrangements have sensitive lists which prohibit tariff concessions on them. On these products the MFN rate applies. Hence the data has to be sourced for the following tariff preferences/barriers.

1 SAFTA preferential tariffs for LDCs and non-LDCs.
2 Sensitive lists for LDCs and non-LDCs under SAFTA.
3 Preferential tariffs under bilateral trading arrangements, wherever applicable (India-Sri Lanka Free Trade Agreement, Pakistan-Sri Lanka Free Trade Agreement, India-Afghanistan Preferential Trading Agreement).
4 Negative list for India by Pakistan.
5 MFN rates on imports in the case of products under sensitive lists.

The information was obtained from several sources. The preferential tariffs under the SAFTA Trade Liberalisation Programme were obtained from the SAARC secretariat website. The bilateral preferential tariffs and list of sensitive products were obtained from the Department of Commerce websites of India and Sri Lanka. The list of products under negative list for India was obtained from the Ministry of Commerce website of the Government of Pakistan. Thus a complex web of tariff barriers/general and preferential were identified criss-crossing overlapping regional/bilateral FTAs were analyzed.[7]

Afghanistan

It will be seen that except for oilseeds, Bangladesh's tariffs on food imports from Afghanistan are generally in excess of 10%. It has no food product in its sensitive list for Afghanistan. It may consider removing spices-seeds of cumin (090930) from its sensitive list. Also it may consider reducing its tariff on dried grapes (080620), which is quite high under its TLP.

India's imports of all identified products are duty-free and none of them are under its sensitive list. The situation is similar for Maldives. Pakistan has no sensitive list for Afghanistan, while preferential rates under SAFTA are down to 5%. Pakistan could consider making its imports for these products duty-free in line with India and Maldives.

Sri Lanka has four products in its sensitive list on food products imports from Afghanistan. It might consider removing these from its sensitive list.

Bangladesh

Afghanistan has 27 products in its sensitive list for Bangladesh. It may consider removing some of them. There are 18 of them having tariff rates 10% and above. Afghanistan could target these products for their removal from their sensitive list.

Under SAFTA India has offered duty-free access to Bangladesh on all its food products. Maldives too offers duty-free access to Bangladesh on these products. Pakistan imposes a modest duty of 5% to Bangladesh and could offer duty-free access as offered by India and Maldives. Pakistan has two products under its sensitive list on which high tariffs apply. Those products under vegetables (081090)[8] and non-alcoholic beverages (220290) could be removed from its sensitive list for LDCs.

Sri Lanka has a sensitive list of 30 products on its food imports from Bangladesh. Of these, Bangladesh has high AMAF on processed foods (190590), fruits and vegetables (070190) and oilseeds (120740). Sensitive lists on these products could be removed on a priority basis.

India

India has the largest number of food products with potential for export to the SAR. Afghanistan has 127 products in its sensitive list for India. Of these, 44 of them have tariffs of 10% and above. These products could be removed from Afghanistan's sensitive list for India. Among these, products with high AMAF for India include processed foods, (210690, 190490), fruits and vegetables (080610), sugar and related products (170490), honey and non-alcoholic beverages (220290).

There are 44 products in Bangladesh's sensitive list for India under SAFTA. There are 35 products under this list having tariffs of 37.5%. Among these products those having high AMAF for India include among others, sugar and related products (170199) and processed foods (190531, 201309, 200980). These may be prioritized for liberalization under TLP.

Maldives does not have any product in its sensitive list. And most SAFTA rates for India are nil. The rate is 15% only in the case of two products, viz., processed foods (201320, 220210).

In general, India faces additional restrictions in entering the Pakistan market since the latter country has a negative list of 1,209 items for Indian products prohibiting their entry. Fortunately, not many food products are included under Pakistan's negative list. The remaining products that are on Pakistan's positive list come under the country's TLP under SAFTA excluding those that are in their SAFTA sensitive list. The latter products face Pakistan's MFN duties. The products listed in the for Pakistan as a market excludes the products under its negative list.

It will be seen that there are 30 products under Pakistan's SAFTA sensitive list for India's food products. These may be considered by Pakistan for their removal. Among these products, India has high AMAF in sugar and related products (170111, 170199), fodder (230990) and oils and fats (151620, 151590).

There are 153 products in the combined sensitive lists for food products under SAFTA and ILFTA for Sri Lanka. This is the largest list of sensitive products on which India is faced with sensitive list. There is the need to prune this large list by Sri Lanka. Food products in which India has AMAF include milk products (040210), processed foods (190590) and fruits and vegetables (080620).

Maldives

The mainstay of Maldives exports are marine products. Afghanistan does not have any sensitive list on Maldives potential food exports. Afghanistan's both MFN and preferential rates are low varying from 2.5–9%. It may consider reducing its tariffs processed meat and fish (160414) under its SAFTA TLP.

Bangladesh does not have any sensitive list on Maldives identified food products. However, its SAFTA preferential rates still remain high varying from 14% to 25%. These products could be brought under Bangladesh's TLP.

India offers duty-free market access to all Maldives identified food export products. Pakistan has no product under its sensitive list for Maldives. Its SAFTA preferential rates are 55 on all products. It may consider making all such products duty-free in line with India.

Sri Lanka has only two products under meat and fish which come under its sensitive list for Maldives, attracting 15% duty on them. These may be considered for removal from Sri Lanka's sensitive list.

Pakistan

Afghanistan has a list of 61 food products in its sensitive list for Pakistan. Its preferential tariffs range from 2.5% to 25%. There are ten products in with tariffs 16–25%. These products may be considered for removal in its sensitive list. Among some of these products in which Pakistan has high AMAF are: processed foods (190590, 210690) and sugar and related products (170490).

Bangladesh has 31 products under its sensitive list for food products for Pakistan. Except for two products, all the rest have 37.5% tariffs on them. These products could be removed from their sensitive list. Among these products Pakistan has high AMAF for sugar and related products (030379) processed foods (210690) and sugar and related products (170490, 170199).

India has a sensitive list of 25 food products on Pakistan's exports to India. Among these products, Pakistan has high AMAF in processed foods (190590), sugar and related products (170199) and fruits and vegetables (080450, 070190).

Maldives does not have food product on its sensitive for food imports from Pakistan. Except for fodder (230990) it provides duty-free access to all other food product imports from Pakistan.

Sri Lanka has only five products in its sensitive list for food products for Pakistan if the SAFTA and PSFTA lists are combined. These products attract MFN rates varying from 15% to 25% on them. Removal of these products from either of the lists will enable Pakistan to access Sri Lankan market free from all products in the latter's sensitive lists.

Sri Lanka

Afghanistan has 30 food products in its sensitive list for Sri Lanka. Of these, 14 products have MFN rates 10% and above. Afghanistan could consider removing these from its sensitive list for Sri Lanka. Some of these products in which Sri Lanka has high AMAF are processed foods (210690, 190531) and fruits and vegetables (070900).

Bangladesh has 14 products in its sensitive list for Sri Lanka. Of these, 11 have MFN rate of 37.5%. Among products attracting 37.5%, Sri Lanka has high AMAF in processed foods (190531) and in honey and non-alcoholic beverages (220210). In spices (090411) Sri Lanka has high AMAF. Bangladesh could consider removing these products from its sensitive list.

India has six products in its sensitive list for SAFTA but none of these are in India's bilateral free trade agreement with Sri Lanka. Hence taking both the regional and bilateral free trade agreements with Sri Lanka, India does not have any negative list for Sri Lanka's food products exports to India. Besides, under its bilateral free trade agreement with India, these products are duty-free for the Indian market.

Maldives has only two food products, viz., meat and fish (030741) and processed foods (200819), which are in its sensitive list for Sri Lanka on which tariffs of 25% are being applied. It may consider removing these from its sensitive list.

Pakistan has nine food products under its sensitive list with Sri Lanka under SAFTA, of which only two are under oils and fats (151190, 151790) and are in its bilateral PSFTA with Sri Lanka. These two products carry high incidence of specific duties which Sri Lanka could consider removing from its sensitive list. Except for these two products, the others enter the Sri Lankan market duty-free as provided under its bilateral free trade agreement with Pakistan.

South Asia

Table 3.6 summarizes the sensitive list faced by each supplier in the region and Figure 3.2 illustrates the same. The incidence of sensitive lists faced by each regional supplier of their high potential food products in South Asian markets is presented in Table 3.6 and illustrated in Figure 3.2. It will be seen that the incidence of sensitive products is the highest in Sri Lanka and the lowest in Maldives. India and Pakistan too have relatively low incidence of sensitive lists on the potential food export products of other partner countries in the region. The incidence of trade restrictiveness in terms of sensitive lists is also higher for Afghanistan and Bangladesh.

TABLE 3.6 Sensitive list faced by each regional supplier from their high AMAF food products

Market	Supplier	No. of products with AMAF > $1 million	SAFTA		Bilateral	
			No. of sensitive list in SAFTA	Share (%)	No. of sensitive list in Bilateral Agreement	Share (%)
Afghanistan	Bangladesh	44	26	59	n/a	n/a
	India	183	117	64	n/a	n/a
	Maldives	6	0	0	n/a	n/a
	Pakistan	98	61	62	n/a	n/a
	Sri Lanka	60	30	50	n/a	n/a
	Gross Total	391	234	60	n/a	n/a
	Net Total	223	136	61	n/a	n/a
Bangladesh	Afghanistan	7	1	14	n/a	n/a
	India	183	62	34	n/a	n/a
	Maldives	6	0	0	n/a	n/a
	Pakistan	98	36	37	n/a	n/a
	Sri Lanka	60	24	40	n/a	n/a
	Gross Total	354	123	35	n/a	n/a
	Net Total	217	69	32	n/a	n/a
India	Afghanistan	7	0	0	n/a	n/a
	Bangladesh	44	0	0	n/a	n/a
	Maldives	6	0	0	n/a	n/a
	Pakistan	98	24	24	n/a	n/a
	Sri Lanka	60	10	17	1	1.70
	Gross Total	215	34	16	1	0.50
	Net Total	147	27	18	1	0.70
Maldives	Afghanistan	7	0	0	n/a	n/a
	Bangladesh	44	0	0	n/a	n/a
	India	183	7	4	n/a	n/a
	Pakistan	98	3	3	n/a	n/a
	Sri Lanka	60	2	3	n/a	n/a
	Gross Total	392	12	3	n/a	n/a
	Net Total	225	8	4	n/a	n/a
Pakistan	Afghanistan	7	0	0	n/a	n/a
	Bangladesh	44	7	16	n/a	n/a
	India★	183	30	16	4	2.20
	Maldives	6	0	0	n/a	n/a
	Sri Lanka	60	9	15	3	5.00
	Gross Total	300	46	15	7	2.30
	Net Total	205	32	16	6	2.90

(Continued)

TABLE 3.6 (Continued)

Market	Supplier	No. of products with AMAF > $1 million	SAFTA		Bilateral	
			No. of sensitive list in SAFTA	Share (%)	No. of sensitive list in Bilateral Agreement	Share (%)
Sri Lanka	Afghanistan	7	4	57	n/a	n/a
	Bangladesh	44	29	66	n/a	n/a
	India	183	145	79	170	92.90
	Maldives	6	2	33	n/a	n/a
	Pakistan	98	69	70	1	1.00
	Gross Total	338	249	74	171	50.60
	Net Total	218	165	76	170	78.00

Source: Author's calculation based on UN COMTRADE data

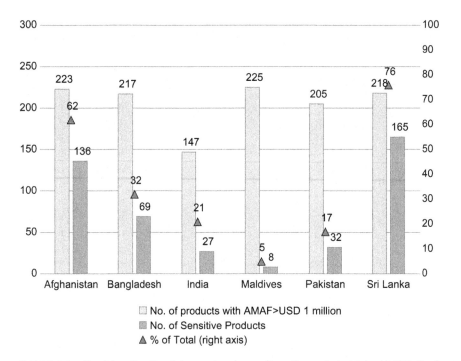

FIGURE 3.2 Sensitive list faced by regional suppliers from their high AMAF food products

Source: Author's calculation based on UN COMTRADE data

Summary and major recommendations

In the SAR agriculture is more protected than non-agriculture. Given the nature and composition of trade flows in FPT in SAR, the study highlights that the three major sectors that need to be targeted for trade liberalization are fruits and vegetables, cereals, sugar and related products and spices. By adding the processed foods and meat and fish sectors, almost the entire food sector would be covered.

From an analysis of food product categories, the study moves deeper to analyze the underlying products under each product category for each regional member country.

This study has highlighted the incidence of tariff barriers facing South Asian countries. Even though the level of protection of food products trade has come down through the SAFTA TLP and bilateral arrangements between India and Sri Lanka and between Pakistan and Sri Lanka, a large number of products are still contained in their sensitive lists. The study has identified these and highlighted particularly those that the supplying countries have export potential.

It has been observed that the incidence of trade restrictiveness in terms of the prevalence of sensitive lists is far higher in Sri Lanka, Afghanistan and Bangladesh. These countries must take the lead to prune their sensitive lists.

While moving under the path of trade liberalization, SAARC Contracting States need to prioritize agricultural products for their removal from each country's sensitive lists. This study could help negotiators to identify their request list to include those in which they have high AMAF. Given the complexity of crisscrossing and overlapping bilateral and regional trading arrangements, it is hoped that this study would help in the identification of such products for trade liberalization.

While identifying the possibilities and path to trade liberalization in agricultural products, the study has further brought out some anomalies in the notifications on sensitive lists and the corresponding prevalence of preferential tariffs on food items thus restricted. Normally products under a sensitive list must be subject to MFN and not preferential tariffs. This study identified a number of products in sensitive lists that were being offered not MFN but preferential rates. The countries in this region must address such anomalies if uncertainties in regional food trade are to be avoided. While it is not clear which notification is given precedence, the study recommends that the de jure preferential tariffs be made de facto to intensify the process of trade liberalization in food products in the region.[9]

The study further recommends that the various notifications issued by the SAARC Secretariat could be accessible at the Secretariat's website preferably in uniform harmonised 6-digit HS format and made available both in PDF and Excel format for ease of negotiation and in facilitating research on regional trade liberalization.

The study further recommends that the format for data classification for notifications issued by the SAARC Secretariat needs to be uniform preferably at 6-digit HS classification for ease in negotiations. This is not the case as some are in the 6-digit, others at 8-digit level. For the sake of transparency and simplicity the HS classifications should be harmonized at 6-digit level and negotiations be held at this level. Further, the format of presentation of data for each country's list of sensitive products and trade liberalization programme is provided in different formats, being mostly in PDF, but in some cases in Word, some as picture, but rarely in Excel. For ease of data analysis by researchers as also for business involved in trade, it is suggested that all presentations should be in PDF format, with an option for access to the excel version.

In terms of food categories, cereals have the highest AMAF, followed by sugar and related products. However, in terms of actual trade flows, the most important items traded are fruits and vegetables, cereals and sugar and related products. Standardization of these products should be given priority. A list of products that could be added by SARSO for further standardization has been highlighted in this study. The study has identified the major food suppliers of different product categories having high AMAF.

Further, collective effort should be made by cereal surplus countries of this region to assure certainty of supplies to regional deficit countries in times of scarcity. India is already doing this in terms of its two neighbours – Nepal and Bhutan. As a goodwill gesture it may extend the same to other LDCs in the region.

In addition, the Agreement on South Asian Food Bank should be activated by improving its operability along the lines suggested in this study.[10] The study suggests the Agreement should keep in mind three windows:

1   Those that relate to emergencies – natural or human generated. Such emergencies should be dealt with as being in the nature of public good and in non-commercial terms.
2   Emergencies that are in the nature of shortages in which case market-oriented pricing principle could be adopted with some discount.
3   A window to be linked to food aid with such agencies such as the World Food Programme. The SAARC Food Bank would be an ideal agency to attract food aid to the countries suffering acute shortages in the region.

The trigger mechanism that entitles a Member State to draw grains from the reserve asks for too high a threshold for eligibility. It will be more appropriate to apply this mechanism for seasonal shortfalls since it may be too late when an annual shortfall is assessed. Further, looking at the experience on the ground, a 3% shortfall over the average seasonal production in the past three years may be a better indicator for a Member State to seek food supply from the Bank.

Further, the criterion of acute shortage, defined in terms of quantitative shortfall in production, needs to be supplemented by price trigger resulting from shortages. Price volatility beyond 10%, irrespective of production shortfall could entitle Member States to seek supplies from the Food Bank.

On institutional arrangements, it appears that the Food Security Board (FSB) has been saddled with too many responsibilities. Can the FSB undertake judicial functions for adjudicating disputes? It may be more appropriate to assign this function to the SAARC Arbitration Council. Noting that the composition of the SFB changes every two years, it may be more appropriate to assign most of its functions to an institutional organization such as the SAARC Agricultural Centre with appropriate capacity building for dealing with its functions.

As in the case of SAARC Food Bank, the SAARC Seed Bank also suffers from a number of operational limitations. The agreement has no provision about how to conserve genetic resources to empower local farmers to benefit from local seed systems.

There is limited focus on agriculture research and development, including breeding of varieties that enhance food security and effective climate change adaption.

The Seed Board needs to develop a set of guidelines to promote linkages between the seed bank and the farming communities under the community seed banks to ensure that farmers also contribute to its operationalisation through exchange of their materials.

The role of the traditional seed system in ensuring seed and food security as well as promoting the conservation and sustainable use local genetic resources should not be undermined. The Bank could consider the setting up of regional conservation and development funds.

Further, the seeds included include those of 'common variety'. It is not clear what is included under it. Member States are required to collaborate with each other in the development of a list of common varieties of major priority/identified crops while recognizing the need to preserve local/indigenous varieties as may be appropriate (Art. IV). This process has to be initiated to reduce any ambiguity on this score.

Besides, the common varieties are currently limited to include wheat, maize, pulses and oilseeds. There is need to add millets that are gluten free and add to nutrition security. Besides, given that fruits and vegetables constitute the largest food category in FPT, it may be worthwhile to include their seeds to enrich intake of vitamins and promote more balanced nutrition given that these products are become more important with growing incomes.

Acknowledgements

This paper chapter is an abridged version of a more comprehensive study under the same title, submitted to UNESCAP SSWA, New Delhi, as Development Papers 1404, October 2014, available at www.unescap.org/sites/default/files/Development%20Paper_Agricultural%20Trade_1405.pdf.

Annex tables attached to this paper chapter giving detailed product level analysis not available on the website, can be had on request from UNESCAP SSWA office, New Delhi.

The author of this chapter is a former professor of South Asian Studies and Dean, School of International Studies, Jawaharlal Nehru University, New Delhi. I express my thanks to Dr. Subrata Kumar Behera for his valuable comments while drafting the report on this study. Similarly, I convey my thanks to Mr Subash Sharma, then Programme Coordinator, SAARC Secretariat for providing me clarifications on various relevant notifications issued by the Secretariat.

Notes

1 According to Mukherji (2012), intraregional exports among six South Asian countries in agricultural products in relation to the region's world exports was 9% and the same for intraregional imports was 17% in 2010.
2 Available at wits.worldbank.org.
3 This concept was first used by Mukherji (2002) under the term 'potential trade'. Subsequently the concept was used in other studies such as Mukherji (2005), and Bano, Takahashi and Scrimgeour (2013). In this study the same concept is being used under the term Additional Market Access Frontier (AMAF) to better reflect a country's market access frontier. If AMAF is the minimum of exports of the reporting country to RoW and regional imports from RoW, it is assumed that reporting country's exports and regional imports are of the same quality and are similarly priced, which may not hold true for a large number of product categories. This concept only sets the outer limit for mutual trade expansion among partner countries offering trade preferences to the supplier country (tariff/non-tariff). The actual trade expansion will be much more modest depending on price and substitution elasticities of the liberalised products being exchanged. In this study this concept is being used to identify agro products having high market access frontier for the supplying countries that could be considered for elimination from the sensitive lists of major importing countries in the region. It is assumed that the larger the supply capability and the wider the market of the partner countries, and smaller the existing trade flows, the greater the possibility of trade expansion with the easing of mutual trade restrictiveness among them.
4 Country-wise tables for each product category are available in UNESCAP Development Papers 1404, the main Report of this study, op cit, n1. The Annex tables for each product category, giving details of each product under this group can be made available, on request, from UNESCP SSWA office, New Delhi.
5 These include refined sugar, biscuits, sugar-free biscuits, cream filled biscuits, instant noodles, black tea, *vanaspati* and skimmed milk powder.
6 The data in this section has been culled from the customs notifications of SAARC Member States as posted on SAARC Secretariat's website as also from national customs notifications issued by respective Member States governments as of 2014. No new notifications have been posted on SAARC website since then. For detailed product level analysis, see Annex tables, see op cit, n6.
7 See op. cit. n 6.
8 All products codes discussed in this section are in 6-digit Harmonised System of Coding.
9 This would further the process of reducing the trade liberalisation imbalance between India and Pakistan-a long standing demand made by Pakistan.
10 The salient features of SAARC Food Bank and seed Bank, suggestions for improving their operational efficiency, have been brought out in op cit, n1. This section brings out the main recommendations of these two institutional arrangements, even though they are not discussed in the main text of this chapter.

References

Adhikari, K. (2012), 'Seed Banking in South Asia', SAWTEE Policy Brief, No. 24, South Asia Watch on Trade, Economics and Environment.

Bano, S., Y. Takahashi and F. Scrimgeour (2013), 'ASEAN-New Zealand Trade Relations and Trade Potential: Evidence and Analysis', *Journal of Economic Integration*, Vol. 28(1), pp. 144–182.

FAO (2012a), 'Regional Trade Agreements and Food Security in Asia', Food and Agriculture Organisation. Available at: www.fao.org/docrep/018/i3026e/i3026e00.htm

FAO (2012b), 'SAFTA and Food Security in South Asia: An Overview', Food and Agriculture Organisation.

FAO (2013), 'State of Food Insecurity in the World: The Multiple Dimensions of Food Security', Food and Agriculture Organisation.

FAO (2014a), 'Food Outlook: Biannual Report on Global Food Markets', Food and Agriculture Organisation. Available at: www.fao.org/docrep/019/i3473e/i3473e.pdf

FAO (2014b), 'Global Information and Early Warning System (GIEWS)', Food and Agriculture Organisation. Available at: www.fao.org/giews/english/index.htm

FAO (2014c), 'State of Food and Agriculture (2014)', Food and Agriculture Organisation.

Government of India (2002), 'Establishing of the SAARC Regional Seed Bank', Department of Agriculture & Cooperation, Ministry of Agriculture.

IFPRI (2013), 'Global Hunger Index 2013', International Food Policy Research Institute.

Iqbal, M. and R. Amjad (2010), 'Food Security in South Asia: Strategies and Programmes for Regional Collaboration', MPRA Paper, No. 38077, Munich Personal RePEc Archive.

ITC (2012), 'Enhancing Pakistan's Agricultural Sector Exports to India', Trade Related Technical Assistance (TRTA II) Programme (2012), International Trade Centre.

Mukherji, I. N. (2002), 'Charting a Free Trade Area in South Asia: Instruments and Modalities', in *Trade, Finance and Investment in South Asia*, T. N. Srinivasan (Ed.), pp. 78–121, Social Science Press, New Delhi.

Mukherji, I. N. (2005), 'The Bangkok Agreement: A Negative List Approach to Trade Liberalisation in Asia and Pacific', *Asia-Pacific Trade and Investment Review*, Vol. 1(2), pp. 27–53, United Nations Economic and Social Commission in Asia and Pacific, Bangkok.

Shrestha, P. K. (2012), 'Regional Approach to Food Security in South Asia: SAARC Seed Bank', Paper presented at Regional Consultation on Trade, Climate Change and Food Security in South Asia, South Asia Watch on Trade, Economics and Environment (SAWTEE), Kathmandu, 20–21 December 2012.

WTO (2014), 'Market Access: Tariffs and Tariff Quotas', World Trade Organization, Geneva. Accessed at: www.wto.org/english/tratop_e/agric_e/negs_bkgrnd10_access_e.htm#back1

TECHNICAL APPENDIX

Additional Market Access Frontier (AMAF) for Product i:

$$AMAF = \sum_{i=0}^{n} \min\left(SEi, MIi\right) - ETi$$

Where:
SEi = Supplier's Global Exports;
MIi = Market's Global Imports;
ETi = Supplier's Existing Exports to Partner's Market.

It is the minimum of supplier's world exports and market's world imports less supplier's current exports to the specified market.

Summation over products gives the total or sectoral AMAF over all products/sectors.

4

AGRICULTURAL TRADE IN SOUTH ASIA

Issues, challenges and the way forward

Sachin Chaturvedi

Introduction

There have been several initiatives in South Asia to address the issue of food insecurity at the regional level, particularly through enhanced trade and regional cooperation. For instance, the SAARC Declaration on Food Security (SAARC-DFS) adopted by the Extraordinary Session of the Agricultural Ministers in November 2008 recognised the strategic importance of making available quality seeds and essential agricultural inputs to the farmers. This initiative led to renewed commitment towards opening up of regional markets for such inputs. There also exists a joint commitment by SAARC nations to cooperate and collaborate in order to mitigate the risks associated climate change and movement of agricultural goods across boundaries.

This chapter discusses the potential of agricultural trade in facilitating the right to food in South Asia. To what extent has the existing stringent food standards been a trade impediment? What is the relative significance of food products in intra-regional trade of South Asia? What is the scope of regional cooperation for enhancing agricultural trade? In the following sections, we attempt to answer these questions and discuss the broad state of affairs in the framework of food security in South Asia. The third section explores intra-regional food trade followed by identification of key factors imposing barriers to regional trade. In the fourth section we take up detailed analysis of impact of SPS and TBT as key barriers while the last section draws key conclusions and policy recommendations.

Intraregional trade and impediments

Evidence of informal trade in the region

Informal trade across borders is a unique and prominent feature of the South Asian trade scenario. The food sector occupies a major place in these transactions. Major impetuses for the informal trade occurs because of localized marketing of village produce by border communities as well as illicit trade through circuitous routes involving third countries as transit ports. Various estimates differ widely on the exact volume of informal trade; some researchers have put it as high as or more than the volume of formal trade.[1] Rao et al. (1997) discuss India's border trade with selected neighbouring countries where they mention the unofficial trade data of India with selected neighbouring countries (Bangladesh, Bhutan and Myanmar) for the year 1995.

The study mentions that unofficial and official exports from India to Bangladesh have more or less been equal. The value of unofficial exports to Bangladesh was US$ 368 million whereas the official exports was US$ 300 to 500 million in the 1990s. Taneja (1999) mentions that food and live animals accounted for three-fifths of the informal trade between India and Bangladesh as compared to 7% of the formal trade. It further elaborates on the fact that unofficial trade is dominated by essential commodities (food mostly) whereas official trade is dominated by manufactured goods. Therefore, the main argument boils down to the magnitude of informal trade in South Asia being considerably high and the food element in the same holding a significant proportion.[2] An assessment of the magnitude of intraregional food trade is therefore important to understand the larger dynamics of the importance of food sector in the intraregional trade regime of South Asia.

Intraregional food trade in South Asia

It has been empirically demonstrated that increased agricultural trade among economies play a significant role in achieving food security.[3] It, therefore, becomes imperative to examine the level of regional trade in food sector[4] across the South Asian economies and the various impediments that affect the scope of regional integration in this area.

As South Asia is one of the most populated regions in the world where per capita income of the region is growing fast, food trade within the region has been growing at a high pace during the last decade. However, due to recessionary pressure, total food exports of the region decreased from US$ 3,736.8 million in 2008 to US$ 3,640.6 million in 2016. In 2008, the food sector was 28.33% of the total intra-regional exports and 35.78% of the total intraregional imports in South Asia. However, since 2008, a declining trend is discernible as share of the food sector declined to 20.36% for intraregional exports by 2016 and 23.53% for imports in the same period. This includes both processed and non-processed food.

In the case of South Asia, the non-processed food sector comprised 17.64% of the total intraregional exports in the year 2008. The share of non-processed food decreased slightly to 14.04% in 2016, as evident in Table 4.1. The share of the processed food export was 10.7% of the total intraregional exports in 2008, which subsequently declined to 6.3% of the total intraregional export, but the absolute value of the exports increased from US$ 981.5 million in 2008 to US$ 1,181.5 million in 2016. The economic literature indicates that SPS and other tariff barriers

TABLE 4.1 Importance of food sector in the overall intraregional trade (%)

Year	Exports			Imports		
	Non-process	Process	Overall	Non-process	Process	Overall
2008	17.64	10.70	28.33	10.71	25.07	35.78
2009	16.59	7.07	23.66	6.89	10.79	17.68
2010	17.59	10.20	27.79	8.02	13.05	21.06
2011	16.05	9.58	25.63	8.64	22.19	30.83
2012	13.40	8.73	22.13	8.02	16.25	24.26
2013	12.99	7.88	20.86	9.83	17.95	27.77
2014	15.75	7.06	22.81	10.56	16.12	26.68
2015	15.47	7.94	23.41	11.56	15.92	27.48
2016	14.04	6.32	20.36	9.84	13.70	23.53

Source: Author's estimation using Comtrade, 2017 based on the classification of Athukorala and Jayasuriya (2005) and Mohanty (2007)

Note: Share indicates as a percentage of total (intra-regional exports/imports).

affect more severely the processed food sector than the non-processed food sector, though the latter constitutes a large segment of trade in many developing countries.

National experiences and intraregional food exports

Interesting results come up when one analyzes the intraregional food exports and national experiences (Table 4.2). It can be seen that India and Pakistan constitute almost 77% of overall intraregional food exports in South Asia in 2016. Afghanistan has the third highest share of 8.6% followed by Sri Lanka with a 7.1% share. Nepal is a marginal player and constitutes 4.4% of the overall intraregional food exports in South Asia. Bangladesh, Bhutan and Maldives have small and negligible shares of 1.8%, 1% and 0.4%, respectively. India and Pakistan continue to be the leading players in the case of both processed and non-processed food, but the proportion of non-processed food exports is higher in the case of India and that of processed food is higher in the case of Pakistan.

India constitutes 45.5% of processed food export in the region and Pakistan's share is 42.3%, in 2016. In the case of non-processed food exports to the region, India has the highest share of 53.7%. This is followed by Pakistan with a share of 18.5%. Out of India's total exports of food to the region, 71.1% is non-processed and 28.9% is processed food. Afghanistan, Sri Lanka, Bhutan, Bangladesh and Nepal perform better in the non-processed food sector and only Maldives and Pakistan perform better in the processed food sector. Intraregional trade in non-processed food constitutes almost 67.5% of the food sector exports and processed food constitutes 32.5%.

TABLE 4.2 Intraregional exports of South Asian countries in 2016: by broad food sectors

Exports in US$ million

Var	AFG	BGD	BTN	IND	LKA	MDV	NPL	PAK	South Asia
Non-processed	292.14	41	29.97	1,321.03	218.18	0.57	101.72	454.49	2459.1
Processed	1.09	23.89	6.62	537.25	40.17	13.94	58.65	499.85	1,181.46
Total	293.23	64.89	36.59	1,858.28	258.35	14.51	160.37	954.34	3,640.56

Share in regional exports (in %)

Var	AFG	BGD	BTN	IND	LKA	MDV	NPL	PAK	South Asia
Non-processed	11.9	1.7	1.2	53.7	8.9	0.0	4.1	18.5	100.0
Processed	0.1	2.0	0.6	45.5	3.4	1.2	5.0	42.3	100.0
Total	8.1	1.8	1.0	51.0	7.1	0.4	4.4	26.2	100.0

Share of exports of non-processed and processed in each country's intraregional food exports (in %)

Var	AFG	BGD	BTN	IND	LKA	MDV	NPL	PAK	South Asia
Non-processed	99.6	63.2	81.9	71.1	84.5	3.9	63.4	47.6	67.5
Processed	0.4	36.8	18.1	28.9	15.5	96.1	36.6	52.4	32.5
Total	100.0	100.0	100.0	100.0	100.0	100.0	100.0	100.0	100.0

Source: Author's estimation using UN COMTRADE database

Product-level analysis and intraregional food exports

A peculiar feature of intra-regional trade in the food sector is that it is concentrated around very few products (Table 4.3). In 2016, over 90% of the regional food exports is taking place in eight items viz. vegetables, fruits and nuts, vegetable oils and fats, dairy products, processed rice, sugar, other crops, other food products and other cereal grains. However, vegetables, fruits and nuts account for the highest share of 28% followed by food products and other crops with 21.5 and 11.6% respectively. The other food sectors, including beverages and tobacco products, oil seeds, wheat, bovine meat products, fishing, paddy rice, animal products, chemical, rubber, plastic products, bovine cattle, sheep and goats, horses and meat products, together contribute nearly 10% of the region's overall trade in the food sector.

Intraregional trade indicates that intensity of trade in food items has been asymmetric not only across products and sectors but also across countries within the region. In major products, participation of some countries like Afghanistan, Bangladesh, Bhutan and Maldives is extremely limited. At times, it is so low that their combined share is only at 2%. The most important food products traded in the region are vegetables, fruits and nuts, other food products, crops, processed rice and sugar, which are largely exported by India and Pakistan. Maldives is only trading in fishing and food products, and Afghanistan's exports are concentrated in vegetables, fruits and nuts. Bangladesh's exports focus on vegetable fruits and nuts and other food products. Sri Lanka's exports are mostly in other crops, vegetables, fruits, nuts and other food products. India is the only country engaged in exports of all the products with high concentration in vegetables, fruits and nuts, food products, other

TABLE 4.3 Intraregional trade in broad food sectors in 2016 (in US$ million)

Product category	AFG	BGD	BTN	IND	LKA	MDV	NPL	PAK	South Asia
Beverages and tobacco products		10.9	3.43	62.02	14.15		9.12	1.34	100.92
Bovine meat prods		0.12		28.87	0.53			7.67	37.19
Chemical, rubber, plastic products		0.44		19.16	1.99				21.59
Bovine cattle, sheep and goats, horses			0	10.58			1.58		12.16
Fishing		5.49		20.74	0.49	5.69	0	0.44	32.85
Cereal grains n.e.c.	32.81			114.1	0.01		0.07	1.97	148.96
Dairy products	0.14	0.11	0.11	66.03	2.72		1.22	44.61	114.94
Animal products n.e.c.		0.34		9.75	1.57		0.06	11.85	23.57
Crops n.e.c.	40.46	1.21	8.67	222.6	76.22		65.35	7.72	422.21
Food products n.e.c.		12.6	7.73	342.8	74.13	8.82	46.86	291.2	784.15
Meat products n.e.c.			0	2.76	1.96			0.12	4.84
Oil seeds	17.8	0.02	0.01	42.51	1.73		0.38	2.49	64.94
Processed rice		0.01		178.7	0.16			132.6	311.44
Paddy rice		0	0	25.31	0.07			0	25.38
Sugar		0.06		143.9	0.17		1.84	114.8	260.75
Vegetables, fruit, nuts	202	25.9	16.5	393.4	74.64		27.19	280.7	1,020.22
Vegetable oils and fats		7.8	0.16	136.8	7.81		6.69	55.34	214.56
Wheat				38.32				1.54	39.86
Total	293.2	64.9	36.6	1858	258.4	14.5	160.4	954.3	3,640.53

Source: Author's estimation using UN COMTRADE database

Note: GTAP product classification is used to define broad food sectors.

crops and processed rice. Pakistan is also engaged in the export of the majority of the products with high concentration in other food products, vegetables, fruits, nuts, processed rice and sugar. India and Pakistan collectively represent 77.3% of the intraregional food exports. However, vegetables, fruits and nuts have been the most dominant products exported by most of the regional countries.

Extra regional focus of food trade in South Asia

The analysis of the intraregional food trade in South Asia in the previous section hints towards the extra regional focus of food trade by countries in the region. This point is analyzed at several instances in the literature that focusses on the source and destinations of food imports and exports by South Asian countries, which in most cases lies outside the region. As Weerahewa (2009) highlights, there is evidence of a high magnitude of food trade with trade partners lying outside the South Asian region by showcasing the top exporters and importers of the SAARC members in the year 2006. It clearly shows that for most of the South Asian countries the import sources and export destinations of food and agricultural trade lies outside the region.[5] This point is further elaborated by Chatterjee and Khadka (2011) where it has been argued that SAARC countries export 92% and import 95% of food products from non-SAARC countries.[6] Similarly, an analysis of the top 20 commodities (2-digit HS) traded by South Asia including the food sector for the years 2010–12 showcase a narrow concentration of intraregional trade.[7]

A detailed analysis of the food trade within and outside the South Asian countries reveals interesting aspects. India accounts for nearly 51% of the total intraregional food exports and 17.43% of the total intraregional food imports in the region. One of the reasons for the similarity is that most South Asian countries do not share a common border with each other. India shares its borders with all the countries in the region except Afghanistan, Sri Lanka and Maldives. This is also reflected in regional orientation of trade flows of food products.[8]

The share of regional trade in food export is low for most countries except Pakistan and Sri Lanka. The import scenario is relatively distributed with Bangladesh, Nepal, Maldives, Pakistan and Sri Lanka being significant importers. Since India accounts for more than half of the intraregional food trade, it is important to understand the source and destinations of food imports and exports by South Asian countries and demystify the quantum of this extra regional focus.

Amongst the South Asian economies, Bhutan, Nepal and Afghanistan are the countries whose top exporters are South Asian partners (Table 4.4). In the case of Bhutan, 99.3% of its total food exports were to South Asia in 2016 and only 0.7% of total foods exports were extra regional. It also has the largest share of intraregional imports of 97.5% in 2016. Similar is the case for Nepal, where South Asia counts for 90% of the total food trade by Nepal in 2016. In Afghanistan, 86.4% of its total foods exports are to the region.

TABLE 4.4 South Asian countries' intraregional trade and extra regional trade of food product, 2016

Country	Exports		Imports	
	% share of Intraregional	*% share of extra regional*	*% share of intraregional*	*% share of extra regional*
AFG	86.37	13.63	25.15	74.85
BGD	7.96	92.04	15.35	84.65
BTN	99.32	0.68	97.45	2.55
IND	6.55	93.45	3.46	96.54
LKA	10.12	89.88	20.62	79.38
MDV	10.55	89.45	29.94	70.06
NPL	90.32	9.68	63.64	36.36
PAK	25.29	74.71	8.00	92.00

Source: Author's estimation using UN COMTRADE database

TABLE 4.5 Estimated food product gains (US$ '000')

	Bangladesh (2011)		Pakistan (2011)	Sri Lanka (2011)
	If imports from Pakistan	If imports from India	If imports from India	If imports from India
Total gain (processed food products)	7,019.247	72,336.99	143,338	37,925.21
Total gain (non-processed food products)	0	3,4667.18	1,147,322	18,288.18
Total gain (food products)	7,019.247	10,7004.2	1,290,660	56,213.39

Source: Author's calculation based on data from World Integrated Trade Solutions (WITS)

Note: Estimated gains are calculated on the basis of unit cost of import.

On the contrary, in Pakistan, the share of intraregional export in total food exports is 25.3%. The majority of food products are exported outside the region. For Maldives, the focus of exports is extra regional, with South Asia constituting for only 10.6% of the total food exports by Maldives. Similarly, for Bangladesh exports, major destinations are outside the region and only 8% of total food exports is intraregional. In the case of Sri Lanka, 89.9% of total exports are to outside the region. India, which is a major player in the food trade, also exports to countries outside the region. It is interesting to note that despite India being responsible for more than half of South Asia's food trade, its intraregional food export share is merely 6.6%, the other 93.5% is extra regional, explaining for the low magnitude of intraregional food trade within the region.

As already discussed, most of the countries in the region trade outside the region except Afghanistan, Bhutan and Nepal, who export heavily within the region. However, the cost of such non-cooperation is immensely high. It can be noted from the table that follows that gains from food trade within the region are very high (Table 4.5). In the case of Bangladesh, which heavily imports from countries like Indonesia, Brazil and Thailand, the high gains of import from the South Asian partners including India and Pakistan, as mentioned here, identify the large scope of cooperation or rather the cost of non-cooperation on the food trade frontier. Similar is the case for Pakistan and Sri Lanka.

Reasons for low intraregional trade in South Asia

Import tariffs in South Asia

The import tariff is considered as one of the most conventional instruments used to protect domestic production of goods. Despite the global trend of declining tariffs, agricultural goods continue to face high tariffs, particularly in the developed regions. Considering the relatively low import duty on agricultural goods in South Asian countries, the average tariff on food products is high in the case of

TABLE 4.6 Average preferential tariffs on food products, 2012

Exporting country	Importing country							
	AFG	BGD	BTN	IND	MDV	NPL	PAK	SL
AFG	–	–	–	16.68	–	–	–	–
BGD	–	–	–	19.96	30	8.25	13.75	15.89
BTN	–	–	–	23.43	–	7.5	6.75	–
IND	0	19.95	–	–	15.04	7.31	11.03	5.32
MDV	–	–	–	13.75	–	7	4.25	4.5
NPL	–	23.75	57	19.26	–	–	9	7.41
PAK	9.86	20.89	–	21.5	14.6	7	–	3.28
SL	–	17.87	–	2.87	15.3	7	2.39	–

Source: WITS database

Note: The tariff figures are simple averages of preferential tariffs. In some cases tariff figures for the latest year were not available, figure for earlier year was considered.

India, Bangladesh and Sri Lanka. Since Bhutan is not yet a WTO member, it has no binding commitment to lower its tariff (evident in the high tariff with Nepal). It is interesting to note that while Bangladesh faces the highest average import tariffs in Nepal, Nepal also faces the highest average import tariffs in Bangladesh (Table 4.6).

The other two high tariff imposing countries, India and Sri Lanka, have one interesting similarity. These countries have maintained trade surpluses in recent years. It appears that countries with high trade deficits impose lower tariffs due to food security concerns. Bhutan, however, is an exception in this regard.[9] Furthermore, the South Asian countries continue to impose several para-tariff measures that also affect food trade within the region.

Non-tariff barriers

Non-tariff measures are legitimate means to regulate bilateral trade for achieving health, safety, environmental and other socio-economic objectives. However, they are often used in disguise to restrict trade and hence are often termed non-tariff barriers. This practise is well recognized in global trade negotiations and as a result, Agreement on Technical Barriers to Trade (TBT) and the Agreement on Sanitary and Phytosanitary (SPS) Measures were signed to ensure that such measures are used for legitimate purposes and not to restrict trade. Nevertheless, the agreements are not easy to impose since legitimacy is often a matter of subjective assessment. While TBT relates to both agricultural and industrial goods, SPS are largely applied on agricultural goods. NTMs affecting agricultural trade relate to standards, testing and certification procedures. For instance, in India, there are biosecurity and SPS requirements. Nearly all agricultural imports, including livestock and food products, require some kind of SPS certificate and import permit.

As compared to both developed and other developing countries, incidences of NTMs is relatively low in South Asia. This is largely due to a low development of standards in the region.

However, it must also be noted that there is significant inequality with respect to development of standards and testing procedures across South Asian countries. As one would expect, in India, standards and testing procedures are better developed compared to its regional neighbours. Hence, other South Asian countries often find it difficult to meet Indian standards. On the other hand, some of these countries are often so dependent on essential commodities that they have limited options and cannot afford to impose high standards on agricultural imports. (Nanda, 2012).

A detailed discussion on the state of SPS and TBT mechanisms is done in the later section of the chapter, since it constitutes a major part of the existing non-tariff barriers in the South Asian region.

High unit cost

There has been little progress when it comes to lowering the export and import costs in the South Asian countries. Both export and import costs are higher in the region as compared to the world average. In 2005, the average import cost in South Asia was substantially lower compared to the world average, whereas the average export cost was marginally lower. In 2011, costs to import became marginally lower, while the export costs became substantially higher. It is also interesting to note that, globally, export costs are relatively lower compared to import costs. However, the same is not true for South Asia and more specifically for India, which does not provide such cost-effective policies to boost international trade.[10]

State of SPS and TBT mechanisms in South Asia

In order to ensure food security, it cannot be denied that international and regional trade in food play an important role. However, there are several impediments in this aspect, specifically the trade barriers that have emerged as points of conflict and disagreement affecting regional trade. As mentioned earlier, food safety has moved to the centre stage of international trade, wherein rising food standards have proven costlier for the developing world. In this context, it is important to analyze the existing SPS and related issues that have become a source of friction in the international trade in the South Asian region.

Prior to discussing the existing level of non-tariff barriers and the various forms of restrictions faced by the South Asian economies, it becomes imperative to first have a sense of certain key areas with respect to food safety in South Asia such as the institutional architecture and the legislative frameworks in place. The following tables give a brief picture of these aspects (Tables 4.7 and 4.8).

TABLE 4.7 Institutional architecture for food safety mechanism in South Asian countries

Institutional Architecture	Bangladesh	India	Nepal	Sri Lanka
Key Agency	Ministry of Health and Family Welfare	Food Safety and Standards Authority of India (FSSAI)	Ministry of Agricultural Development	Ministry of Health/ Directorate General of Health Services
Other Agencies	Ministry of Agriculture, Ministry of Food, Ministry of LGRD, Ministry of Fisheries and Livestock, Ministry of Industries, Ministry of Science, Information and Communication technology; Ministry of education, Ministry of Information, Ministry of Home and Ministry of Law, Justice and Parliamentary Affairs	Ministry of Consumer Affairs, Food and Public Distribution, The Bureau of Indian Standards and the Ministry of Food Processing Industries, Export Inspection Council (EIC)	Department of Food and Technology and Quality Control, Food Standardization Fixation Committee	Sri Lanka Standards Institution, Ministry of Agriculture, Ministry and department of Agriculture, Department of Animal Production and Health, Department of Fisheries, excise and Consumer Affairs Authority
TBT Nodal Point	Bangladesh Standard and Testing Institution (BSTI)	International Relations and Technical Information Services Department, Bureau of Indian Standards (BIS)	Nepal Bureau of Standards and Metrology (NBSM)	Technical Standards Director General of Sri Lanka Standards Institute and Director of Commerce, Department of Commerce (DOC)
SPS Nodal Point	Ministry of Commerce (MOC)	Trade Policy Division, Ministry of Commerce (MOC)	WTO Section Agribusiness Promotion and Statistics Division, Ministry of Agricultural Development	Ministry of Health

Source: (a) Key agencies and other agencies complied from country reports on 'Laws and Regulations to Food and Food Additives'; (b) TBT and SPS Nodal Points: WTO

TABLE 4.8 Legislative framework for food safety

Legislations	Bangladesh	India	Nepal	Sri Lanka
Key Legislation	"The Bangladesh Pure Food Ordinance", 1959 Under Ministry of Health and Family Welfare and "The Bangladesh Pure Food Rules", 1967	The Food Safety and Standards Act, 2006	Food Act 1966 and Food Rules1970	The Food Act No. 26 of 1980
Related Framework	The Bangladesh Standards and Testing Institution Ordinance, 1985 Amended by The Bangladesh Standards And Testing Institution (Amendment) Act, 2003 Under Ministry Of Industry, The Foodgrain Supply Ordinance, 1956

The Radiation Protection Act, 1987

The Iodine Deficiency Disorders Prevention Act, 1989

Fish and Fish product (Inspection and Quality Control) Rules, 1997 | The Prevention of Food Adulteration Act, 1954, The Fruit Products Order, 1955, The Milk and Milk Products Order, 1992, The Meat Food Products Order, 1973, The vegetable Oil Products (Control) Order, 1947, The Edible Oils Packaging (Regulation) Order, 1998, The Solvent Extracted Oil, De-oiled Meal and Edible, Flour (Control) Order, 1967, Any other order issued under the Essential Commodities Act, 1955 relating to Food.

All these eight acts have been repelled in India from 5 August 2011 and replaced by a single Act which is The Food Safety And Standards Act, 2006 | Nepal Standards Act (1980, as amended), Nepal Standards Regulations (1982), Nepal Seeds Act (1988), The Seed regulation (1997), Plant Protection Rules (2010), Feed Act (1966), Animal Health and Livestock Services Act (1998) | Miscellaneous Regulations under section 32 of the Food Act including regulations on multiple aspects such as Food Hygiene, Food standards, Food Labelling, Iodized salt, Food sweeteners, Bread standards, Preservative and milk, Colouring and many others included in the section in various years |

Source: Compiled from country reports on 'Laws and Regulations to Food and Food Additives'

The South Asian region has witnessed falling tariffs in the recent years.[11] The success of the South Asian Free Trade Area (SAFTA) would therefore depend, among other factors, on the level of cooperation among the South Asian countries on issues concerning sanitary and phytosanitary (SPS) measures and Technical Barriers to Trade (TBT) that constitute a major proportion of the non-tariff barriers in the South Asian region.

As evident from the Table 4.9, NTMs in multiple forms faced by the South Asian countries come across as a major challenge. Particularly the food exports from India and Afghanistan among South Asian countries faced highest number of bilateral NTMs. Most of the bilateral NTMs imposed on these countries are in the SPS category (i.e. 93% of total bilateral NTMs imposed followed by antidumping measures (ADP)). These SPS measures are considered a major hindrance for market access by many developing countries, as trade barriers are no longer a major concern. These measures are not in favour of developing countries because of complexity in its numbers and nature of requirement (i.e. standards) that these countries have to meet in order to access developed countries and other global markets. In addition to it the poor capacity to these standards by developing countries adds up to this problem (Doherty, 2010).

In the case of Sri Lanka, where Europe has taken the league in terms of exports of food products leaving the US and Japan behind, which formed the second and third largest markets respectively until 2003, upon which there was a contraction of the share of the US market. The Japanese market continued to expand, absorbing 23.7% of processed food exports of the country until 2010. In 2010, the share of the EU in Sri Lankan exports was 38.5%, whereas Japan and the US constituted 11.2% and 3.6% respectively in the total processed exports. Beverages, fish products, fruits and vegetables and cereals constitute most of the exports of Sri Lanka. Non-tariff barriers have increasingly gained an important space in these markets. Rejections from Sri Lanka have increasingly been rising from 2002 to 2010. A look at the bilateral export profile to the US highlighted the fall in Sri Lankan exports from

TABLE 4.9 Number of bilateral NTBs faced by SAARC countries

PRTISO	ADP	CV	SPS	Total
AFG			2,738 (42.4)	2,738 (42.4)
BGD	7 (0.1)		75 (1.2)	82 (1.3)
BTN			83 (1.3)	83 (1.3)
IND	256 (4)	115 (1.8)	2,843 (44.1)	3,214 (49.8)
LKA	16 (0.2)	14 (0.2)	20 (0.3)	50 (0.8)
NPL	4 (0.1)		50 (0.8)	54 (0.8)
PAK	24 (0.4)	7 (0.1)	201 (3.1)	232 (3.6)
Total	307 (4.8)	136 (2.1)	6,010 (93.1)	6,453

Source: Author's estimation based on WTO I-TIP database

TABLE 4.10 Trends in FDA rejections in South Asia and their causes, 2011–13

Reason for refusal	Multiple	Filth	Salmonella	Labelling 2008–11	Labelling 2011–13	Others	Total (2011–13)
Bangladesh	102	38	169	21	13	88	410
India	1,340	390	678	742	22	2,430	4,860
Nepal	3			3		6	9
Pakistan	254	40	68	281		1,440	1,802
Sri Lanka	136	27	37	263		57	257

Source: Author's compilations from various sources

US$ 34.8 million in 1990 to US$ 22.9 million in 2010 with a decadal CAGR of −2.1% from 1990 to 2010.

It shall be important to look into the US FDA rejections for multiple reasons that reflect certain emerging challenges that South Asian countries are experiencing in the global market. Table 4.10 provides details for rejections on various grounds for the South Asian countries for 2011–13. The trend is similar to what was witnessed in the initial years of the decade. The number of rejection cases due to salmonella has gone up from 186 in 2008 to 325 in 2010 to 402 in 2012, along with 'filth' increasing to 236 in 2012 as compared to 189 in 2010. Labelling rejections has been constant more or less, with the statistics being 248 in 2008 and 254 in 2010. For instance, in the case of Sri Lanka's rejected consignments, the share of labelling as a cause of rejection has gone up tremendously, with a mere 17% share in 2000–01 to 53% in 2002. Though in later years it was also been consistent with 52% in 2008 and the same thereafter. The other category that saw expansion was 'filth' (as named by US FDA).

Another important dimension to be analyzed focusses on the barriers within the SAARC region. There are multiple issues faced by the region. For instance, Bangladesh faces multiple issues in terms of its export restrictions to India. The Bangladesh Economic Outlook (2010) has mentioned the following impediments:

- The export of agriculture products to India faces several impediments related to risk analysis in context of 'human, animal or plant life or health'.
- India also insists on shelf life to be not less than 60% of original shelf life at the time of import as per the Food Adulteration (Prevention) Act 1954.
- Rule 32 of the Prevention of Food Adulteration Rules (PFA), 1955, of India deals with packing and labelling of foods. This rule alone has 30 provisos, and provisos within provisos. In addition there are also cross-references to other rules. These rules prescribe the contents to be specified on the label, the size of the label, the design of the label, the areas specified for display panels, details

of colours and flavours, trade name or description of food contained in the package, names of ingredients used in the product by weight and volume etc. Goods are cleared only on receipt of the test report. No certificate from the country of origin is accepted. The results of the laboratory tests cannot be challenged. Separate regulations have been enacted for different food items.
- India has banned the export of betel nut from Bangladesh through land customs stations by their notification No, 49/2006, dated 20 February 2007.

India is a major trading partner to Nepal and accounts for nearly 80% of its agricultural trade. The Indian government imposes several laws and standards for agro commodities trade, and its compliance by the trading partner is a must. Among the various restrictions, the Indian Plant Quarantine Order (PQO) 2003, is regarded as one of the major issues as far as trade of agro commodities is concerned.

Even in the case of exports, multiple issues prevail in the Indian landscape. A report from the Federation of Pakistan Chambers of Commerce (FPCCI) pointed towards the multiplicity of standard industries (nearly 25 agencies) in India that act as a major hurdle in terms of quality approval of exports. Non-tariff measures have emerged as one of the foremost areas for joint action among the policy makers of India and Pakistan.[12]

In addition to multiplicity of institutions, another area of concern in the case of the South Asian region is the differentiation in the food standards. This acts as a major barrier towards increased regional trade. As is clear from Table 4.11, standards vary from country to country as illustrated through specific products and the related food standards in each country in the region.

There are certain policy options available to the South Asian economies to overcome the issues regarding NTBs. The South Asian economies need to come together in unison to address the challenges with respect to compliance with food standards in South Asia. In this particular context there are lessons to be learned from the ASEAN region, which is led by the Committee on Food, Agriculture and Forestry (COFAF) and ASEAN Consultative Committee on Standards and Quality (ACCSQ), which adopted Good Agricultural Practises (GAP), Good Collection Practises (GCP) and Good Agriculture and Collective Practises (GACP), which actually facilitated adoption of common approach and common baselines. In a similar context, it would be beneficial to analyze the policy measures adopted by other regional trading blocs such as EU and NAFTA with respect to food security (Table 4.12).

With the increasing share of food trade in the South Asian region, an agreement on harmonization of various elements may be explored. The inclusion of various aspects like principles governing inspection and certification may be involved following the Codex, or any other international organization with open access to membership.

TABLE 4.11 Specific product standards in the South Asian countries

Product specific standards	Bangladesh	India	Nepal	Sri Lanka
Cow's milk	The standards include cow's milk along with other local processed milk products manufactured and traded in the country. The main descriptions include 1) cow milk, 2) buffalo milk 3) milk or mixed milk	There are standards for Milk in the categories such as 1) Mixed Milk, Standardized Milk, Recombined 2) Milk, Toned 3) Milk, Double Toned Milk 4) Skimmed Milk 5) Full Cream Milk	There are standards for processed milk including 1) standards for pasteurization 2) sterilization	There are definition and standards for Cow's Milk. There are individual definitions for Milk and Milk categories such as 1) standardized milk 2) pasteurized milk 3) sterilized milk 4) flavoured milk 5) reconstituted milk and others
Prepared frozen foods	No provision	Standards available for commodities like dessert, fruits, vegetables, meat and meat products and fish and fish products	No provision	No provision
Carbonated water	Standards available specifically for 1) aerated water 2) Soda water available	Standards for 1) Non-alcoholic beverages 2) carbonated water	There are specifications for carbonated water (non-alcoholic beverages)	Standards available for carbonated soft drinks
Instant noodles	No Provision available	No provision	Standards available for instant noodles	No provision

Source: Based on International Life Sciences Institute (ILSI), India, 2013

TABLE 4.12 Policy framework for food safety in select regional trading blocks

RIA	ASEAN	EU	NAFTA
key agency	ASEAN Consultative Committee on Standards and Quality (ACCSQ)	European Food Safety Authority	(a) US Food and Drug Administration (FDA) except for meat and poultry products (b) The Food and Safety Inspection Service (FSIS) for Meat and Poultry products
Dispute settlement mechanisms	Self Dispute Settlement Mechanism through Consultation or matter being raised to Senior Economic Officials Meeting (SEOM)	Follows WTO Dispute Settlement Mechanisms	Follows WTO Dispute Settlement Mechanism
Harmonization in agricultural products	(a) Codex standards for labelling of pre-packaged food, Food Additives, Guidelines on Claims and Nutrition Labelling (b) International Standards for phytosanitary Measures, Standards Number (c) Organisation of Animal Health Guidelines for disease reporting, import, export risk analysis and surveillance	(a) None of the Mutual recognition Agreements signed by the EU relates to the food sector (b) EU is also reluctant to recognise the general equivalence of food safety standards	(a) The NAFTA signatories have agreed to work toward "equivalent" SPS measures without reducing national levels of desired, appropriate protection. (b) NAFTA allows countries to determine their own level of appropriate protection
TBT-related initiatives	The Prepared Food Stuff Product Working Group (PFPWG) under the ACCSQ undertakes several activities such as (i) Exchange of Information on standards, rules (ii) Review and analyze the comparative study of regulatory regime among member countries (iii) Identify areas for possible harmonization and MRAs (iv) Develop sectoral MRA (v) Identify technical infrastructure needs and build up mutual confidence in conformity assessment		(a) In total, there are more than 30 NAFTA Committees and Working Groups in areas such as technical standards, rules of origin, and government procurement.
SPS-related initiatives	Working Group on SPS under the SOM AMAF includes following action plans including compiling information on NTMs affecting agricultural-products and developing MRA of SPS standards to liberalise intra-ASEAN trade in agricultural-products		NAFTA committee on sanitary and phytosanitary measures which was created to facilitate the enhancement of food safety and sanitary conditions and to promote the equivalence of SPS measures within the NAFTA countries

Also, it may be analyzed that multiple inspections and certification systems may be capable of meeting similar objectives and can therefore cater to the idea of equivalence. Although it is mandatory for all products to meet the same safety standards as domestically produced foods, international trade rules allow each foreign country to apply its own differing, regulatory authorities and institutional systems in such standards under an Internationally recognised concept known as equivalence. The Codex Committee on Food Import and Export Certification and Inspection System (CCFICS) has articulated guidelines with respect to equivalence, as many developing countries did not have a clear picture about it.[13] As per the Codex guidelines, it was clear that the agreement on equivalence did not have a mandated duplication of measures, but it pointed to the acceptance of alternative measures that fulfil an importing partner's accepted level of sanitary and phytosanitary protection provisions.

At the international level, MRAs (Mutual Recognition Agreements) have also emerged as instruments to lessen the scope and role of NTB in trade. They serve as a crucial alternative to address limitations with respect to standards for countries. It benefits in multiple ways, including lesser cost of retesting or recertification and reducing the time for trade approvals. In this context, India has taken several initiatives. To recognise its conformity assessment procedures, The Export Council of India has entered into several agreements with different countries (Table 4.13).

TABLE 4.13 Existing recognition arrangements by India

Country	Products covered	Year of agreement/ recognition
USA	Black pepper	1988
European Commission	Fish and Fishery products, Basmati rice	1997
Australia	Fish and Fishery products	2002
Korea	Frozen marine products, processed spice goods, processed nuts, tea, honey, jam, preserved goods, sauce, sugar	2004
Turkey	Food products, food packaging materials and stainless steel utensils	2004
Sri Lanka	Around 164 products under the Import Inspection Scheme of Sri Lanka namely milk products, edible oil, packaged water, preserved food, toiletries, bicycle tyres and tubes, steel section and wires, electric goods and PVC cables and cords, etc.	2005
Singapore	Food and Agriculture (egg products, dairy products, drinking water), Electric & electronic products, Telecommunication equipment and drugs and Pharmaceuticals	2005
Japan	Poultry and marine products	2005
Italy	Marine sector (Technical cooperation)	2005
Russia	Fish & Fishery products	2009
Brazil	Fish & Fishery products	2010

Source: Compiled by the author from various ECI Reports

Table 4.13 gives a description of the Existing Recognition Agreements for India. One can see that Sri Lanka is the only country with which India has entered into a recognition agreement, involving 164 products that constitute several food items as well. It is also exploring Technical Cooperation Agreement (TCA) as an alternative instrument, which is *de facto* recognition of a third party. India has also taken several initiatives with respect to institution building for standard setting for trade – for instance, The National Accreditation Board for Testing and Calibration Laboratories (NABL), under the Department of Science and Technology, which is also a part of an International network, namely The International Laboratory Accreditation Corporation (ILAC) and Asia Pacific Laboratory Accreditation Corporation (APLAC).

There is an urgent need for the establishment of accredited laboratories to cater to standard related issues acting as impediments in the South Asian region. Also, a need for capacity building for accreditation infrastructure development is felt especially for Bangladesh, Nepal and Sri Lanka. Several initiatives are being undertaken by the local governments with cooperation of advanced countries.

The success of the South Asian Free Trade Area (SAFTA) would depend, among other factors, on the level of cooperation among the South Asian countries on issues concerning sanitary and phytosanitary (SPS) measures and Technical Barriers to Trade (TBT). The trade in food, plants, animals and other products can be expanded to a large extent by greater mutual understanding on regulations and procedures relating to SPS measures, which is crucial for regional trade facilitation in South Asia. It is also important to realise that these South Asian countries may have shared concerns with respect to standards, as most of them export common products. While each WTO member has an option to fix their own 'Appropriate Level of Protection' (ALOP), it would benefit immensely the countries if they appropriately address issues related to SPS in the right earnestness. A region-wide coordinated position at the international standards setting bodies particularly, at the forums like Codex Commission etc., may be considered in this regard.

In South Asia, the external sector lays the foundation for growth, with the processed food sector contributing the most to it in recent years. Despite a negative trade deficit with the rest of the world, it has been successful in registering an overall trade surplus in the processed food sector, though with a declining volume of exports in the later years. Recent trends reveal an interesting aspect where South Asia is emerging as an exporter to the regional economies, i.e., the developing countries more significantly than the outside world. With a shrinking share of exports to the US and Japan, its processed food sector exports including sugar, egg, cereals and dairy products have been confined to the region. However, there is still immense potential that remains untapped. This clearly calls for strengthening of cooperation among the South Asian economies on multiple fronts, with an aim of enhancing regional trade in agricultural exports. In order to realize the existing potential, strengthened SPS and TBT measures are a must.

Way forward

The post green revolution era has posed multiple challenges pertaining to food security in the South Asian region. There are myriad challenges pertaining to different dimensions as discussed in the chapter. However, there is ample scope for cooperation within SAARC countries such as collaboration in agricultural research which along with financial and infrastructural commitments can substantially overhaul the food and agricultural production system in the region. This will also augment the returns for the large number of people who depend on the agriculture sector for their livelihoods. Following are certain specific policy recommendations for issues pertaining to food security and food safety in South Asia.

Amidst these considerations, it cannot be denied that a farmer's access to and right over seeds lays the foundation of agriculture and therefore represents an important component of food security. While the idea of privatizing living matter (seeds, genes, breeds etc.) was germinated by the WTO's Intellectual property agreement on Trade Related Aspects of Intellectual Property Rights (TRIPS), the *sui generis* option (meaning one of its own kind) it gave to countries, has not been fully used due to several implementation issues. With India being the only country amongst the South Asian nations to have a PVP law in motion (other countries have drafts or the same), there are multiple challenges in terms of implementation of farmer's rights and therefore food security in the times to come.

Given the magnitude of informal trade in South Asia being large and the dominance of the food sector in this informal trade, there is immense opportunity for regional cooperation in this regard. Since the magnitude of processed food exports by the developing world to the developed countries has increased manifold, there is immense potential for export growth for the South Asian nations. Achieving food safety that composes a component of the tier of food security issues, therefore, becomes an area of utmost importance, especially since food safety has moved to the forefront of international trade.

However, exploiting these opportunities poses multiple challenges. In particular, the capacity of the developing countries' exporters to penetrate these markets depends critically on their ability to meet the stringent food safety standards. In this respect, impediments faced with regard to international trade in seeds, fertilizers and strategic grains, especially due to food safety standards that were in dispute over SPS and TBT mechanisms, pose a major challenge for the trade in food for the South Asian countries. Therefore, the need for an effective integration amongst the South Asian economies for mutual benefit is primary.

Regional coordination on food safety issues

In the case of South Asia, a multiplicity of agencies may often lead to various issues including difficulties in coordination. There is a lack of one single competent authority to monitor for quality and standards of exports and imports in the South Asian region. For instance, for import related regulation India has 'The Food

Safety and Standards Authority of India' (FSSAI), which consolidates various acts and orders that have hitherto handled food related issues in various Ministries and Departments. It also has the Export Inspection Council (EIC), which was established in order to ensure sound development of the export trade in India through quality control and inspection and for matters connected thereof. Therefore a convergence of such authorities into one competent authority could be beneficial as also seen in the case of the western economies. The USA, for instance, has the USFDA, which is the nodal institution for regulation and supervision of food safety standards.

South Asian Regional Standards Organisation (SARSO)

In this regard, the members of SAARC established a specialised body called the South Asian Regional Standards Organization (SARSO) in the year 2011 to facilitate coordination in standard development and conformity assessment in order to improve the intraregional trade as well as increase market access globally. The major objective of this specialised body is to promote and undertake harmonisation of national standards of the SAARC members in order to remove the trade barriers and enhance the flow of goods and services in the region. In SARSO, there are six sectoral technical committees (STCs) on (a) food and agricultural products; (b) jute, textile and leather; (c) building materials; (d) electrical, electronics, telecom and IT; (f) chemical and chemical products; and (g) conformity assessment. These STCs develop draft SAARC regional standards through consensus among SAARC countries, and finally these standards are then endorsed by the governing board of SARSO. All standards developed by SARSO have a unique identity and are marked as SAARC Regional Standards (SARS) with a specific number like SARS 0001. In this particular context – SARSO as a new entity in the area of trade related standards – there are lessons to be learned from the ASEAN region.

Scope for enhanced technical cooperation

Technical cooperation holds much significance especially for developing regions like South Asian where regional cooperation can strengthen national structures by means of transfer of skills and knowledge systems. It is essentially a process where two or more developing countries pursue their individual or collective development through cooperative exchanges of knowledge, skills, resources and technical know-how. For instance, The Indian Technical and Economic Cooperation (ITEC) is a step towards greater technical cooperation amongst the South Asian economies. The ITEC programme is a successful bilateral assistance programme by the Indian government that focusses on addressing the needs of the developing countries through innovative technical cooperation for developing countries in Asia, Africa, Latin America, Eastern Europe, Central Asia, Gulf countries and small islands in the Pacific and the Caribbean region. The programme makes a special recognition of regional grouping such as ASEAN, BIMSTEC and AU by providing additional slots.

Similarly, there is wide scope for regional cooperation on the safety front where technical cooperation can serve as an effective tool to reduce the costs of compliance of emerging complex food safety standards. The India-Bhutan MoU is an example for the same. In order to ensure better safety standards in Bhutan's imports from India, a Memorandum of Understanding was signed in the year 2011 wherein it was agreed by both the parties that the Bhutanese imports from India would come under the inspection purview of the Export and Import Council (EIC) of India and Bhutan Agriculture and Food Regulatory Authority (BAFRA) to ensure quality and safety. Given the magnitude of imports from India to Bhutan, the agreement serves as a win-win situation for the countries. In the case of any non-compliance with respect to safety, labelling and packaging, the Bhutanese authority can report the same to EIC which shall undertake necessary investigation. The second aspect of this MOU is the technical cooperation that involves an exchange of experts, training of the staff on important aspects like accreditation regulation and a certification system that shall generate further efficiency.

Revisiting SAFTA rules of origin

While regional economic integration has intensified in Asia and the Pacific, particularly in Southeast and South Asia regions, where a number of bilateral and regional FTAs are in place and many more under negotiations, intraregional trade has not picked up accordingly. One of the reasons for this is the complication brought about by the different Rules of Origin (ROO) agreed to in these FTAs, resulting in the reluctance of private sectors to avail of the provisions under these 'free trade agreements'.

The differences of preferential ROOs from one FTA to another creates complications and inefficiency for the business sector, since manufacturers in an exporting country must adjust their production operations to different sets of ROO in order to benefit from tariff preferences under those FTAs. It is therefore important to simplify and harmonise these ROOs in order for the various FTAs signed and being negotiated, as well as future ones, to result in lower transaction costs and greater intraregional trade in goods as well as trade with trading partners outside the region. The SAFTA ROO, most relevant amongst which is the Generalized System of Preferences (GSP), an autonomous tariff preferential schemes offered mainly by OECD countries to eligible products originating in designated developing countries, agreed at UNCTAD in 1964, is a combination of change in tariff heading rules and a specific value added rule, with regional cumulative rules. With the widening of product coverage under SAFTA, stringent ROO elements could be introduced. Since the finalisation of a comprehensive agreement will be in 2016, still there will be time to examine other preferential ROO and work on policy options on SAFTA ROO and its possible simplification and improvement. To organise a technical workshop exclusively for the SAARC Member States will be an effective capacity building activity as requested by participants from SAARC during the workshop on simplification and harmonization of ROO, March 2008.

Substantive mutual recognition agreements

With the increasing cost of compliance of emerging complex food safety standards, regional cooperation serves as an effective tool in sharing costs related to the compliance of such standards. Regional initiatives in the form of increased numbers of Mutual Recognition Agreements should be one such measure that can help in minimizing the costs of setting up infrastructure facilities and sharing costs of compliance, along with other policy options like agreements on equivalence and recognition of conformity assessment. The India and Sri Lanka MRA for 164 products gives the sense of reduction in trade barriers in the South Asian context. Such success stories can be realized with other trading partners as well.

Gains from strengthened food trade in South Asia

In order to achieve food security in South Asia it is important to realize the role of agricultural trade between the nations. Although the region trade is impeded by multiple tariff and non-tariff barriers, as discussed in the third section of this chapter, there is immense potential that can be realized in order to promote regional agricultural trade. For instance, the existing demand-supply gap in high yielding varieties of rice seeds in India and Bangladesh provides a huge scope for cooperation between the two countries that could be realized through trade and knowledge sharing. Lack of formal cooperation is causing difficulties in terms of availability and access to quality rice seeds, a critical input for production of the most important staple food in both the countries. This non-cooperation is also facilitating the informal exchange of low-quality seeds. There are multiple projects initiated in this regard including the project titled 'Addressing Barriers to Rice Seeds Trade between India and Bangladesh' supported by the Bill and Melinda Gates Foundation and the 'Stress Tolerant Rice for Africa and South Asia' (STRASA) project. In order to formalize the cooperation, signing a memorandum of understanding has been the suggestion by the representatives of the seeds association of both the nations.[14] A memorandum would initiate long-term cooperation in other seeds as well, enhancing the overall agricultural productivity in the region. A need for identification of existing gaps in agricultural cooperation and robust estimation of informal trade in HYV seeds are other critical dimensions in this regard.

Notes

1 See Annexure 1 to 5 of Rao et al. (1997). See also Taneja (1999 and 2005) that mentions the level of official and unofficial trade of India with other South Asian countries for multiple years.
2 Ibid.
3 Mittal and Deepti (2009). See also Schutter (2009).
4 In this study, processed food includes live animals, beverages and tobacco, animal and vegetable oils and fats, oil seeds and oleaginous fruit, unmanufactured tobacco and refuse. Non-processed food includes meat products, dairy products, dried or preserved eggs, fish products, meal and flour of wheat, meslin and other cereals, fruits and vegetables, flour

or starch preparations, macaroni, malt extract, prepared or preserved vegetables, tapioca, sago, substitutes from starches, fruit preparations, nuts, jams, jellies, sugar preparations and honey, coffee extracts, instant tea, edible products and preparations and processed vegetable oils. The classification was used by Athukorala and Jayasuriya (2005) using the SITC product classification, and the classification was further expanded using HS classification by Mohanty (2007).

5 See Tables 4.1, 4.2 and 4.3 indicating relatively low levels of intraregional food trade in South Asia.
6 Several sources indicate South Asia's heavy reliance on external markets for food trade. See Weerahewa (2009) and Nanda (2012).
7 See Table 4.3 representing South Asia's main food commodities which are traded within the region.
8 See Nanda (2012).
9 Ibid.
10 See Chatterjee and Khadka (2011).
11 See Table 4.6 on average preferential tariffs on food products in 2012.
12 Pakistan Today (2011).
13 See Codex (1999) for details.

References

Athukorala, P. C. and S. Jayasuriya (2005), 'Processed Food Exports from Developing Countries and Food-Safety Related Market Access Issues: Aims and Scope of the Research Project', Research and Information System for Developing Countries (RIS), New Delhi, India.

Bach Friis, C. and A. Matthews (1999), 'Development Aid and Food Security', Second Annual Conference on Global Economic Analysis, Danish Institute of Agricultural and Fisheries Economics, Denmark.

Banerjee, A. (2010), 'Challenges to Food Security in South Asia', RIS Policy Brief, No. 47, Research and Information System for Developing Countries, New Delhi.

Bhutani, S. (2013), 'Re-Searching Agriculture in South Asia: The Law and Policy Context for Agricultural Research and Development and Its Impact on Smallholder Farmers', IIED, London.

Chatterjee, B. and M. Khadka (2011), 'Climate Change and Food Security in South Asia', CUTS International, Jaipur.

Chaturvedi, S. (2004), 'Regional Cooperation for Poverty Alleviation and Food Security in South Asia', RIS Discussion Paper, No. 87, Research and Information System for Developing Countries, New Delhi.

Chaturvedi, S. and S. K. Mohanty (2011), 'South Asia and Trade of Safe and Quality Foods: Role of Equivalence, MRAs and Other Policy Options', FAO Regional Office for Asia and the Pacific.

Codex Alimentarius Commission (1999), 'Guidelines for the Development of Equivalence Agreements Regarding Food Import and Export Inspection and Certification Systems', CAC/GL 34–1999, Geneva.

Doherty, M. (2010), 'The Importance of Sanitary and Phytosanitary Measures to Fisheries Negotiations in Economic Partnership Agreements', International Centre for Trade and Sustainable Development (ICTSD): 21–23.

FAO, IFAD and WFP (2013), 'The State of Food Insecurity in the World 2013: The Multiple Dimensions of Food Security', FAO, Rome.

FICCI (2014), 'The South Asian Century: Progressing Towards Regional Integration', Federation of Indian Chambers of Commerce and Industry, New Delhi.

IFPRI (2013), 'Global Hunger Index Report', International Food Policy Research Institute, Washington, DC.

Jiongwanich, J. (2009), 'Impact of Food Safety Standards on Processed Food Exports From Developing Countries', Asian Development Bank Working Paper Series, No. 154, Asian Development Bank, Philippines.

Mitchell, D. (2008), 'A Note on Rising Food Prices', Policy Research Working Paper, No. 4682. Development Prospects Group, World Bank.

Mittal, S. and S. Deepti (2009), 'Food Security in South Asia: Issues and Opportunities', Indian Council for Research on International Economic Relations. New Delhi.

Mohanty, S. K. (2007), 'Trade and Environment Dimensions in the Food and Food Processing Industries in Asia and the Pacific', Regional Study, UNESCAP, Bangkok.

Nanda, Nitya (2012), 'Agricultural Trade in South Asia: Barriers and Prospects', SAWTEE Working Paper, No. 03/12, South Asia Watch on Trade, Economics and Environment, Nepal.

Narasimhan, S. M. (2008), 'Towards a Balanced "Sui Generis" Plant Variety Regime', UNDP, New York.

Pakistan Today (2011), 'Non Tariff Barriers Hampering Pakistan's Exports to India', Lahore, Friday, September 2.

Peschard, K. (2013), 'Farmer's Rights and Food Sovereignty: Critical Insights From India, Food Sovereignty: A Critical Dialogue', *The Journal of Peasant Studies*, International Conference, Yale University.

Plahe, J. (2011), 'TRIPS Downhill: India's Plant Variety Protection System and Implications for Small Farmers', *Journal of Contemporary Asia*, Vol. 41(1), pp. 75–98.

Pray, C. E. and A. Naseem (2007), 'Supplying Crop Biotechnology to the Poor', *Journal of Development Studies*, Vol. 43(1), pp. 192–217.

Ragavan, S. and J. Mayer (2007), 'Community-based Rights and IPR REgime: Revisiting the Debate', RIS Discussion Paper, No. 122, Research and Information System for Developing Countries, New Delhi.

Ramasundaram, P., S. Kurup and R. Chand (2011), 'Maneuvering Technology for Surplus Extraction: The Case of Bt Cotton in India', NCAER Policy Brief, No. 37, National Centre for Agricultural Economics and Policy Research, New Delhi.

Rangnekar, D. (2013), 'The Cunning State of Farmers' Rights in India: Aligning with Global Law or Emancipating Farmers?', Food Sovereignty: A Critical Dialogue International Conference, Yale University, United States.

Rao, V., S. Baruah and R. U. Das (1997), 'India's Border Trade with Select Neighbouring Countries', Research and Information System for Developing Countries, New Delhi.

Santilli, J. (2012), *Agbiodiversity and the Law*, Routledge, London.

Sastry, K., H. Rashmi and J. Badri (2011), 'Research and Development Perspectives of Transgenic Cotton', *Journal of Intellectual Property Rights*, Vol. 16(March), pp. 139–153.

Schutter, O. D. (2009), 'International Trade in Agriculture and the Right to Food', Occasional Paper, No. 46, Dialogue on Globalisation, Friedrich-Ebert-Stiftung, Geneva.

Sharma, P., and Gulati, A. (2012), 'Approaches to Food Security in Brazil, China, India, Malaysia and Nigeria', Indian Council for Research on International Economic Relations, New Delhi.

Spielman, D. J., D. Kolady, A. Cavalieri and N. Chandrasekhara Rao (2011), 'The Seed and Agricultural Biotechnology Industries in India', IFPRI Discussion Paper, No. 01103, International Food Policy Research Institute, Washington, DC.

Taneja, N. (1999), 'Informal Trade in the SAARC Region', Indian Council for Research in International Economic Relations, New Delhi.

Taneja, N. (2005), 'Informal Trade in the SAARC Region: Implications for Free Trade Agreements', in *Towards South Asian Economic Integration and Unity*, S. Soz, S.K. Sahni, and R.N. Srivastava (Eds.), Foundation for Peace and Sustainable Development, New Delhi.

UNESCAP-SSWA (2013), 'Regional Cooperation for Strengthening National Food Security Strategies in South Asia: A Policy Agenda', United Nations Economic and Social Commission for Asia and the Pacific, South and South-West Asia Office, New Delhi.

USAID and EAT (2014), 'Regional Trade in Seed, Fertilizer and Strategic Grains. A Review of the Legal, Regulatory, and Institutional Constraints to Growth Across South Asia', United States Agency for International Development (USAID) and Enabling Agricultural Trade (EAT), United States.

Weerahewa, J. (2009), 'Impact of Trade Facilitation Measures and Regional Trade Agreements on Food and Agricultural Trade in South Asia', ARTNET Working Paper Series, No. 69, Asia-Pacific Research and Training Network on Trade.

Wise, T. and S. Murphy (2012), 'The Continuing Food Crisis', *Economic and Political Weekly*, Vol. 47(08).

World Bank (2006), 'Intellectual Property Rights: Designing Regimes to Support Plant Breeding in Developing Countries', Agriculture and Rural Development Department, Report No. 35517-GLB.

5

SAARC FOOD BANK

Raising operational efficacy

*Mustafizur Rahman, Estiaque Bari
and Sherajum Monira Farin*

Introduction

This chapter seeks to contextualise the current food security scenario in South Asia with a view to operationalise the idea of a collective regional initiative to improve food security situation in South Asia as embedded in the concept of the SAARC Food Bank (SFB). It goes without saying that the modality of ensuring food security through regional collective action ought to take as its reference point the dynamics of production, distribution, trade, stock and reserves of rice and wheat. Common topography, ecology and geography, significantly large border areas, shared risks of trans-border environmental damages of high frequency and intensity and susceptibility to production shortfall – all these factors add to South Asia's concerns regarding food security.

There is also a spatial dimension to this vulnerability which emanate from similar nature of calamities and adverse environmental impacts in South Asia. This reinforces the need for common region-wide initiatives to tackle the attendant challenges. Since the impacts of disasters and calamities, whether human-made or natural, could transcend national boundaries and give rise to cross-border problems, there is an added justification to take appropriate collective measures to forestall such possibilities. In view of this, an effective response mechanism to address the challenges ought to be multilateral, relying on regional cooperation among countries that share common geography, history and culture, and whose economies are increasingly interconnected (Ingram et al., 2010). It is pertinent to recall here that the need for collective endeavours to ensure regional food security, with participation of regional countries, was recognised by the SAARC early on. Indeed, this recognition led to the establishment of the SFB in 2007. The task at hand is to identify appropriate institutional architecture and operational modalities to enable SFB to service its mandate of helping SAARC member countries to address food-emergency situations through efforts based on partnership and sharing.

This chapter is based on a review of relevant secondary evidence, use of quantitative tools, key informant interviews (KIIs) and focus group discussions (FGDs). KIIs and FGDs were participated in by representatives of key stakeholder groups. Review of relevant literature was carried out to glean the needed information from secondary sources, which included published materials and relevant documents, agreements, regulations and meeting minutes pertaining to the SFB. Review of cross-regional experiences in ensuring collective food security was undertaken with a view to gain learnings; the possibility of replicating some of the pertinent measures was examined to draw insights for the SFB. An analytical exercise was conducted by using the most updated secondary data available from the World Development Indicators (WDI), UNCTAD stat (statistical database of the United Nations Conference on Trade and Development) and Trade Map. Quantitative assessments (meta-analyses) were based on latest FAO (Food and Agriculture Organisation of the United Nations) data set. Estimates of production shortage at the country level were made on the basis of certain assumptions (spelt out in the Annex). Reserve adequacy for the SFB were estimated on the basis of possible production shortages at the country level.

This introductory section is followed by three sections. The second section provides a brief overview of the state of production, demand and trade in foodgrains and draws relevant insights from the review of literature and cross-regional experiences. The third section lays out the background of setting up the SFB, its structure and challenges of its operationalisation. The fourth section comes up with a number of recommendations towards raising operational efficacy of the SFB.

Stylised facts and review of literature

Some stylised facts

It is to be kept in mind that South Asia is a major player in global foodgrains production. According to the FAO statistics, in 2014, South Asia alone produced 30.4%, 17.9% and 3.3% of global production of rice, wheat and maize, respectively. India's share in production of foodgrains is understandably the highest in the region. As per the authors' calculation, South Asia as a region is a net importer of foodgrains, with India and Pakistan being the only two net exporting countries (Table 5.1). In terms of adequacy of food at the disposal of citizens, Bangladesh, India and Pakistan are countries with food surplus; Afghanistan, Nepal and Sri Lanka have deficit in foodgrains availability. Bangladesh is a net importer of foodgrains despite having a surplus in terms of rice production.

However, intraregional trade of the SAARC countries has remained at very low levels, at about 6.2% of their global trade (Table 5.2), in spite of the fact that South Asian countries have opened up their economies significantly over the past years, as evidenced by the relatively higher degree of openness (Table 5.3). India and Pakistan are major exporters of foodgrains in the region; while the majority of SAARC members have significant trade in foodgrains with India, Afghanistan's trade is mostly with Pakistan (Rahman et al., 2017). Several features of foodgrains

TABLE 5.1 Food production deficit/surplus of South Asian countries, 2013

Country	Population (million)	Domestic supply[1] ('000 MT)	Production ('000 MT)	Food gap[2] ('000 MT)	Net import ('000 MT)
Afghanistan	31	6,453	5,511	−942	1,292
Bangladesh	157	33,929	35,606	1,677	3,128
India	1,252	181,226	199,696	18,470	−18,473
Nepal	28	5,148	4,732	−416	532
Pakistan	182	27,313	28,746	1,433	−4,261
Sri Lanka	21	3,423	3,082	-341	831

Source: Authors' calculation using data from FAOSTAT (2016)

Notes
1. Domestic supply = Foodgrains production + Net import + Change in stock.
2. Food gap = Production − Domestic supply (negative sign demarcates 'Deficit').

TABLE 5.2 Percentage of intraregional trade to the region's global trade (five-year average)

Region	1996–2000	2001–2005	2006–2010	2011–2015
SAARC	4.6	6.1	6.1	6.2
ASEAN	22.9	24	25.0	25.4
ASEAN Plus Three	32.7	34.8	34.6	35.5

Source: Authors' compilation using UNCTADstat (2016)

TABLE 5.3 Trade openness of South Asian countries

Country	2016			2014	
	Trade openness	Import (% of GDP)	Export (% of GDP)	Time to import (days)	Time to export (days)
Afghanistan	55.9	49.0	6.9	91	86
Bangladesh	38.0	21.3	16.6	34	28
Bhutan	81.5	52.1	29.4	37	38
India	39.8	20.6	19.2	21	17
Maldives	182.8	89.0	93.8	22	21
Nepal	50.0	39.4	10.7	39	40
Pakistan	24.5	15.8	8.7	18	21
Sri Lanka	50.5	29.1	21.4	13	16
South Asia	38.9	20.9	18.0	34	33

Source: Authors' compilation from World Bank (2016)

production and trade in South Asia are pertinent in the context of the subsequent discussion on SFB in this chapter: first, the status of South Asian countries varies with regard to the correspondence between demand and supply of foodgrains. Second, surplus/deficit status tend to change in view of production performance in particular periods. Third, bottlenecks in the movement of foodgrains between origin and destination involves significant delays. Fourth, both tariff and non-tariff barriers inform the nature of trade in foodgrains. Fifth, a price of the foodgrains that tend to evolve through regional trade could serve as a reference point for price fixation in operationalising the SFB.

All SAARC countries have a number of policies in place to address food and nutrition concerns and reduce market uncertainties.[1] Common core elements of these policies are: raising agricultural productivity, development of functional market structure, adoption of sustainable technological options, investment in agricultural research and trade and tariff policies relating to foodgrains and distribution of food among vulnerable groups. Crop insurance policies are in place in some SAARC countries to provide safeguard to foodgrains-producing farmers against possible crop losses; however, concerns remain about the effectiveness of those schemes. Agricultural policies pursued by SAARC countries in general aim to create a conducive and stable environment towards production, availability and accessibility of food. Nutrition security is specifically addressed through various safety net programmes. All major crop-producing South Asian countries (India, Pakistan, Bangladesh and Sri Lanka) maintain national buffer stocks through market-based procurement policies. In addition, all SAARC members have functioning public food distribution systems (PFDSs) with built-in networks, storage facilities, and entry and exit mechanisms for foodgrains albeit on a limited scale (Rahman et al., 2017).

In spite of the previous information, as past experiences reveal, there is a need for collective efforts in South Asia to ensure food security at times when emergencies lead to largescale disruption in foodgrains production, transportation, accessibility and availability. Hence the rationale for the SFB and importance of raising its operational efficacy.

Theoretical framework

In general, three sets of countries are involved in foodgrains trade: (a) countries that almost always export foodgrains – these rarely suffer from lack of food availability and are capable of mitigating temporary supply shock because of production failure, (b) countries that almost always import foodgrains – variability of foodgrain price in the world market determines the rate of inflation in their domestic market – and (c) countries that are normally self-sufficient in foodgrains production; however, these are in need of import if natural disasters cause significant production shortages. Evidently, second and third sets of countries are not adequately capable of mitigating temporary supply shocks (Gilbert, 2011). The argument is that a temporary negative supply shock causes a fall in supply (in this case, e.g., production shortfall of foodgrains due to natural calamity or export restriction), which then results in a rise in commodity prices, which in turn has negative implications for access and availability of foodgrains. More precisely, a temporary negative supply shock will shift the

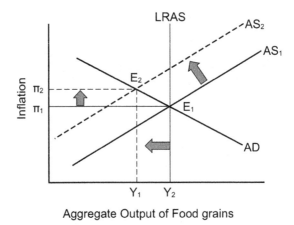

FIGURE 5.1 Effect of production failure due to natural disaster: a negative supply shock scenario

aggregate supply curve upward and intersect the aggregate demand curve at the new equilibrium E_2 (Figure 5.1). As a consequence there will be food price inflation and equilibrium aggregate output of foodgrains will come down. Due to lack of availability of foodgrains, marginally non-poor households and households below the poverty line will be afflicted by food insecurity. There is a possibility that even a non-poor, food-secure household could find itself falling into the poverty trap with no, or inadequate, access to food. During emergencies, high import bills for foodgrains create balance of payment pressure in import-dependent countries.

Evidence from literature

Food reserves are usually geared to protecting consumers from possible adverse impacts of price volatility (Rojko, 1975; Briones, 2011; Gilbert, 2011). Most common such reserves are: (a) *Food Emergency Reserves*, with an objective to guarantee availability, accessibility and utilization of food in situations of natural disasters or external shocks; and (b) *Price Stabilisation Reserve*, which involves buying foodgrains through future short sales when prices are low and selling at a reduced rate when prices are high in the commodities market (Briones, 2011). For instance, national food reserves – or buffer stocks – are built up through domestic procurement and imports and are intended to influence price transmission from international to domestic markets and deal with interseasonal price fluctuations.

In times of national food crisis, be it originating from production shortage or price volatility, movements of foodgrains across borders get disrupted (Joerin and Joerin, 2013). Dependency on global markets for staple foods proves to be largely ineffective in the face of outright export bans, minimum export prices, fiscal-monetary policies to incentivize or disincentivize trade (as may be needed) and other non-tariff barriers (NTBs) that tend to be put into action with a view to ensuring national food security by major net exporting countries (Childs and Kiawu, 2009).

Oftentimes, such policies tend to aggravate an already volatile situation and unsettle the global foodgrains market. For instance, in the wake of the 2007–08 global food crisis, many foodgrains-exporting countries such as Argentina, China, India, Indonesia, Kazakhstan, Russia, Thailand, Ukraine and Vietnam had taken measures in an attempt to reduce respective risks, assuage apprehension of the populace and ensure stability in the domestic market (Joerin and Joerin, 2013; Childs, 2009). On the other hand, importing countries had to encounter a situation where supply of foodgrains in the world market was severely constrained.[2] As a consequence, it was the marginalized sections of the society that suffered the most (Dawe, 2010). Experience in the global food crisis of 2007–08 demonstrates that reliance on market mechanisms alone is not adequate to ensure regional food security in times of crisis (Belesky, 2014). In addition, variability in agricultural production originating from climate impact has added new dimensions to the food insecurity concerns (Ahmed and Suphachalasai, 2014).

In this backdrop, for a production-deficit and importing country, relying solely on trade in foodgrains in times of emergency may not be enough to maintain food security. It is to be noted that even in normal times trade in foodgrains is adversely impacted because of transport and trade facilitation-related constraints that lead to delays and cost escalation. As is known, during periods of food shortages and natural disasters speed of foodgrains delivery is of paramount importance. Thus proximity between supply-demand locations assumes high importance. During emergencies, time needed to ensure access to foodgrains could indeed mean the difference between life and death. For example, Bangladesh, one of the net food-importing countries in SAARC, needs two to three months of turnaround time (depending on the distance) to import foodgrains from abroad, mostly from Thailand, Vietnam or Russia through international tender. Importing foodgrains from most competitive source during times of crisis is not a viable option for a country in need of urgent food supply. The main objective of a regional emergency reserve is to improve the timeliness of emergency food aid transfers to meet urgent needs following a disaster.

There is a wide recognition in relevant literature that regional food reserves could play an important role in parallel with local (as well as international) reserves in alleviating food insecurity in emergency situations and times of crisis (Toyoda and Suwunnamek, 2011). Historically, stockpiling agricultural commodities – particularly staple grains – has played an important role as a buffer to address the likely adverse impact of natural disasters, calamities, seasonal discrepancies and market turbulences (Murphy, 2009). Such food reserves function as a safeguard mechanism to tackle after-effects of major production failures and global and local price upsurge and trade restrictions in the backdrop of the inelastic nature of demand for staple foodgrains. The economic rationale of having regional food reserves includes taking advantage of economies of scale and enhanced scope for price stabilization through access to larger reserves and balancing demand-supply mismatches and a wider scope of supply and distribution systems within particular regions. Such reserves are able to function as an emergency food supply that could help to speed up food assistance response and enhance outreach to the needy. Emergency food reserves are aimed at making food available to vulnerable groups in times of crisis;

their objective is to function effectively without disrupting regular private market operations. Food stocks, therefore, do appear to be a potentially effective means of protecting poor and vulnerable households from low food availability and high food prices (Gilbert, 2011; Curtis, 2014). Price stabilization and government buffer stocks play an important role in food import-dependent countries (von Braun and Torero, 2009; De Castro et al., 2013). Thus the issue of a collaborative approach to safeguard food security is both relevant and important.

Lessons and learnings from other cross-regional experiences

A number of regional groupings have set institutional arrangements to address food security concerns through cross-country collaborative initiatives. The modalities prevalent in these regional structures and their experiences could provide useful information for the purposes of raising operational efficacy of SFB.

Regional food reserve in ASEAN has been in place since 1979 in the form of the ASEAN Food Security Reserve (AFSR) and the ASEAN Emergency Rice Reserve (AERR). AFSR's objectives were to address regional food emergencies and offset any urgent food crisis with the earmarked 50,000MT of rice reserves (which was raised to 87,000 MT under the pilot project titled East Asia Emergency Rice Reserve (EAERR)). However, neither AFSR nor AERR/EAERR addressed an emergency situation prior to 2006, when EAERR provided 100 tonnes of rice to flood victims in Indonesia (Briones, 2011).

In 2011, EAERR was transformed into the ASEAN Plus Three Emergency Rice Reserve (APTERR). With the inclusion of China, Japan and South Korea as part of the agreement, this gave a new lease on life to this regional food security initiative. The three new entrants provided an additional 700,000 MT of rice. The APTERR was to be governed by a council, with day-to-day management to be carried out by a secretariat. The APTERR was formally launched in March 2013. To facilitate the operationalization of the reserve fund, the 13 members of APTERR have agreed to create a fund worth US$4 million (with 75% contribution from China, Japan and South Korea) (APTEER, 2011).

Salient features of the APTERR are (a) unlike AFSR, the reserve is owned by APTERR and funds have been made available for operationalization and maintenance of the reserve; (b) rice is stored in three donor countries and also in the rice-importing countries of APTERR, to offset the consequences of likely export ban that was experienced by AFSR during the 2007–08 food price crisis; (c) unlike the AFSR, APTEER is not only an emergency food reserve, but it also aims to smooth price volatility in the market; (d) there are provisions of dispute settlement in the arrangement; (e) definition of emergency is clearly articulated; (f) the modality for price trigger is still being discussed and developed, and it was decided that the transactions should be based on international market price on a cash basis; (g) the forward contract is valid for three years (Lines, 2011; Briones, 2011; Jongskul, 2012). Operational efficacy of APTERR has increased significantly since 2013, benefitting its member countries.

RESOGEST was set up by Sahel countries of West Africa, along with the Permanent Interstate Committee for Drought Control in the Sahel (CILSS), as a food reserve system to provide guaranteed access to food in the event of scarcity. The primary objective of the RESOGEST is to facilitate cereal trade among and between countries with net surplus and net deficit through triangular operations (purchase/sales/loans) and stimulation of subregional trade in agricultural produce and food products (Lines, 2011). Member countries pledge 5% of their national food stock to the regional food reserve (RESOGEST, 2012). The RESOGEST network is mandated to establish an extensive information system (Rahman and Khaled, 2012). Initiatives are in place to improve capacity on technical and financial management and use of all available resources to mobilize food stock during emergencies, taking advantage of each other's information system, including existent early warning and surveillance systems. In cases of emergency the network is to ease the process of inter-country cereal transfer beyond the regulations of regular trade. This is geared to reducing operational cost.

However, the reserve has never been used by the member countries mainly because of the following constraints: (a) lack of a clear definition of emergency situation; (b) absence of an well-established reference price and modalities for cereal trading; (c) diverse nature of staple food in the region which varied across member countries; (d) absence of quality control mechanisms for cereal trading (in cases of loan and grants); (e) inadequate size of the committed reserve at national level to address regional emergency food crisis; and (f) no early warning system (Lines, 2011; The Rural Hub and ECOWAS, 2012).

The Caribbean Community (CARICOM) was established in 1973 as a framework to promote cooperation among the 11 Member States. Unlike APTERR and RESOGEST, the regional initiative of CARICOM is not only limited to ensuring food security, but it also covers broader economic issues (Byron, 2014). CARICOM has a unique Regional Food and Nutrition Security Policy (RFNSP). CARICOM countries have low domestic food production capacity and are highly dependent on food import. Countries' vulnerability was particularly exposed during the financial crisis of 2007–08. They are susceptible to food price volatility and climate-induced shocks.[3] In order to reduce food- and nutrition-related vulnerabilities, the community has developed a 15-year (2012–2026) regional food and nutrition security action plan to help implement the objectives of the RFNSP. Two main objectives of the RFNSP are to: (a) create regional and national 'value chains' by establishing links between small- and medium-sized farmers and food industries in the region and (b) reduce imports of key commodities from the United States such as feed corn (Wilson, 2016). In this backdrop, the food- and nutrition-related programmes of CARICOM are closely interlinked with greater regional agricultural management initiatives that go beyond the limited focus of addressing and mitigating food security-related efforts. CARICOM experience is relevant for operation of SAARC Agricultural Centre (SAC), which is geared to improving the overall food security situation in South Asia. CARICOM also puts emphasis on developing a strong regional Information System for Food and Nutrition Security (ISFNS) and a regional information system on water-sharing in order to improve water resource management for better agricultural production.

The experience of regional food security initiatives mentioned earlier is pertinent for operationalizing the SFB both in terms of what to do and what not to do.

For example, for the SFB to be effective, size of the reserves need to be adequate and exchange of information is critically important in times of emergency. On the other hand, in absence of well-crafted definitions of emergency situation, trigger price, repayment arrangement and a proper early warning system, it is difficult to operationalize food reserve systems such as the SFB.

Evolution of SFB and challenges of its operationalization

Issues of operationalisation of the SFB are discussed henceforth by drawing insights from the earlier discussion and with a forward-looking perspective. This section reviews the background of the SFB initiative, summarizes its evolving mandates and portrays the current structure of the SFB, while highlighting the operational challenges.

Background of the SFB initiative

SAARC Food Security Reserve (SFSR), which predates the SFB, was established in 1987 as a collective endeavour to address the concerns of food insecurity in South Asia. This initiative faced implementation challenges and failed to get off the ground owing to a number of reasons: (a) structural flaws; (b) lack of specific provisions regarding financing of the costs involved; (c) absence of guidelines to attain the objectives; (d) absence of an appropriate monitoring authority to supervise, execute and follow up the agreed activities; and (e) failure of net food-importing countries to contribute to the reserves to the extent needed (Mittal and Sethi, 2009; Rahman and Khaled, 2012; Raihan, 2011; Pant, 2014). In view of this, decision was taken to establish the SFB at the 14th SAARC Summit held in Islamabad in 2007. SFB's evolving mandate at present includes: (a) inclusion of food shortage as an eligibility criterion for withdrawal of foodgrains in addition to emergency; (b) specification of procedures regarding withdrawal and release of foodgrains; (c) clear indication of the amount of reserve to be earmarked; (d) specific requirements in maintaining quality of foodgrains; (e) instructions for proper storage; and (f) guidelines on price negotiations (Rahman and Khaled, 2012; Pant, 2014). SFB is expected to act as a regional food security reserve for the SAARC member countries during both normal times and at times of food shortages and emergencies, provide regional support to national food security efforts and foster country partnership and regional integration. A pictorial presentation of the procedural flow of actions as regards eligibility, withdrawal, release and replenishment of foodgrains from the SFB is presented in Figure 5.2.

Challenges of operationalising the SFB

Regrettably, the SFB could not be operationalized despite some of the subsequent amendments to facilitate its operationalization.

Stringent rule for withdrawal of foodgrains from SFB

According to Article V (3) of the SFB Agreement, for a member country to be eligible to seek help from the SFB, production of foodgrains of that country in

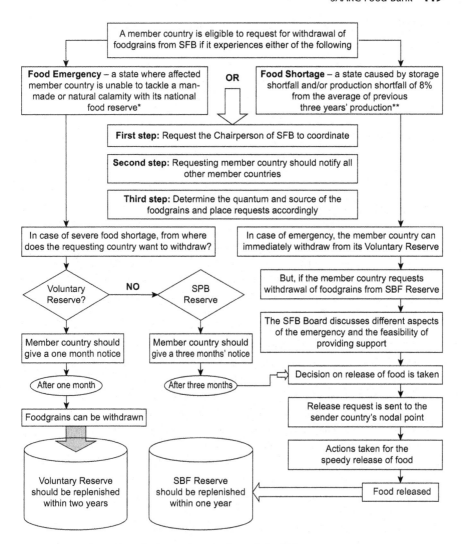

FIGURE 5.2 Flow chart depicting functioning of the SFB

Source: Prepared by the authors based on information gleaned from the SFB Agreement

Note
*At the 9th SFB Board Meeting it was agreed that 'food emergency' will be replaced by 'emergency'.
**The provision has been modified with the deletion of the trigger criteria (8% production shortfall from the average of previous three years' production). However, these amendments are to be approved at the next meeting of the Council of Ministers.

the concerned year had to be 8% lower than the average of the production of the previous three years. This stringent rule for withdrawal of foodgrains from SFB reserves is stated to be a major stumbling block towards effective operationalisation of the SFB. Review of the SFB Board meeting minutes suggests that this issue of reassessing the minimum threshold criteria has been an agenda for discussion since the 2nd SFB meeting in 2009. At the 18th SAARC Summit, the leaders gave directions to eliminate the threshold criteria. At the most recently held 9th Meeting, the SFB Board has decided to amend Article V (3), with a view to delete the trigger criteria relating to withdrawal of foodgrains from the SFB. However, this amendment is yet to be approved at the meeting of the Council of Ministers. The results presented in Box 1 justify the decision of the board to do away with the trigger threshold.

BOX 5.1 RESULTS OF META-ANALYSIS

Results of meta-analysis (5) based on production data for foodgrains at the country level (FAOSTAT) suggest that if production shortfall of foodgrains in 2015 was 8% lower than the average of the production of the previous three years (2012, 2013 and 2014), the entire SFB reserve would be adequate to support the needs of Afghanistan, Bhutan and Sri Lanka only. Estimates also indicate that the SFB has reserve adequacy to support only 2% of India's admissible production shortage (of the 8% mentioned here), while it is equivalent to only 12% and 20% of shortfalls in cases of Bangladesh and Pakistan, respectively (Table 5.4).

Similar exercises have been carried out with varying extents of possible production shortfalls (5%, 3% and 1%). Results are presented in Table 5.4. The results are similar as in the earlier cases concerning major agricultural countries (India, Pakistan and Bangladesh) of SAARC. At the level of 5% admissible production shortfall, the SFB would have reserve adequacy to support only 4% of India's production shortage, while it would be equivalent to only 18% and 31%, respectively, for Bangladesh and Pakistan. Similarly, if the shortfall criteria is set at 3%, it is observed that the SFB would have reserve adequacy to support only 6% of India's admissible production shortage, while for Bangladesh and Pakistan these would be 31% and 52%, respectively. Furthermore, if the shortfall criteria is set at 1%, the SFB would have reserve adequacy to support only 19% of India's admissible production shortfall, while it will be able to cater to 92% of Bangladesh's admissible production shortfall (Table 5.4). Thus, one finds that the reserve was not adequate enough to address the production shortfall estimated on the basis of three years' average production.

Another dimension of the previous conditionality was tested by comparing the production of 2015 with the average of the previous three years (2012 to 2014), five years (2010 to 2014) and seven years (2008 to 2014), juxtaposed against the criteria of production shortfall of variable percentages (8%, 5%, 3% and 1%). The results are presented in Tables 5.4, 5.5 and 5.6, respectively. Here also, similar patterns of inadequacy of reserve were observed.

TABLE 5.4 Reserve adequacy status of the SFB for different levels of production shortfall of foodgrains compared to previous three-year average, 2012–2014

Country	Average production (last 3 years)	Production shortfall				Reserve amount	Reserve adequacy (at different % shortfalls)			
		(Metric tonnes)					Percentage (of 486,000 MT)			
		8%	5%	3%	1%		8%	5%	3%	1%
Afghanistan	5,733,333	457,029	286,667	172,000	57,333	2,840	106	170	283	848
Bangladesh	52,666,667	4,207,484	2,633,333	1,580,000	526,667	80,000	12	18	31	92
Bhutan	82,962	6,637	4,148	2,489	830	360	7,317	11,716	19,527	58,581
India	250,000,000	20,166,667	12,500,000	7,500,000	2,500,000	306,400	2	4	6	19
Maldives	–	–	–	–	–	400	–	–	–	–
Nepal	6,666,667	535,478	333,333	200,000	66,667	8,000	91	146	243	729
Pakistan	31,000,000	2,480,075	1,550,000	930,000	310,000	80,000	20	31	52	157
Sri Lanka	3,933,333	315,945	196,667	118,000	39,333	8,000	154	247	412	1,236

Source: Authors' calculation using data from FAOSTAT (2016).

TABLE 5.5 Reserve adequacy status of the SFB at different levels of production shortfall of foodgrains compared to previous five-year average, 2010–2014

Country	Average production (last 5 years)	Production shortfall				Reserve amount	Reserve adequacy (at different % shortfalls)			
		8%	5%	3%	1%		8%	5%	3%	1%
		(Metric tonnes)					*Percentage (of 486,000 MT)*			
Afghanistan	5,300,000	422,441	265,000	159,000	53,000	2,840	115	183	305	916
Bangladesh	52,200,000	4,165,479	2,610,000	1,566,000	522,000	80,000	12	19	31	93
Bhutan	82,078	6,566	4,104	2,462	821	360	7395	11833	19721	59163
India	242,000,000	19,620,000	12,100,000	7,260,000	2,420,000	306,400	2	4	7	20
Maldives	–	–	–	–	–	400	–	–	–	–
Nepal	6,360,000	509,870	318,000	190,800	63,600	8,000	95	153	255	764
Pakistan	31,000,000	2,478,768	1,550,000	930,000	310,000	80,000	20	31	52	157
Sri Lanka	4,000,000	320,695	200,000	120,000	40,000	8,000	151	243	405	1214

Source: Authors' calculation using data from FAOSTAT (2016)

TABLE 5.6 Reserve adequacy status of the SFB at different levels of production shortfall of foodgrains compared to previous seven-year average, 2008–2014

Country	Average production (last 7 years)	Production shortfall				Reserve amount	Reserve adequacy (at different % shortfalls)			
		8%	5%	3%	1%		8%	5%	3%	1%
		(Metric tonnes)					Percentage (of 486,000 MT)			
Afghanistan	5,057,143	403,961	252,857	151,714	50,571	2,840	120	192	320	960
Bangladesh	51,142,857	4,079,103	2,557,143	1,534,286	511,429	80,000	12	19	32	95
Bhutan	80,641	6,451	4,032	2,419	806	360	7527	12044	20073	60218
India	237,142,857	19,071,429	11,857,143	7,114,286	2,371,429	306,400	3	4	7	20
Maldives	–	–	–	–	–	400	–	–	–	–
Nepal	6,228,571	498,352	311,429	186,857	62,286	8,000	97	156	260	780
Pakistan	31,428,571	2,522,025	1,571,429	942,857	314,286	80,000	19	31	52	155
Sri Lanka	3,942,857	315,087	197,143	118,286	39,429	8,000	154	246	411	1232

Source: Authors' calculation using data from FAOSTAT (2016)

Conditionality met, but SFB never made use of

A meta-analysis was undertaken to examine whether the threshold criteria alone was responsible for the non-functionality of SFB. The exercise was based on country-level production data retrieved from the FAOSTAT. The analysis reveals that there were four cases where production of foodgrains dropped by 8% compared to the average of previous three years' production. In 2008 and 2011, Afghanistan experienced 29.1% and 13.9% production shortfall in foodgrains, respectively, compared to the average production level for the preceding three years. Similarly, Pakistan experienced a 9.6% production shortfall due to the prolonged flood experienced in 2012 (Table 5.7). Most recently, in 2014, Sri Lanka had experienced

TABLE 5.7 Change in paddy and wheat production compared to previous three-year average (%)

Country	2008	2009	2010	2011	2012	2013	2014
			Change in paddy production				
Afghanistan	16.4	13.6	11.4	4.5	−24.6	−16.7	−4.3
Bangladesh	13.3	10.5	8.8	4.8	1.8	2.2	2.7
Bhutan	8.0	−11.2	−1.5	9.6	8.0	3.4	−2.4
India	5.4	−5.7	0.8	10.8	8.2	3.9	−0.7
Nepal	5.9	11.3	−3.5	4.2	17.0	−0.3	7.9
Pakistan	26.0	15.1	−25.4	−34.0	−30.0	7.7	13.6
Sri Lanka	19.6	5.9	21.1	−1.2	−2.6	15.1	−18.0
South Asia	7.8	−0.9	2.0	6.6	5.1	3.7	0.5
			Change in wheat production				
Afghanistan	−35.0	45.1	11.7	−16.8	16.7	19.6	18.4
Bangladesh	3.4	10.0	11.3	12.4	9.7	31.2	21.2
Bhutan	−40.3	−43.5	−23.8	23.8	−3.2	−1.5	−6.6
India	10.3	8.2	3.1	8.6	14.6	6.9	3.0
Nepal	8.4	−10.0	5.4	17.1	19.2	0.7	6.2
Pakistan	−5.0	10.0	2.4	10.7	−3.0	0.9	6.9
Sri Lanka	–	–	–	–	–	–	–
South Asia	−1.8	9.1	3.9	5.0	7.5	4.9	4.0
			Change in paddy and wheat production				
Afghanistan	−29.1	40.7	11.7	−13.9	11.2	15.1	15.9
Bangladesh	13.1	10.5	8.8	4.9	1.9	2.7	3.1
Bhutan	2.2	−14.3	−3.3	10.6	7.2	3.1	−2.7
India	7.0	−1.0	1.7	10.0	10.5	5.0	0.7
Nepal	6.6	5.6	−1.1	7.5	17.6	−0.1	7.4
Pakistan	3.5	11.5	−5.9	−2.3	−9.6	2.3	8.3
Sri Lanka	19.6	5.9	21.1	−1.2	−2.6	15.1	−18.0
South Asia	4.3	2.7	2.7	6.0	6.0	4.1	1.8

Source: Authors' calculation using data from FAOSTAT (2016)

Note: (a) Production data on wheat was missing for Sri Lanka. (b) Maldives does not produce wheat and rice.

nearly 18% production shortfall due to the drought in most parts of the country before the main harvesting season (Table 5.7). Thus, the notion that SFB could not be operationalized because no SAARC member has yet experienced the particular level of emergency food situation that meets the high threshold of eligibility is not fully corroborated by the evidence on the ground.

Inadequate quantum of reserve

Initially, at the time of the first meeting of the SFB Board in Colombo in 2008, members agreed to have a reserve of 243,000 metric tonnes (MT) for the SFB.[4] Later, as per endorsement at the 36th Session of the Standing Committee, the quantum of reserves was doubled at the 3rd SFB Board meeting.[5] Despite this, analysis in Box 1 shows that even at 1% admissible production shortfall compared to the previous three years' average, India and Bangladesh cannot be adequately supported even if the entire SFB reserve of 486,000 MT was put at the disposal of respective countries (Table 5.4). In view of the previous analysis, the SFB reserves will need to be significantly raised for its operational relevance.

Absence of agreed pricing modality

At the 4th Board Meeting of the SFB in Dhaka, modalities of *deferred payment* were discussed highlighting specific equations (Rahman and Khaled, 2012; Pant, 2014). However, members were not able to reach an agreement about the pricing modalities. The reference export price has not been specified either. The price to be paid by the receiving (affected) country also includes trans-portation and administrative costs in addition to costs incurred on account of other logistical supports. Determination of all these costs require access to certain information, and time is rather scarce in times of emergency. Arriving at an acceptable, reasonable, humane and concessional price level continues to remain a significant challenge in determining the price at which food is to be accessed.

Lack of dedicated funds for SFB

No dedicated fund is available for undertaking the operational costs of the SFB. Costs incurred in the operations of the SFB are to be financed by the SAARC Secretariat. The storage systems across countries for rice and wheat are differ-ent and involve divergent technical requirements. The system of maintaining the storage of foodgrains and ensuring that required quality standards are main-tained[6] involves significant amount of funding along with administrative- and infrastructure-related resource allocation, which further contributes to cost escalation. Budgetary allocations (as a share of respective national budgets) for ensuring food security vary across South Asia; not all countries are well-endowed to underwrite the expenditures involved. Thus in the absence of earmarked funds for the SFB, issues concerning its operationalization have remained unaddressed.

Lack of information sharing

Detailed information in regard to the quantum of reserve, godowns/storage facilities and locations was first presented at the 2nd meeting of the SFB Board. At the 9th meeting, Bhutan, Maldives and Nepal shared detailed information on their respective storage methods. Currently, there are 43 earmarked warehouses (Rahman et al., 2017). India, being the largest contributor, has earmarked its reserve in 23 warehouses, which are spread across the country. Although members have reported the locations of their respective warehouses designated for SFB reserves, a lack of readiness is observed on the part of member countries to share information as regards quantum of respective reserves of rice and wheat. As both rice and wheat are considered to be politically sensitive items, countries tend to be reluctant to report about actual amounts of national reserve. The SAARC Food Bank Information System (SFBIS) had been launched at the 9th SFB Board meeting to address this particular issue. Hopefully this laudable step will facilitate inter-governmental sharing of information in this connection. There is no 'implementation/regulatory plan' document that would articulate how the SFB is to function. Moreover, formulation and circulation of a set of guidelines on storage methods, practices and quality control measures have remained long overdue.[7]

Servicing the mandate: recommendations for operationalization of the SFB

Based on the experience of the progress made with respect to the SFB, review of literature, consultations with relevant stakeholders and experts and review of cross-country best practices, a number of recommendations have been proposed in the following section with a view to raising the efficacy of the SFB and towards its effective operationalization.

Policy amendments

1   The SFB Board has agreed to amend the definition of 'food emergency' and 'food shortage' (Article V (2)). In addition, if the amendment of Article V (3), as agreed at the 9th SFB Board meeting, is approved by the SAARC General Assembly, then the current threshold criteria of 8% admissible production shortfall will no longer be there. These decisions will make it easier for member countries to receive support from the SFB reserve when food crisis or emergency situation

originates from price volatility. These decisions will hopefully contribute to making the SFB an effective institution, and help it serve its mandate.

2   The provision for dispute settlement should be included in the SFB Agreement with a view to settling possible disputes between two or more SFB members through negotiations or through a set of rules agreed upon by all parties.

Enhancing regional trade

3   Although overall intraregional trade is not significant in the SAARC region, it is observed that the amount of intraregional trade in foodgrains in the region is not negligible (Rahman et al., 2017). Freer movement of foodgrains and removal of non-tariff bottlenecks will contribute towards better availability of foodgrains across various SAARC countries. This will contribute towards mitigating food security concerns and will thus reduce the need for dealing with food-related emergencies that SFB-type institutions are geared to address in the first place.

4   SAARC countries should come to an agreement that trade-related restrictions of the type seen during the 2007–08 economic and food crises, in the form of minimum export price or outright ban, will not be enforced in cases of intra-regional trade in foodgrains during times of crisis. For a start, such a commitment may be made with respect to export of foodgrains to the least developed country (LDC) members of the SAARC.

Pricing strategy

5   Thanks to the regional trade in foodgrains, there does exist a *reference price* for comparison purposes and for determining price of foodgrains. Besides, up-to-date and reliable international market prices of rice and wheat are readily available from various global data sources. During incidents of natural disasters or emergency food crisis, such prices could be taken to serve as the *reference price* for the purposes of the payment of foodgrains received by any country under the SFB mechanism. It is to be noted that 'deferred payment' has been proposed as a pricing modality at the 4th SFB Board Meeting.

Need for additional provisions

6   Designated testing laboratory for the purpose of SFB is now in place. To eliminate procedural constraint regarding quality standards, SFB Board should develop a system of issuing 'No Objection Certificate' in collaboration with the CGAL. This will ensure that the required quality of foodgrains is maintained. These may be included as a provision under Article IV of the SFB Agreement.

7   As a forward-looking strategy, SFB could include a provision to keep a certain share of the reserves in the form of biofortified rice. This nutritionally rich rice may be targeted to the most vulnerable groups during periods of emergency. In

this regard, World Food Programme's (WFP) existing mechanism of distributing specialized fortified nutritious foods could be taken advantage of.[8]

New institutional mechanisms

8 To ensure smooth functioning of the SFB, the option of establishing a dedicated fund for the SFB should be considered with utmost urgency. The SFB Board may take inspiration from the practices pursued by the APTERR, which maintains an endowment fund as an operational fund. Countries such as Maldives, which hardly produces any foodgrains, may be allowed to make their contribution to the SFB in monetary terms. As mentioned in the preceding section, the current SFB reserve is not adequate to support food emergencies in countries such as India.[9] In view of this, an operational fund could be set up to provide the needed support.

9 In South Asia, the network of weather stations belonging to the meteorological departments of different countries is rather weak. This problem is compounded by lack of high-quality weather data for locations smaller than the district level. At present, the SAARC Meteorological Research Centre (SMRC), which was previously responsible to project possible shocks and natural calamities and alert the countries under threat via targeted policy briefs, along with three other centres, has been merged into SAARC Environment and Disaster Management Centre (SEDMC). It remains unclear which entity will be responsible to undertake agricultural forecasting. An agricultural forecasting committee should be constituted with the needed capacity to undertake forecasting work (by using latest available technology of satellite images) concerning foodgrains production and likely food shortages.

Options for institutional tie-up

10 As was noted earlier, ASEAN's capacity as well as flexibility was significantly enhanced with the entry of China, Japan and South Korea in the food reserves system. This indicates that greater access to foodgrains could make operationalization of food security mechanisms such as the SFB more effective. It is conceivable that the SFB, at some point in time in future, could think of coming to an understanding with ASEAN food reserves from which both the food security systems could stand to benefit. In this regard, it is important to highlight that at the 9th SFB Board meeting members have agreed to add a provision that allows the board to explore the implementation of regional food security projects in collaboration with international development partner organizations under MoUs with the SAARC Secretariat.

11 SFB may consider collaborating with the WFP. This could benefit the SFB in three major ways: (a) SFB may use the Vulnerability Analysis and Mapping (VAM) assessment developed by the WFP as an eligibility criterion for countries to seek

help; (b) SFB may make use of the logistics architecture of the WFP to ensure better distribution of foodgrains during times of emergency; (c) SFB may utilize WFP's early warning and early impact analysis mechanisms to forecast weather.

Distribution mechanism

12   All SAARC member countries have well-functioning PFDS, which are mandated to distribute foodgrains under various social safety net programmes and are also deployed to stabilise markets at times of price volatility (Rahman et al., 2017). The nodal agencies designated with the responsibility to interact with the SFB Board are mainly the national agencies in place which are involved with the task of distribution and maintenance of the foodgrains reserves for the SFB. There is a need for closer interaction between SFB and PFDSs in the architecture of operationalization of the SFB, so that in times of emergency, the foodgrains from the nearest storage facilities can be made available to the national PFDS of (affected) countries for distribution to the needy households and individuals in affected areas.

The need for political commitment

13   There is a need for demonstrated and strong political support towards raising the efficacy of the SFB as an important tool to ensure region-wide food security and to attain the ambitions articulated in Agenda 2030 in the context of South Asia. Political commitment will give clear direction to concerned officials in the member countries to share the needed information and will encourage the involved parties in member countries to undertake the needed initiatives to make the SFB effective and to raise its operational efficacy. Adequate resources will need to be deployed to ensure that an appropriate SFB architecture is in place, the decision-making procedures are transparent, the food reserves, in quantitative and qualitative terms, are in place and the networks have the capacity to work efficiently during times of emergencies. Only through a strong political commitment can all these be implemented in a time-bound manner.

Acknowledgements

The authors would like to acknowledge the generous support received from UNESCAP SSWA, New Delhi, India, for conducting this study. They would like to put on record their deep appreciation of the valuable cooperation extended by Dr Nagesh Kumar, Head of UNESCAP-SSWA and his colleague Mr Matthew Hammill, and Mr J. H. Jabed, Director of Agriculture and Rural Development, SAARC Secretariat, Kathmandu, Nepal. This chapter draws significantly on Working Paper 113 published by the Centre for Policy Dialogue (CPD), Dhaka, Bangladesh, based on an earlier version of the report submitted to SSWA.

Notes

1 Bangladesh: National Food Policy Plan of Action 2008–2015 (PoA 2008), National Food Policy (2006); Bhutan: Food and Nutrition Security Policy of the Kingdom of Bhutan 2014 (FNSP 2014); India: National Food Security Act 2013 (NFSA 2013); Maldives: Agricultural Development Master Plan 2006–2020 (ADMP 2006); Nepal: Agriculture and Food Security Project's Country Investment Plan (AFSP 2010); Sri Lanka: National Agricultural Policy (NAP-SL) and the National Nutrition Policy 2010 (NNP 2010).
2 One has to keep in mind that the traded amount of foodgrains, particularly of rice, as share of total global production, unlike many other commodities, is rather small (for rice this was about 9% in 2015). Consequently, any shortage in the global tradable supply tends to give rise to disproportionate and knee-jerk responses on the part of governments in anticipation of any speculative behaviour in the market.
3 The food price volatility arising from the food and financial crises of 2008–09 and 2011–12 has forced the region to confront serious financial, food security and health-related consequences of such high dependence on food imports.
4 As would be expected, India's contribution was the largest (63%), while Maldives and Bhutan contributed the lowest (0.1%) (Rahman et al., 2017).
5 In the reserve allocation, rice accounts for 60%, mostly contributed by India and Bangladesh, while share of wheat was 40%. Sri Lanka's reserves include only rice and Afghanistan's reserves include only wheat.
6 At the 4th SFB Meeting, the Board designated Central Grain Analysis Laboratory (CGAL), New Delhi, India as SAARC Foodgrain Testing Reference Laboratory.
7 As per the 9th SFB Board meeting minutes, the necessary information (according to a format circulated in the 6th/7th meeting) has been submitted only by Bangladesh, Bhutan, India, Maldives, Nepal and Sri Lanka, whereas Afghanistan and Pakistan committed to provide the information as soon as possible.
8 WFP already has this mechanism in place for South Asian countries such as Bangladesh, India, Nepal, Sri Lanka etc.
9 Indeed, 8% production shortfall of foodgrains for India is estimated to be nearly 2.5 times higher than the combined shortfall for all other SAARC member countries. In the global context, India's 8% shortfall in foodgrains production is estimated to be 1.4% of global production of foodgrains.

References

Ahmed, M. and S. Suphachalasai (2014), 'Assessing the Costs of Climate Change and Adaptation in South Asia', Asian Development Bank (ADB), Manila.

APTEER (2011), 'ASEAN Plus Three Emergency Rice Reserve Agreement', Association of Association of Southeast Asian Nations.

Belesky, P. (2014), 'Regional Governance, Food Security and Rice Reserves in East Asia', *Global Food Security*, Vol. 3(3–4), pp. 167–173.

Briones, R. M. (2011), 'Regional Cooperation for Food Security: The Case of Emergency Rice Reserves in the ASEAN Plus Three', ADB Sustainable Development Working Paper, No. 18, Asian Development Bank (ADB).

Byron, J. (2014), 'Developmental Regionalism in Crisis? Rethinking CARICOM, Deepening Relations With Latin America', *Caribbean Journal of International Relations and Diplomacy*, Vol. 2(4), pp. 23–50.

Childs, N. W. and J. Kiawu (2009), 'Factors Behind the Rise in Global Rice Prices in 2008', US Department of Agriculture, Economic Research Service.

Curtis, M. (2014), 'Why Wait Until the Next Crisis? Improving Food Reserves Strategies in East Africa', Agency for Cooperation and Research in Development (ACORD).

Dawe, D. (Ed.) (2010), 'The Rice Crisis: Markets, Policies and Food Security', Earthscan and Food and Agriculture Organization of the United Nations (FAO), London.

De Castro, P., F. Adinolfi, F. Capitanio, S. Di Falco and A. Di Mambro (Eds.) (2013), *The Politics of Land and Food Scarcity*, Routledge, Abingdon.

DFPD (2016), 'New Delhi: Department of Food and Public Distribution (DFPD), Government of India'. Available at: http://dfpd.nic.in/saarc-food-bank.htm. Accessed: 27 February 2016.

FAO (2015), 'FAO Statistical Pocketbook 2015: World Food and Agriculture', Food and Agriculture Organization of the United Nations (FAO), Rome.

FAO, IFAD and WFP (2002), 'Reducing Poverty and Hunger: The Critical Role of Financing for Food, Agriculture and Rural Development', Conference Paper. Available at: www.ifad.org/documents/10180/8ccc7684-0775-4745-a10a-3afe98ab12bd

FAOSTAT (2016), 'Food Security'. Available at: http://faostat3.fao.org/browse/area/*/E. Accessed: 4 April 2016.

GFSI (2016), 'Global Food Security Index'. Available at: http://foodsecurityindex.eiu.com/Index. Accessed: 16 April 2016.

Gilbert, C. L. (2011), 'Food Reserves in Developing Countries: Trade Policy Options for Improved Food Security', International Centre for Trade and Sustainable Development (ICTSD).

Ingram, J., P. Ericksen and D. Liverman (Eds.) (2010), *Food Security and Global Environmental Change*, Earthscan, London.

Joerin, J. and R. Joerin (2013), 'Reviewing the Similarities of the 2007–08 and 1972–74 Food Crisis', Swiss Federal Institute of Technology, Zurich.

Jongskul, A. (2012), 'Current Operations of ASEAN Plus Three Emergency Rice Reserve (APTERR)', Proceedings of the Presentation Delivered at the Asia Pacific Economic Cooperation (APEC) Food Emergency Response Mechanism Working Meeting, 10–11 April, Taipei, Taiwan.

Lines, T. (2011), 'The Potential Establishment of Emergency Food Reserve Funds', United Nations Conference on Trade and Development (UNCTAD), Geneva. Available at: www.tomlines.org.uk/FoodReservesLinesDec11.pdf

Mittal, S. and D. Sethi (2009), 'Food Security in South Asia: Issues and Opportunities', ICRIER Working Paper, No. 240. Indian Council for Research on International Economic Relations (ICRIER). Available at: http://icrier.org/pdf/WorkingPaper240.pdf

Murphy, S. (2009), 'Strategic Grain Reserves in an Era of Volatility', Institute for Agriculture and Trade Policy (IATP), Minnesota. Available at: www.iatp.org/files/451_2_106857.pdf

Pant, K. P. (2014), 'The SAARC Food Bank for Food Security in South Asia', Discussion Paper. South Asia Watch on Trade, Economics and Environment (SAWTEE). Available at: www.sawtee.org/publications/DiscussionPaper18.pdf

Rahman, M., E. Bari and N. Farin (2017), 'SAARC Food Bank (SFB) Institutional Architecture and Issues of Operationalisation', CPD Working Paper, No. 113, Centre for Policy Dialogue, Dhaka. Available at: http://cpd.org.bd/cpd-working-paper-113-saarc-food-bank-sfb-institutional-architecture-and-issues-of-operationalisation/

Rahman, M. and Khaled, N. (2012), 'LDC Issues for Operationalisation of the SAARC Food Bank: Bangladesh Case Study', SAWTEE Working Paper, Kathmandu. Available at: www.sawtee.org/Research_Reports/R2012-04.pdf

Raihan, S. (2011), 'SAARC Food Bank and Food Security in Bangladesh', in "Food Security: Can Trade Address It?" *Trade Insight*. Special Issue, Vol. 7(1), R. Adhikari, K. Adhikari, P. Sharma and P. Kharel (Eds.), Kathmandu: South Asia Watch on Trade, Economics and Environment (SAWTEE).

RESOGEST (2012), 'Cooperation Framework'. Available at: http://portails.cilss.bf/archives CILSS/IMG/pdf/RESOGEST_COOPERATION_FRAMEWORK.pdf. Accessed: 10 April 2016.

Rojko, A. S. (1975), 'The Economics of Food Reserve Systems', *American Journal of Agricultural Economics*, Vol. 57(5), pp. 866–872.

The Rural Hub and ECOWAS (2012), 'Regional Food Security Reserve', Economic Community of West African States (ECOWAS), Abuja. Available at: www.inter-reseaux.org/IMG/pdf/Faisabilite_Reserve_Regionale_EN.pdf

Toyoda, T. and Suwunnamek, O. (2011), 'Regional Cooperation for Food Security in East Asia: From Rice Reserve APTERR and Information System AFSIS to Common Agricultural Policy', Conference Paper. Available at: http://7thasae.ipsard.gov.vn/ppt/presentation/A4/A4_ASAE_Takeshi%20Toyoda.pdf

UNCTADstat (2016), 'Data Center'. Available at: http://unctadstat.unctad.org/wds/ReportFolders/reportFolders.aspx?sCS_ChosenLang=en. Accessed: 2 March 2016.

von Braun, J. and M. Torero (2009), 'Implementing Physical and Virtual Food Reserves to Protect the Poor and Prevent Market Failure, IFPRI Policy Brief, No. 10, International Food Policy Research Institute (IFPRI).

von Grebmer, K., J. Bernstein, A. de Waal, N. Prasai, S. Yin and Y. Yohannes (2015), '2015 Global Hunger Index: Armed Conflict and the Challenge of Hunger', International Food Policy Research Institute (IFPRI), and Concern Worldwide.

Wilson, M. (2016), 'Food and Nutrition Security Policies in the Caribbean: Challenging the Corporate Food Regime?' *Geoforum*, Vol. 73, pp. 60–69. doi.org/10.1016/j.geoforum.2015.05.005.

World Bank (2016), 'World Development Indicators (WDI)'. World Bank Group, Washington, DC. Available at: http://databank.worldbank.org/data/reports.aspx?source=poverty-and-equity-database. Accessed: 5 March 2016.

PART II

National food security strategies

Leveraging regional cooperation

6

ENSURING FOOD SECURITY IN BANGLADESH

Issues beyond production and challenges ahead

Mustafizur Rahman and Towfiqul Islam Khan

Introduction

Being the most densely populated country in the world,[1] ensuring food security has continued to remain a key challenge in Bangladesh's developmental journey. This journey has seen Bangladesh making a transformation from a chronic and persistent food deficit country to one nearing food self-sufficiency over the post-independence period since 1971. It may be recalled here that efforts to achieve MDG-1 relating to halving the poverty level by 2015 has brought commendable success to Bangladesh, in the backdrop of her sustained 6% plus economic growth rate over the past decade and targeted poverty reduction initiatives (Rahman and Khaled, 2012). Indeed, Bangladesh is one of the successful countries in terms of reducing hunger. According to GHI, Bangladesh was able to move from 'high alarming' to 'serious' group over the past years (IFPRI, 2016). Implicit in this categorization, however, is the fact that ensuring food security still remains a major concern in the Bangladesh context, more so because Bangladesh is under performing and lagging when MDG target for nutrition is taken cognizance of.

Bangladesh has already committed to deliver the sustainable development goals (SDGs) including 'SDG 2: End hunger, achieve food security and improved nutrition, and promote sustainable agriculture' at the country level. Besides, the current Seventh Five Year Plan (FY2016-FY2021) includes ensuring food security as one of its core development objectives (GED, 2015). Thus, ensuring food security is present on Bangladesh's agendas both from the national development plans and as part of global commitment.

The core objectives of this chapter are to: (a) assess the present food security situation of Bangladesh and trace the improvement over time in order to identify the key gaps; and (b) identify the challenges associated with food security in Bangladesh, which can help formulating future national policies.

Food security is a complex phenomenon manifested in numerous physical conditions with multiple causes.[2] This study has undertaken an analysis of the issues involved from four dimensions: food availability, economic and physical access to food, food utilization and stability over time. Food and Agricultural Organization of the United Nations (FAO) introduced a set of food security indicators in its 'The State of Food Insecurity in the World 2013' report (FAO, 2013), which measures separately the four dimensions of food security to allow a more nuanced assessment of food insecurity. This chapter assesses the state of food security in the context of Bangladesh based on these indicators. The progress has been examined both from country as well as regional contexts. A detailed literature review has also been undertaken to identify the key challenges facing Bangladesh in going forward.

Following this introduction, the next section provides an assessment of food security in Bangladesh based on indicators developed by the FAO. The third section outlines the future challenges facing food security in Bangladesh, while the fourth section concludes the chapter.

State of food security in Bangladesh

The issue of food security includes food production, actual availability and the access, stability and utilization of resources. As the following discussion will indicate, despite the commendable foodgrains production growth, Bangladesh still has to be concerned with food security because of developments in the other elements of the food security equation. Although Bangladesh has graduated into a lower-middle-income economies (LMICs) from its low-income-country (LIC) status in June 2015, poverty, hunger and malnutrition remain serious concerns in Bangladesh.

Food security in Bangladesh is challenged by a host of factors ranging from the country's ever-increasing population, climate change impacts, scarcity of natural resources with nearly no fallow land for cultivation, vulnerability to price shocks and the low purchasing power of a significant proportion of population. In spite of these constraints, Bangladesh has met the MDG hunger target. This remarkable feat was achieved in the context of rapid economic growth in the 1990s spurred by significant growth in agricultural productivity and driven by a combination of factors including macroeconomic stability, liberalisation of agricultural-input markets and opening up of the economy and targeted incentives to stimulate agriculture production.

Bangladesh's foodgrains production has almost doubled between 1990 and 2014. Both increased yield rate and higher cropping intensity have contributed to this. Higher foodgrains production has also contributed to higher per capita availability of foodgrains in Bangladesh.[3] However, in order to ensure food security and to guard against unforeseen circumstances, Bangladesh maintains some measures of public food stocks on a continuing basis. Public food stockholdings allow the government to intervene in the market towards price stabilisation as well as to undertake various food security programs on a regular basis. Import, mainly of wheat, is carried out both by public and private sectors to meet domestic demand for foodgrains.

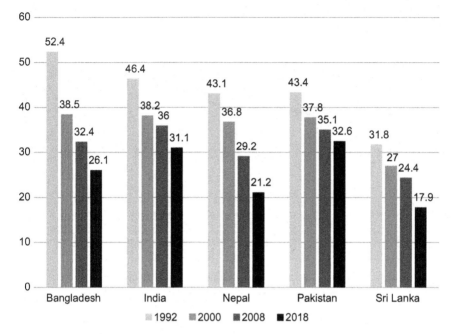

FIGURE 6.1 GHI for South Asian countries

Source: IFPRI (2016)

Bangladesh also pursues regular public foodgrains procurement programme that is used for servicing the public food distribution system in the country.

Among five South Asian countries, Bangladesh is ranked third according to the Global Hunger Index 2016,[4] with a score of 27.1 ahead of India (28.5) and Pakistan (33.4), but behind Sri Lanka with 25.5 points and lastly Nepal with 21.9 points (Figure 6.1). However, Bangladesh has been able to make notable improvement in the index during last two decades.

Food availability

Food availability is ensured through domestic production, national food stocks and distribution. One of the indicators of food availability is adequacy of food that is at the disposal of citizens as per consumption requirements. Over the past years, agricultural productivity has increased significantly in Bangladesh, with average yields and the value of food production per capita rising notably since the mid-1990s (Figure 6.2). Private seed firms have been encouraged to enter the agricultural seed sector and regulatory frameworks have been strengthened.

Foodgrains (cereals, roots and tubers) dominate the food consumption basket in Bangladesh providing about 80% of total dietary energy supply. Thus, adequacy of foodgrain deserves priority attention in ensuring food security of Bangladesh.

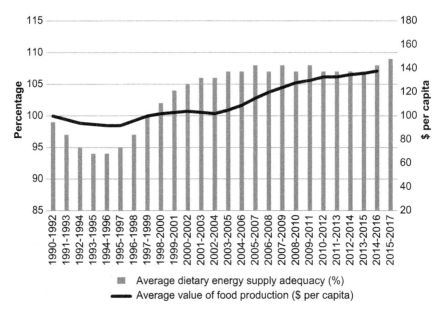

FIGURE 6.2   Food production and dietary energy supply adequacy in Bangladesh

Source: Compiled by authors from FAOSTAT

In 2009–11, cereals still provided 80% of all calories consumed, the highest in the world (Table 6.1). However, a negative growth of cereals and vegetative food as share of calorie energy intake is discernible since 2000. Moving away from cereals and into a variety of high-value food products was likely to not only make more nutritious food available but would also create an opportunity to increase farmers' incomes.

Protein intake per capita per day was 55 grams in 2009–11 in Bangladesh.[5] This is the lowest among the countries of South Asia region[6] and even lower than LDCs and LICs.[7] In Bangladesh, 82% of protein intake was from vegetative food. About two-thirds of protein came from cereals, 15% from non-cereals such as pulses, potatoes and oilseeds and oil, and the other 18% (12 gr/caput/day) came from animal food like fish, milk and meat. Low proportion of animal foods as a source of calorie and protein intake is likely to have an adverse impact on country's nutrition and health of population. There has been a positive change in terms of the contribution of animal food in total protein intake,[8] but this is rather inadequate and was the lowest among countries in the South-Asian region.

Access to food

As is well-recognised, even when aggregate food supplies are adequate, a number of factors can prevent poor households or individuals from accessing the food. Income levels may not be adequate to purchase the necessary food at prevailing market price; access to land for cultivation may be limited, or the household may lack the necessary

TABLE 6.1 Share of dietary energy supply derived from cereals, roots and tubers (%) in Bangladesh

Regions/subregions/countries	1990–92	2000–02	2009–11
World	58	55	52
South-Asia	67	64	60
Afghanistan	74	77	77
Bangladesh	85	84	80
India	66	63	59
Maldives	51	43	41
Nepal	77	74	69
Pakistan	55	51	50
Sri Lanka	60	56	58
Least developed countries (LDCs)	72	72	68
LICs	71	71	68
LMICs	65	63	60
Low-income-food-deficit countries (LIFDCs)	67	65	63

Source: Compiled by authors from FAOSTAT

assets or access to credit to help cope with difficult times. Furthermore, the situation could be aggravated by not being included in programmes which are geared to providing in-kind or cash transfers to supplement food acquisition capacity (WFP, 2015).

Economic and physical constraints that undermine access to food render many households incapable of meeting minimum food-dietary needs. Physical constraints often play an important role. Bangladesh has the lowest percentage of paved roads in transport networks and a large part of these are of poor quality. This compares unfavourably within the South-Asian region as a whole. The country's rail lines density in 2012 was about 2 km per 100 square km of land area, as compared to an average of 1.4 km per 100 square kilometres in South-Asia as a whole. Besides, domestic food level price index[9] has been on an increasing trend since 2001; however, this is currently found to be at levels consistent with longer-term trends for Bangladesh and other countries of South-Asia.

Bangladesh has been able to reduce the prevalence of undernourishment since the 1990s. In 1990–92, 32.8% of the population was undernourished, which stood at 16.4% in 2014–16. However, some 26 million people remain undernourished as the progress stalled since the mid-2000s. Prevalence of food inadequacy is conceptually analogous to the prevalence of undernourishment, but this is calculated by setting the caloric threshold to a higher level. The measure estimates the percentage of population that is at risk of not covering the food requirements associated with normal physical activity. This, therefore, includes also those who, even though they cannot be considered chronically undernourished, are likely to be constrained to undertake economic activities because of food-related insufficiencies. Figure 6.3 shows that although the rate of food inadequacy has decreased since mid-1990s, still around 26% of the total population lacks food adequacy.

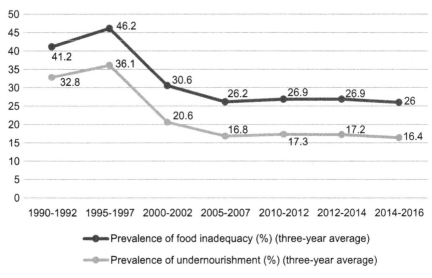

FIGURE 6.3 Prevalence of undernourishment and food inadequacy in Bangladesh

Source: Compiled by authors from FAOSTAT

TABLE 6.2 Depth of the food deficit (kcal/caput/day) in Bangladesh

Regions/subregions/ countries	1990–92	2000–02	2012–14	2014–16
World	138	111	84	81
South-Asia	169	130	116	114
Afghanistan	202	326	158	173
Bangladesh	247	139	122	116
India	165	122	110	109
Maldives	69	75	45	34
Nepal	149	147	50	51
Pakistan	179	172	170	172
Sri Lanka	228	268	209	192
LDCs	306	273	207	208
LICs	299	274	214	214
LIMCs	198	164	140	138
LIFDCs	161	123	99	95

Source: Compiled by authors from FAOSTAT

In Bangladesh, poor consumers allocate about seven-tenths of their expenditure to food. In this prevailing situation, a rise in producer prices can significantly reduce the ability of consumers to meet food needs. The depth of the food deficit[10] in 2014–16 indicates that Bangladesh needed 116 kcal per capita per day to lift the 26 million undernourished people; this was by and large similar to the status of deficit in countries of South Asia as a whole (Table 6.2).

Risk exposure and stability

Two types of indicators are used to measure the extent and exposure to risk. Key indicators for exposure to risk include areas equipped for irrigation, which provides a measure of the extent of exposure to climatic shocks such as droughts and the share of food imports in total merchandise exports, which captures the adequacy of foreign exchange reserves to pay for food imports. A second group of indicators captures risks or shocks that directly affect food security, such as swings and volatility in food and input prices, production and supply (FAO, 2013). Here the menu of indicators covers a number of stability measures, including an indicator of political instability available from the World Bank. Figure 6.4 shows that the cereal import dependency ratio has been about 9% to 11% over the last 15 years, which is still higher compared to 5.3% for the South-Asia region as a whole.[11]

Irrigation in Bangladesh has experienced increasing coverage thanks to sustained public infrastructure development programs of the government. As a matter of fact, in the South Asian region Bangladesh had the second-best percentage of arable land equipped for irrigation after Pakistan (Figure 6.5). This proportion has increased over time and reached 68% in 2010–12 from 32.8% in 1990–92. But the focus is now shifting to promoting water-saving farming practices to deal with declining aquifer levels and the increasing cost of irrigation. This has added to the challenge of maintaining food security on a sustained basis.

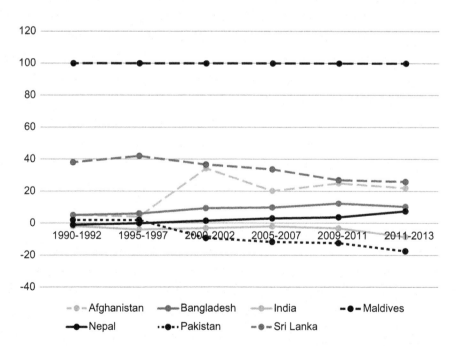

FIGURE 6.4 Cereal import dependency ratio (%)

Source: Compiled by authors from FAOSTAT

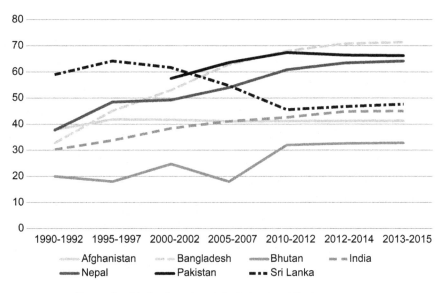

FIGURE 6.5 Share of arable land equipped for irrigation (%)

Source: Compiled by authors from FAOSTAT

TABLE 6.3 Value of food imports over total merchandise exports (in %) in Bangladesh

Regions/subregions/countries	1990–92	2000–02	2011–13
World	7	5	5
South-Asia	11	9	8
Afghanistan	59	187	296
Bangladesh	35	23	20
Bhutan	20	14	16
India	4	5	5
Maldives	48	83	80
Nepal	28	25	81
Pakistan	15	11	16
Sri Lanka	22	13	18
LDCs	31	20	16
LICs	30	25	24
LMICs	15	10	11
LIFDCs	12	9	9

Source: Compiled by authors from FAOSTAT

Capacity to import of a country depends on export earnings, remittances and terms of food import price relative to export unit price. As indicated in Table 6.3, a ratio of food imports to Bangladesh's total exports has been on average 19% during the 2005–07 period; which increased by 5.0 percentage points during 2009–11, but declined by 3.0 percentage points for the period 2011–13. In general, Bangladesh's capacity to import food out of export earnings has been quite manageable.[12]

Although Bangladesh has pursued various policies to promote agricultural research, technology adoption and infrastructure development, in view of the increasing demands to enhance productivity as also quality, much more will need to be done in this respect. State of governance remains much to be desired. Often both efficacy and impact of institutions and initiatives are undermined by confrontational politics, often violent and prolonged (Figure 6.6).

High price volatility has a detrimental impact both for the producers and the consumers. Greater price volatility encourages speculative behaviour. This also discourages investment since price volatility creates uncertainty about investment returns and raises likelihood of losses. This adds to uncertainties about what to produce and how much to produce and for which segments of customers to produce. This in turn could result in higher food prices hurting the consumers. Successive governments in Bangladesh have tried to stabilise food markets through proactive procurement and an open-market sales programme. Table 6.4 shows that domestic food prices had been relatively less volatile in Bangladesh compared to other countries of South Asia.

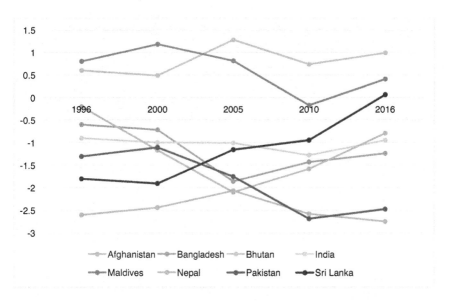

FIGURE 6.6 Index of political stability and absence of violence

Source: Compiled by authors from FAOSTAT

Note: Political stability and absence of violence measures perceptions of the likelihood that the government will be destabilised or overthrown by unconstitutional or violent means, including politically-motivated violence and terrorism. The index value may vary from −2.5 (weak stability) to 2.5 (strong stability). The original source of the data is WorldWide Governance Indicators. For Bangladesh, the index figure was (−) 0.61 in 1996 which deteriorated to (−) 1.84 in 2005 and then somewhat improved to (−) 1.35 in 2012.

TABLE 6.4 Domestic food price volatility in Bangladesh

Regions/subregions/countries	2000	2010	2014
South-Asia	9.9	17.0	13.7
Bangladesh	3.3	4.5	4.5
India	3.9	3.5	8.4
Maldives	57.6	20.8	N/A
Nepal	10.0	9.8	10.2
Pakistan	8.4	9.3	13.2
Sri Lanka	6.2	6.8	8.3

Source: Compiled by authors from FAOSTAT

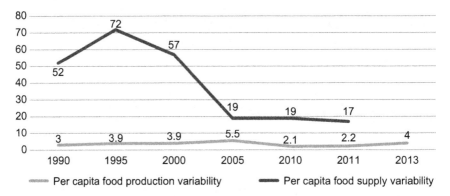

FIGURE 6.7 Per capita food production and supply variability (kcal per day) in Bangladesh

Source: Compiled by authors from FAOSTAT

Food supplies have seen low variability while production variability has somewhat increased in recent years. Per capita food supply variability stood at 17 kcal per day in 2011, which was 72 kcal per capita per day in 1995, meaning from the supply side or distribution side relative stability has been maintained (Figure 6.7). However, production variability was similar to price variability, which indicates that the fluctuation of food production was not significant with respect to price variability.

Utilisation of food

Food utilisation is determined by food safety and quality, how much a person consumes and how a person metabolises food to energy, nutritional status and growth. Adequate food utilisation requires a diet providing sufficient energy and essential nutrients, potable water, adequate sanitation, access to health services, proper feeding practices and illness management (WFP, 2015).

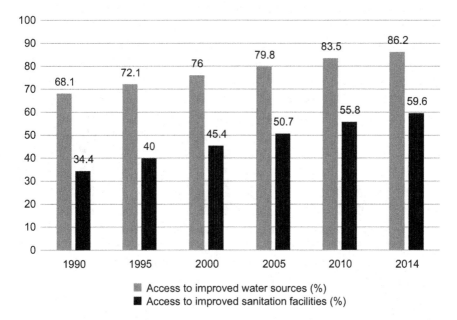

FIGURE 6.8 Access to improved water sources and sanitation (% of population with access) in Bangladesh

Source: Compiled by authors from FAOSTAT

Both access to improved water sources and sanitation facilities has increased in Bangladesh over the years in percentage terms; however, there exist regional disparities. In 2014, around 13.8% of people did not have access to improved water sources and 39.4% of people did not have access to improved sanitation facilities (Figure 6.8).

Bangladesh was on track to achieve the MDG target of reducing the percentage of children who are underweight to 33 by 2015 (Figure 6.9). However, there are considerable regional disparities, and progress in tackling undernutrition shows a slowing trend in recent years. Although progress has been made as regards reducing the percentage of children who are stunted, the situation has deteriorated and reached the level of 1995 as regards percentage of children who are affected by wasting. This indicates that higher incomes alone are not sufficient to reduce undernutrition. Issues of distribution, inequalities and the government's supportive interventions are no less important.

Progress in terms of reducing the proportion of women who are anaemic has not been very promising (48.1% in 2011 compared with 49.5% in 2005); anaemia continues to remain a serious public health problem in the country (Figure 6.10). Gender-based differences, notably in wages and in access to inputs and markets, also have an impact on food security and nutrition. The situation is almost similar as regards prevalence of anaemia among the children. Currently, interventions such as school-time feeding programs are being considered to address this challenge.

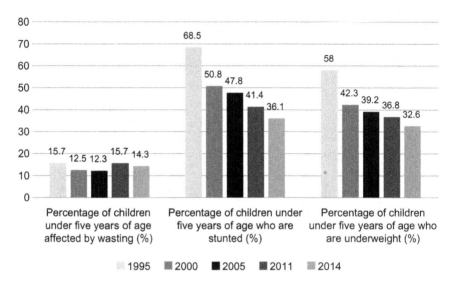

FIGURE 6.9 Wasting, stunting and underweight prevalence among children aged < five years in Bangladesh

Source: Compiled by authors from FAOSTAT

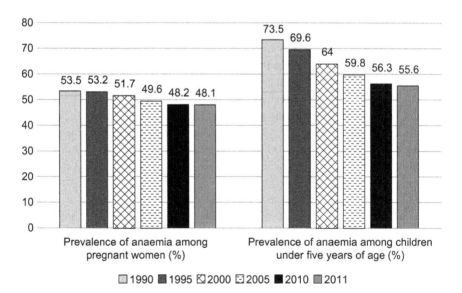

FIGURE 6.10 Prevalence of anaemia among pregnant women and children in Bangladesh

Source: Compiled by authors from FAOSTAT

Lack of dietary diversity results in widespread vitamin and mineral deficiencies; these can have serious and long-lasting consequences for individual welfare and for the country's socio-economic development. Vitamin A deficiency in Bangladesh has increased to 19.6% in 2000 from 4.3% in 1990. The increase in prevalence of vitamin A deficiency was also observed for India between 1995 and 2000. Meanwhile, the prevalence of iodine deficiency has decreased to 42.5% thanks to some awareness building initiatives by the government in the early 2000s.[13]

Overall performance

The previous assessment highlights notable progress made by Bangladesh in addressing the multidimensional features of the food security agenda. For most of the FAO proposed indicators, Bangladesh has made consistent and commendable progress over the past two decades. However, when the state of Bangladesh's food security is compared with the regional (South Asian) average, it is observed that Bangladesh has still some ground to cover. Among the four pillars of food security (availability, access, stability and utilisation), the fourth pillar, utilisation of food, was found to be the weakest link in the Bangladesh context (Table 6.5).

TABLE 6.5 Bangladesh's overall performance according to food security indicators within a comparative South Asian setting

Food security indicators	Better	Worse	Indifferent
Availability			
Average dietary energy supply adequacy		✓	
Average value of food production		✓	
Share of dietary energy supply derived from cereals, roots and tubers	✓		
Average protein supply		✓	
Average supply of protein of animal origin		✓	
Access			
Percentage of paved roads over total roads		✓	
Road density	✓		
Rail lines density	✓		
Gross domestic product per capita (in purchasing power equivalent)		✓	
Domestic food price index		✓	
Prevalence of undernourishment		✓	
Share of food expenditure of the poor			✓
Depth of the food deficit	✓		
Prevalence of food inadequacy		✓	

(Continued)

TABLE 6.5 (Continued)

Food security indicators	Better	Worse	Indifferent
Stability			
Cereal import dependency ratio	✓		
Percentage of arable land equipped for irrigation	✓		
Value of food imports over total merchandise exports		✓	
Political stability and absence of violence/terrorism		✓	
Domestic food price volatility	✓		
Per capita food production variability	✓		
Per capita food supply variability	✓		
Utilization			
Access to improved water sources		✓	
Access to improved sanitation facilities	✓		
Percentage of children under five years of age affected by wasting		✓	
Percentage of children under five years of age who are stunted		✓	
Percentage of children under five years of age who are underweight		✓	
Prevalence of anaemia among pregnant women		✓	
Prevalence of anaemia among children under five years of age		✓	
Prevalence of vitamin A deficiency in the population		✓	
Prevalence of iodine deficiency		✓	

Source: Compiled by authors from FAOSTAT

Except for access to improved sanitation facilities, Bangladesh lags behind the South Asian average for all other eight indicators. In connection to this, it is important for Bangladesh to focus on providing balanced nutrition during the 'first 1000-days of a child'[14] to attain nutrition related targets in the medium term. This is also true for the availability pillar. On a welcome note, Bangladesh's performance as regards food stability has been, to a large extent, satisfactory compared to the South Asian average. In view of the fact that, Bangladesh has now graduated to the lower middle-income country status, she will now have to compare with a new cohort of countries in her (new) group. The challenge of maintaining food security, on a comparable basis, will now become even more challenging.

Food security challenges in Bangladesh

Despite the positive changes in the policy environment and the cropping system, food security is set to continue as a key concern in Bangladesh. Growing population, rising longevity, demographic momentum, higher purchasing power, changing structure of food demand, climate change impact, shrinking arable land and reduced opportunities for further enhancement of cropping intensity, regional and global market situation – all these factors are likely to make addressing Bangladesh's food security challenges in the 21st century quite formidable. A number of issues will call for particular attention in view of this and these have been highlighted in the discussion in this section.

Addressing below poverty line population

Despite significant decline in the national poverty rate – from 48.9% in 2000 to 24.3% in 2016 – about 39 million people are still to cross the minimum threshold line of poverty (GED, 2017). Moreover, only 27.8% of people are covered by social safety nets. In addition, increasing inequality and natural, manmade and seasonal shocks compel people to undergo internal migration and move in and out of the poverty line. The impact of high cereal prices could be devastating for this group with limited purchasing power. CPD (2008) estimated that income erosion suffered by consumers due to high inflation in FY2008 was to the tune of 21.1%. The study also found that an additional 8.5% of the population, or 2.5 million households, had fallen below the poverty line. Characteristics of the ultra-poor also vary across regions. Even within developed regions in the country, there are pockets of poverty where the situation is similar to that of the underdeveloped regions.[15] All this, including the spatial distribution of poverty, makes maintaining food security a challenging task in Bangladesh. Targeted, as well as spatial, coverage of the food distribution system is deployed in Bangladesh to cater to the basic needs of the poor (Rahman and Khaled, 2012). However, these may need to be strengthened particularly in view of the impacts of environmental changes, which will become more visible in the medium term.

Inflationary pressure undermining purchasing power of the poor

Over the last few years Bangladesh has been able to maintain a single digit inflation rate; however, it is still high compared to other South Asian countries. As would be expected, inflation affects the poor relatively more adversely, particularly because food inflation has tended to be significantly higher than non-food inflation and because the poor spend most of their income on food items (Rahman and Iqbal, 2012). Such high inflationary trends have undermined the cause of food security in Bangladesh despite the significant gains in terms of income and production growth. However, this aggregate inflation situation alone does not reflect the real picture. As mentioned earlier, rice comprises about 97% of total foodgrains production in Bangladesh. Rice also accounts for about 50% of total expenditures of the poor. Rising agricultural wages have helped Bangladesh in this respect. Deb (2011) showed that a daily wage that could buy only 3.5 kg of rice in 1990–91 gradually rose to be able to buy 5.9 kg rice in 2006–07. However, the rice-equivalent wage in 2007–08 declined to 4.6 kg/day, owing to a significant increase in the price of rice during this period. This trend has now been reversed thanks to falling rice prices since then. The upshot of the discussion here is that inflationary consequences on purchasing power of the low-income groups, and hence their food security, ought to be kept on the radar screen of the policy makers on a continuing basis.

Mitigating price volatility in a global market

Soaring foodgrains prices in 2007–08 gave rise to serious concerns all over the world. These concerns were most manifest in the case of the low-income groups who spent a significant part of their income on food consumption. Since 2000, global foodgrain prices were showing rising trends with a sharp turn upwards in 2007. In 2007 and 2008, cereal price indices increased by 37.2% and 42.5% respectively. Indeed, between July 2007 and June 2008, cereal price index rose by 76.2%. Rice is the most important cereal for Bangladesh. The international price of rice started to increase since mid-2007. In April 2008, the international price of rice increased by about 53% in a single month (Raihan and Khan, 2013). The price started to ease again since mid-2008, but it did not come down to the pre-crisis level. The price rise in the international market forced countries around the world to take aggressive policy measures, which in turn further aggravated the situation. Sharma (2011) documented that out of 105 countries covered under the study, 33 countries or 31% of the sample resorted to one or multiple export restrictive measures.[16] FAO (2008) also found that roughly one-quarter of the countries imposed some form of export restrictions during the food crisis of 2007–08. Raihan and Khan (2013) emphasised that Bangladesh should think about diversifying her rice import sources. The experience of 2007–08 underpinned the need for Bangladesh to maintain adequate food stocks to face any possible price and supply volatility in the global rice market.

Enhancing productivity and promoting diversity

Improvement in agricultural productivity was particularly important in the Bangladesh context in view of the land scarcity. Productivity gains would allow also resources such as labour to be diverted to non-agricultural sectors, creating employment opportunities and leading to income augmentation that raises purchasing power of the people. Total factor productivity (TFP) indices capture the effect of improvements in technology as well as investments in rural infrastructures.

Empirical evidence indicates that TFP of Bangladesh crop agriculture rose at an annual rate of 0.6% over between 1948 and 2008 (Rahman and Salim, 2013). In post-independence Bangladesh, introduction of high yield variety (HYV) technology and higher cropping intensity have led to higher productivity from which farmers have benefitted notably. Enhancing agricultural productivity, particularly in the crop sector, is important, as arable land in Bangladesh is declining by 0.6% every year due to growing demand for housing, industries and infrastructure (Hossain, 2015).[17] Soil fertility has also been declining due to over exploitation of soil nutrients and imbalanced use of fertiliser.

There is an opportunity to enhance agricultural productivity in Bangladesh since there is significant yield gaps for a number of major crops. Table 6.8 shows yield gaps in Bangladesh for some selected crops. Two most likely options for Bangladesh for enhancing productivity and minimising the yield gap are conversion of area under local to modern varieties and efficient use of the production inputs. The scope for the former appears to be almost exhausted, as Bangladesh is fast approaching the ceiling adoption level (Bera and Kelly, 1990; Baffes and Gautam, 2001). As has been found, the share of HYV rice area in total rice area, after remaining at around 82% during the preceding three years, dropped to 78% in 2013–14 (FPMU, 2013, 2014b, 2015). Almost three-quarters of the total cultivated land is under irrigation at present (Hossain, 2015). All these factors limit the potential for further increase in production through dry season irrigated rice farming in Bangladesh.

The issue of efficient use of the various production inputs including seed, fertiliser, irrigation, pesticides, labour and knowhow has assumed critical importance. Ensuring these inputs, of suitable quality, to farmers requires seed and fertiliser testing, timely access to irrigation and other inputs, credit availability that matches farmers' needs (in terms of collateral, repayment schedule, transaction cost etc.) and transfer of the technical knowhow. Farmers need access to information as regards choice of crop, timing of planting or transplanting and pest management strategies specific to the particular crop or locality. Promoting farm mechanisation is also important as it improves work efficiency, enhances productivity and promotes commercial agriculture. Use of machinery leads to reduced harvest and post-harvest losses and production costs and frees farmers from manual work, ensures timely operation, higher precision and quality produce. There is a need to move towards further mechanisation of commercialisation and productivity enhancement in Bangladesh agriculture. To improve productivity, Bangladesh will also need to encourage crop zoning through targeted policies. Dedicated research programs are required for developing non-rice crop varieties and improving cost-effective technologies. Production of high value crops and introduction of modern varieties of pulses, oilseeds, maize, vegetables and fruits are important from the perspective of broader food security. Agricultural diversification agenda also include scaling up of fish, poultry and livestock production, sectors that have been gaining prominence in Bangladesh agriculture in recent years.

Adaptation strategies in face of growing climate change impacts

Within the South Asian region, Bangladesh is considered to be on the frontline as far as climate change impacts are concerned. In 2007, the Intergovernmental Panel on Climate Change (IPCC) projected that with a business-as-usual scenario of greenhouse gas emission, the global climate may experience 1.1°C rise in average temperature by 2100.[18] Bangladesh's increasing vulnerability originates from its unique geographic location dominated by low floodplains, high density of low-income population and the dependence on nature for agriculture and livelihood. The country has a history of extreme climatic events claiming lives and destroying past developmental gains. Evidence of climate change in the form of warmer summers, irregular monsoons, untimely heavy rainfall over short periods, less rainfall than usual in the dry season, increased frequency, intensity and recurrence of floods and droughts are already visible in the country and have resulted in crop damage (Rahman and Iqbal, 2012). Low flow in the rivers in dry seasons has triggered salinity intrusion undermining crop productivity. Investment in developing climate (draught and salinity) resilient varieties for different crops is of high importance in this context. It is also apprehended that about one-sixth of the land may be submerged with brackish water over the next four decades due to rise in the sea level with an adverse impact on the soil variety (Hossain, 2015). To address the adverse impacts of climate change, the government has prepared the National Adaptation Plan of Action (NAPA) in 2005 and the Bangladesh Climatic Change Strategy and Adaptation Plan (BCCSAP) in 2009. The BCCSAP includes actions to increase resilience through the scaling up of community level adaptation, livelihood diversification, better access to basic services and social protection. To ensure food security in the coming years, Bangladesh will need to give priority importance to implementation of these aforementioned plans.

Ensuring safe food

Another emerging challenge in the context of food security issue for Bangladesh is to ensure safe food. Use of harmful chemicals (pesticides, insecticides) are prevalent in farming practices. This issue has not received the attention that it deserves. Seemingly, 'food first, safety second' has been the dominant mindset in the prevailing context (Hossain, 2015). Indeed, the use of harmful chemicals, particularly by the marketing intermediaries, both in processing and preservation, particularly for perishable foods, has given rise to growing health concerns on the part of consumers. The government has enacted the Food Safety Act, 2013, in view of addressing the attendant problem. There is also a Consumer Rights Act in place. However, enforcement of these measures needs to be strengthened.

Fostering regional cooperation

There are significant opportunities to leverage regional cooperation in the area of food security. In this context, implementation of SAARC Food Bank (SFB) provisions should receive the due priority. The amount available from the Food Bank is not adequate to tackle any large-scale food shortage. Operationalisation of the Food Bank remains a concern though. In its present form, the SFB acts more like an 'emergency relief bank' rather than a 'food bank' (Rahman and Khaled, 2012). The trigger price for accessing food from the Food Bank, amount to be accessed, price and mode of repayment, stock maintenance, contribution by countries – all these issues need to be articulated in clear transparent manner. In order to access the potential benefit from the SFB, the reserve of the Bank can be used as a loan during the lean period and repayment during harvest season in the form of 'receive now and return after'; or 'receive here and return there' (Rahman and Khaled, 2012). Having four tiers of decision making for SFB also makes the decision-making procedures involving SFB a rather lengthy one.[19] Indeed, a well-functioning SFB will need to have fullest support at the highest political level. Availability of reliable food related information and data, and access to the relevant information, remains an important concern in South Asia. This also needs to be addressed through closer cooperation among relevant agencies of the respective countries.

Promoting intraregional trade in food items should be seen as an important aspect of regional and country level food security in South Asia. Intraregional trade in agricultural products is low in South Asia.[20] Trade restrictions imposed on agricultural trade in the form of the SAFTA sensitive list needs to be liberalised at a faster pace.[21] Various trade-restrictive practices also hinder the flow of agricultural trade within the region, including the banning of exports during times of food shortages and the presence of NTBs of various types (Khan, 2013). There is also a need for more efficient and wide-ranging regional transportation connectivity and adequate storage facilities to facilitate trade in agricultural commodities across the national borders in the region.

Resolving water sharing concerns in South Asia is also critical from the perspective of development of agriculture and food security in South Asia. Rivers have become a bone of contention among countries in South Asia including Bangladesh. Increasing drought and flooding and the significant water wastage have the potential to create major water crisis in the region. Collaboration with the South Asian neighbours is required in the areas of water sharing, building dams, joint hydroelectric projects and watershed management and in ongoing river linking projects. A system of joint river basin management, with representations from both upper and lower riparian countries, ought to be considered on an urgent basis.

Joint agricultural research programs with South Asian neighbours for development of abiotic stress tolerant improved varieties (submergence-, drought- and salt-tolerant rice and heat-tolerant wheat etc.) and hybrids and natural resource management techniques (minimum tillage, water saving rice etc.) for similar ecosystems prevalent across national boundaries may be considered. Cooperation is also possible in new sciences such as GIS, remote sensing, water forecasting and systems modelling (Khan, 2013). Free exchange of technology and information such as those relating to germplasm, elite lines, improved animal breed, improved disease management technologies and practices need to be promoted.

WTO food stockholding decision

In Bali, a number of issues concerning the agriculture sector were discussed: proposal of G-33 relating to extension of 'green box' subsidies; submission of G-20 relating to 'export subsidies' and 'tariff rate quota'; the issue of public stockholding for food security purposes (Rahman and Jahan, 2015). As is known, the last issue, the proposal regarding public stockholding, proved to be a most controversial one – negotiations were almost on the verge of collapse when major contending parties failed to arrive at a consensus. The disagreement arose on the grounds of lack of consistency of policies pursued by some developing countries in addressing food security concerns. It was argued by some WTO members that these policies were in contradiction with respect to existing WTO rules and disciplines as agreed under the Agreement on Agriculture (AoA). Spearheaded by India, the G-33 coalition of developing countries, representing sizeable population of small holding farmers, proposed that current WTO farm subsidy rules should be relaxed to allow developing country governments more policy space to buy food from low-income and resource-poor producers at administered prices as part of their food stockholding programs (WTO, 2013). Bangladesh has both offensive and defensive interests in view of this proposal. As a net food importing country, Bangladesh's concerns lie in the possible adverse implications of high food stockholding by some of the foodgrains – exporting countries on global food prices. This could push up the global food prices. On the other hand, release of foodgrains from public stockholding could lead to dumping of foodgrains in the global market, which could undermine the interests of domestic producers in countries such as Bangladesh. In view of these concerns, there is a need to put in place safeguards in the context of the decision regarding public stockholding in the WTO so that food security concerns of countries such as Bangladesh are taken care of.

Concluding remarks

This chapter has argued that in spite of the impressive track record in terms of attaining food security, even when seen from the perspective of multi-dimensionality of the issue involved, formidable challenges remain to be overcome if Bangladesh is to ensure food security for its growing population on a sustained basis. In terms of many of the relevant indicators such as food production, cropping intensity, yield, food intake and availability, Bangladesh's performance, particularly over the past two decades, has been commendable. However, as cross-country comparison in the context of South Asia has shown, Bangladesh lags behind in terms of many of the key indicators of food security. Nutrition, stunting, wasting and under-nourishment continue to remain major concerns although people below the poverty line, both in an absolute and a relative sense, has been on the decline.

Going forward, as the study has identified, Bangladesh will need to strategize carefully to build on her achievements and to ensure the sustainable food security of her young and growing population.

First, the technology frontier appears to have plateaued in Bangladesh and there is a need to infuse higher productivity in agriculture through adoption of higher yielding seeds, mechanisation, adoption of better production practices and technology diffusion.

Second, in view of the possible adverse impact of climate change, Bangladesh will need to undertake formidable restructuring of agro-practices, with significant changes in cropping pattern, rationalisation of water-use and adaptation to climatic impacts. This will call for going for crop-zoning, development and introduction of new types of high yielding variety seeds and adoption of new technological practices. Human resources will also need to be reoriented and developed in view of this.

Third, Bangladesh will need to put in place measures to safeguard against price volatility. This poses a dual challenge for Bangladesh. Domestic prices, particularly of rice, will need to remain stable, and on the other hand production costs should be such that farmers are incentivised. For this to happen, the role of market intermediaries dominating the segments between farm gate and retail outlets will need to be reviewed. Appropriate mechanisms to facilitate marketing by surplus farmers will need to be developed. Government procurement, rice milling and wholesale operations are relevant areas to examine in this context.

Fourth, Bangladesh will need to maintain a careful balance between food security and taking advantage of global markets. Domestic price level, farmers' incentive price, food stock levels and the critical concern of maintaining sustainable food security should inform policy choices in this regard.

Fifth, Bangladesh will need to keep a close eye on the developments in the global trading regime and price movements concerning cereals, particularly rice. The issue of Bangladesh's offensive and defensive interests in view of the Bali Ministerial decision of the WTO as regards public food stockholding has been flagged in the preceding chapter. Bangladesh will need to remain engaged in the process of implementation of this decision, including the 'peace clause'. The peace clause allows concerned developing countries a four-year interim period as a derogation from WTO decision on allowable subsidies. A firm decision in this regard was to be reached by 2017. However, any decision should take into consideration interests of concerned countries including a decision to extend the 'peace clause'. Bangladesh should also urge WTO members to come to an agreement to the effect that during times of high price volatility, foodgrains exporting countries do not take any measures that undermine the interests of net food importing low income countries and LDCs such as Bangladesh. Bangladesh also needs to contribute meaningfully to regional initiatives such as the SAARC Food Bank. Indian price levels have an important significance for domestic price of cereals in Bangladesh. Hence, close cooperation with India should be in the interest of Bangladesh. At the same time, Indian prices should be monitored on a regular basis to understand possible implications and take corrective measures in this regard.

Sixth, sustainable food security will critically hinge on Bangladesh's ability to maintain overall macroeconomic stability, reduce inequality, create employment opportunities and augment income. Raising purchasing power of citizens must be seen as a crucial element in ensuring food security. Success of Bangladesh's strategy to accelerate GDP growth and alleviate poverty will then be important in terms of attaining the goal of sustainable food security.

Last, it is critically important to recognise that the SDGs approach food security from a rights-based perspective. Ensuing food security for its citizens has now become part of a global commitment for Bangladesh. Bangladesh has already prepared a number of strategic documents to address the multidimensional challenges associated with maintaining sustainable food security, ranging from access, availability, stability and utilisation.[22] These strategies will need to be pursued in earnest in order to attain the SDGs related to food security. Bangladesh should remain actively engaged in the SDG process and energetically access global support measures that are expected to be deployed and offered to help developing countries attain sustainable food security over the coming years.

Notes

1 Among the countries with population above 10 million.
2 Food security should not be seen as a mechanical balance between food production (supply) and population (Bayes and Hossain, 2015). Food security is multidimensional, encompassing many issues ranging from food production and distribution to food preferences and health status of individuals. It is often defined as 'access by all people at all times to enough food needed for an active and healthy life. Its essential elements are the availability of food and the ability to acquire it' (Reutlinger, 1985). In a similar vein, FAO (2006) declared, 'Food Security exists when all people, at all times, have physical and economic access to sufficient, safe and nutritious food that meets the dietary needs and food preferences for living an active and healthy life'.
3 Rahman and Iqbal (2012) estimated that per capita food availability between 1992 and 2011 increased from 453 gram/day to 666 gram/day.
4 This calculation results in GHI scores on a 100-point scale where 0 is the best score (no hunger) and 100 the worst.
5 In 1990–92, the comparable figure was only 45 grams.
6 Data on this indicator for Bhutan was not available.
7 Corresponding average figures for South Asia, LDCs and LICs were 61 grams, 57 grams and 56 grams respectively.
8 Contribution of animal food in total protein intake almost doubled between 1990 and 2011.
9 'The indicator is calculated from the 2005 International Comparison Program data from the World Bank as well as general and food consumer price indices from the International Labour Organization (ILO). The ratio of Food and non-alcoholic beverages expenditure to actual individual consumption is calculated in purchasing power parity terms relative to the United States. To control for inflation, this ratio is forecasted and backcasted using the ratio of a country's Food Consumer Price Index (FPI) and General Consumer Price Index (CPI) using a 2005 base year, relative to the United States' (FAO, 2014).

10 'The average intensity of food deprivation of the undernourished, estimated as the difference between the average dietary energy requirement and the average dietary energy consumption of the undernourished population (food-deprived), is multiplied by the number of undernourished to provide an estimate of' the total food deficit in the country, which is then normalized by the total population' (FAO, 2014).

11 This was particularly because of the nearly zero cereal import dependency ratio of India.

12 The share, however, tends to experience considerable volatility in view of fluctuations in global food prices.

13 This was 70.7%in 1995.

14 'The period from the start of a mother's pregnancy through her child's second birthday is a critical window when a child's brain and body are developing rapidly and good nutrition is essential to lay the foundation for a healthy and productive future. If children do not get the right nutrients during this period, the damage is often irreversible' (Save the Children, 2012).

15 The newly emerging pockets of poverty in urban slums and peri-urban areas testify to this.

16 The ban on rice export imposed by India and minimum floor price set by Thailand were of particular relevance from Bangladesh's food security perspective.

17 According to FPMU (2014a), agricultural land availability declined at 0.3% annually between 1976 and 2010.

18 This would eventually cause about 0.6 metre rise in the sea level from thermal expansion and melting of glaciers (IPCC 2007, 2014).

19 The tiers include Board of Governors, Technical Committee on Agriculture and Rural Development, SAARC Standing Committee and SAARC Council of Ministers.

20 Only Nepal, Bhutan and Afghanistan have notable trade interest in food items.

21 There has been an agreement to periodically reduced the Sensitive List by 20%, with many products to be delisted being agricultural items.

22 The documents include National Sustainable Development Strategy (2010–2021), National Food Policy (2006), Bangladesh Country Investment Plan in Agriculture, Food Security and Nutrition, National Agriculture Policy (NAP) 2013, National Nutrition Policy (2015) and National Social Security Strategy (2015).

References

Baffes, J. and M. Gautam (2001), 'Assessing the Sustainability of Rice Production Growth in Bangladesh', *Food Policy*, Vol. 26, pp. 515–542, Elsevier Science Ltd., Washington, DC.

Bayes, A. and M. Hossain (2015), 'Food, Famine and Failures', in *Leading Issues in Rural Development: Bangladesh Perspective*, M. Hossain and A. Bayes (Eds.), A. H. Development Publishing House, Dhaka.

Bera, A. K. and T. G. Kelly (1990), 'Adoption of High Yielding Rice Varieties in Bangladesh: An Econometric Analysis', *Journal of Development Economics*, Vol. 33, pp. 263–285, University of Illinois.

CPD (2008), 'State of the Bangladesh Economy in FY2007-08 and Outlook for FY2008-09', Centre for Policy Dialogue (CPD), Dhaka.

Deb, U. (2011), 'Food Security in Bangladesh: Achievements, Challenges and Way Forward', in *Policy Options to Achieve Food Security in South Asia*, A. Mittal and D. Sethi (Eds.), pp. 77–105, Cambridge University Press, Cambridge.

FAO (2006), 'Food Security', FAO Policy Briefs, Issues 2, Food and Agricultural Organization of the United Nations, Rome.

FAO (2008), 'Soaring Food Prices: Facts, Perspectives, Impacts and Actions Required', Food and Agricultural Organization of the United Nations, Rome. Available at www.fao.org/fileadmin/user_upload/foodclimate/HLCdocs/HLC08-inf-1-E.pdf. Accessed: 16 June 2015.

FAO (2013), 'The State of Food Insecurity in the World: The Multiple Dimensions of Food Security', Food and Agricultural Organization of the United Nations, Rome.

FAO (2014), 'A Core Set of Food Security Indicators', Food and Agricultural Organization of the United Nations, Rome.

FPMU (2013), 'National Food Policy Plan of Action and Country Investment Plan Monitoring Report 2013', Food Planning and Monitoring Unit, Ministry of Food, Government of the People's Republic of Bangladesh.

FPMU (2014a), 'Shrinking Availability of Agricultural Land in Bangladesh: New Evidence', FMU Food Security Policy Brief 10, Food Planning and Monitoring Unit, Ministry of Food, Government of the People's Republic of Bangladesh.

FPMU (2014b), 'National Food Policy Plan of Action and Country Investment Plan Monitoring Report 2014', Food Planning and Monitoring Unit (FPMU), Food Planning and Monitoring Unit, Ministry of Food, Government of the People's Republic of Bangladesh.

FPMU (2015), 'National Food Policy Plan of Action and Country Investment Plan Monitoring Report 2015', Food Planning and Monitoring Unit, Ministry of Food, Government of the People's Republic of Bangladesh.

GED (2015), 'Seventh Five Year Plan FY2016–FY2020: Accelerating Growth, Empowering Citizens', General Economics Division Planning Commission, Government of People's Republic of Bangladesh.

GED (2017), 'Eradicating Poverty and Promoting Prosperity in a Changing World: Voluntary National Review (VNR), 2017', General Economics Division, Planning Commission, Government of People's Republic of Bangladesh.

Hossain, M. (2015), 'Agriculture and Food Security', in *Leading Issues in Rural Development: Bangladesh Perspective*, M. Hossain and A. Bayes (Eds.), A. H. Development Publishing House, Dhaka.

IFPRI (2016), 'Global Hunger Index: Getting to Zero Hunger', International Food Policy Research Institute, Washington, DC.

IPCC (2007), 'Climate Change 2007: Synthesis Report', Intergovernmental Panel on Climate Change, Geneva.

IPCC (2014), 'Climate Change 2007: Synthesis Report', Intergovernmental Panel on Climate Change, Geneva.

Khan, T. I. (2013), 'Regional Co-Operation for Food Security in South Asia', Paper presented at SDPI's Sixteenth Sustainable Development Conference titled Creating Momentum: Today Is Tomorrow, Islamabad.

Rahman, M. and M. A. Iqbal (2012), 'An Analysis of Bangladesh's Food Security Concerns: Nature of the Problem and Potentials of SAFTA-RTA', Food and Agriculture Organization of the United Nations, Regional Office, Bangkok.

Rahman, M. and H. Jahan (2015), 'LDC Issues in Bali MC-9 and the Post-Bali WTO Work Programme: Safeguarding LDC Interests and Addressing the Emerging Tasks', Centre for Policy Dialogue (CPD), Dhaka.

Rahman, M. and N. Khaled (2012), 'LDC Issues for Operationalization of the SAARC Food Bank: Bangladesh Case Study', South Asia Watch on Trade, Economics and Environment (SAWTEE), Kathmandu. Available at: www.sawtee.org/Research_Reports/R2012-04. pdf. Accessed 16 June 2015.

Rahman, S. and R. Salim (2013), 'Six Decades of Total Factor Productivity Change and Sources of Growth in Bangladesh Agriculture (1948–2008)', *Journal of Agriculture Economics*, Vol. 64(2), pp. 275–294.

Raihan, S. and T. I. Khan (2013), 'Impact of Indian Policies on Rice Price in Bangladesh', CPD-CMI Working Paper, No. 4, Centre for Policy Dialogue and Chr. Michelsen Institute.

Reutlinger, S. (1985), 'Food Security and Poverty in LDCs', Finance and Development, Washington.

Save the Children (2012), 'Nutrition in the First 1,000 Days: State of the World's Mothers 2012', Save the Children, London.

Sharma, R. (2011), 'Food Export Restrictions: Review of the 2007–2010 Experience and Considerations for Disciplining Restrictive Measures', Commodity and Trade Policy Research Working Paper, No. 32, Food and Agriculture Organization, Rome.

WFP (2015), 'Food Security at A Glance-Bangladesh', World Food Programme. Available at: http://foodsecurityatlas.org/bgd/country/food-security-at-a-glance. Accessed 16 June 2015.

WTO (2013), '9th WTO Ministerial Conference, Bali, 2013. Briefing note: Agriculture Negotiations – the Bid to "Harvest" Some "Low Hanging Fruit"', World Trade Organization, Geneva. Available at: http://wto.org/english/thewto_e/minist_e/mc9_e/brief_agneg_e.htm. Accessed 16 June 2015.

7

INDIA'S NATIONAL FOOD SECURITY STRATEGIES AND POTENTIAL FOR REGIONAL COOPERATION

S. Mahendra Dev

Introduction

Ensuring food security ought to be an issue of great importance for a country like India, where more than one-third of the population is estimated to be absolutely poor and nearly 40% of the children are malnourished in one way or another. There has been a paradigm shift in the concept of food security from a focus primarily on food availability and stability towards including dimensions of household-level food insecurity and malnutrition. Nutrition security has become more important apart from food availability and accessibility.

The Indian economy has done well in terms of economic growth in the post-reform period, which started in 1991. However, hunger and food insecurity have been high and the reduction in malnutrition among children has been very slow as compared to the rapid economic growth. In fact, the rate of change in the percentage of underweight children has been negligible during 1998–99 to 2005–06. The rank of global hunger index is 55 for India among 76 countries. It may be noted that India is home to one-third of the world's undernourished children. This puzzle of higher economic growth and slower decline in malnutrition shows that many other factors including inequalities across regions and social groups, access to adequate health services, clean drinking water, hygiene, sanitation, women's empowerment, caring capacity and practice, intra-household food security, governance, can determine the changes in food and nutritional status. However, recent numbers show that stunting (height for age) has declined from 48% in 2005–06 to 38.4% in 2015–16, a decline of nearly one percentage point per year. One has to examine the factors responsible for the reduction in malnutrition.

In this paper we examine the strategies followed for achieving food and nutrition security in India: availability, access, absorption and stability. There is a need for regional cooperation in food security in South Asia. Therefore, we also examine in this chapter the potential for regional cooperation, which would enhance the food and nutritional security of India and other countries in the region.

Performance of India in food security

National level food security

National level food security mainly refers to food availability in the country being sufficient stocks of food to meet domestic demand either through domestic supply or imports. Attainment of self-sufficiency of foodgrains at the national level is one of the big achievements in post-independence period. After remaining a food deficit country for about two decades after independence, India has become largely self-sufficient in foodgrains production at the macro level. There were only small occasional episodes of foodgrain imports after the mid-1970s. The foodgrains production increased from about 50 million tonnes in 1950–51 to 273 million tonnes in 2016–17 (GOI, 2017b).

In terms of growth, the performance of agriculture in the post-independence era has been impressive as compared to the pre-independence period. The all crop output growth of around 2.6% per annum in the post-independence period (during 1949–50 to 2014–15) was much higher than the negligible growth rate of around 0.4% per annum in the first half of the last century (GOI, 2017b). As a result, India achieved significant gains in foodgrains and non-foodgrain crops.

The highest growth rate of GDP from agriculture and allied activities of 4.1% per annum was recorded during the 11th Plan period (2007–12), followed by 3.9% during the period 1992–93 to 1996–97 (Table 7.1). There is a significant yield gap between India and many developing and developed countries. For example, paddy

TABLE 7.1 Growth rates in agriculture GDP in all-India

Period	Growth rate (% per annum)
1950–1 to 1964–5	2.51
1967–8 to 1980–1	2.20
1980–1 to 1990–1	3.07
1992–3 to 1996–7	3.85
1992–3 to 2001–2	2.76
1997–8 to 2004–5	1.60
9th Five Year Plan (1997–2002)	2.5
10th Five Year Plan (2002–07)	2.4
11th Five Year Plan (2007–12)	4.1
2012–13	1.5
2013–14	5.6
2014–15	–0.2
2015–16	0.7
2016–17	4.9★

Source: National Accounts Statistics. Various years. Central Statistical Organisation, Government of India and GOI (2014); Economic Survey, 2016–17, Vol. 2.

Note: ★Provisional estimates

yield in India is less than the world average. Yields in China are almost double to those of India for paddy. Within India there is a large yield gap between potential and realised yields.

Changes in consumption patterns and demand for non-cereal food

It is now widely recognized that the food basket is more diversified, and dramatic changes in food consumption patterns have taken place in India in the post-green revolution period. The share of non-food consumption increased significantly. The elasticity is high for non-cereal food and non-food commodities as compared to cereals. A diversified diet is an indication of improved nutrition.

As shown in Table 7.2, the share of cereal consumption declined significantly, while the share of non-cereal food like edible oil, vegetables, fruits etc., has been maintained. On the other hand, the share of non-food consumption increased from 37% in 1993–94 to 51.4% in 2011–12.

TABLE 7.2 Trends in percentage composition of consumer expenditure since 1993–94 (rural areas) in India

Item group	1993–94	1999–00	2004–05	2009–10	2011–12
Cereals	24.2	22.2	18.0	15.6	12.0
Gram	0.2	0.1	0.1	0.2	0.2
Cereal substitutes	0.1	0.1	0.1	0.1	0.1
Pulses and products	3.8	3.8	3.1	3.7	3.1
Milk& products	9.5	8.8	8.5	8.6	9.1
Edible oil	4.4	3.7	4.6	3.7	3.8
Egg, fish & meat	3.3	3.3	3.3	3.5	3.6
Vegetables	6.0	6.2	6.1	6.2	4.8
Fruits and nuts	1.7	1.7	1.9	1.6	1.9
Sugar	3.1	2.4	2.4	2.4	1.8
Salt and spices	2.7	3.0	2.5	2.4	2.4
Beverages etc.	4.2	4.2	4.5	5.6	5.8
Food Total	**63.2**	**59.4**	**55.0**	**53.6**	**48.6**
Pan, tobacco, intoxicants	3.2	2.9	2.7	2.2	2.4
Fuel and light	7.4	7.5	10.2	9.5	9.2
Clothing & bedding	5.4	6.9	4.5	4.9	6.3
Footwear	0.9	1.1	0.8	1.0	1.3
Misc.g. and services	17.3	19.6	23.4	24.0	26.1
Durable goods	2.7	2.6	3.4	4.8	6.1
Non-food total	36.8	40.6	45.0	46.4	51.4
Total expenditure	100.0	100.0	100.0	100.0	100.0

Source: NSS KI (68/1.0), Key Indicators of Household Consumer Expenditure in India

Performance in access to food: household level food security

Achieving food security requires people living in poverty to have sufficient means to purchase food. Individual and household purchasing power to buy food can be ensured through increased consumption capacity from employment intensive growth. Social protection programmes, including the Public Distribution System and employment programmes, can also increase food access through direct food provision, subsidies or increased purchasing power through transfers.

Food inflation

The increase in food prices is a significant negative feature of India's economic environment in the last decade. This trend has a tremendous impact on the quality of life, as people struggle to maintain the food and nutritional standards they had previously achieved, possibly giving up some other forms of consumption to keep themselves well fed.

Food prices were very high from 2006–07 to 2013–14. In the last three years (2014–15 to 2016–17), food prices were low with fluctuations in individual commodities. Food consumption patterns have diversified in recent years. The predominance of cereals in the typical household diet has given way to greater balance across different foods, with a consequent increase in the demand for proteins – pulses, milk, meat, fish and eggs – and for vegetables and fruit. It is no surprise that these items have been the primary causes of food inflation in the recent period.

Food insecurity at household level: poverty ratios

The incidence of poverty may give some indication of the extent to which food is accessible to households. The all-India head count ratio (HCR) has declined from 45.3% in 1993–94 to 37.2% in 2004–05 and to 21.9% in 2011–12 (Table 7.3).

TABLE 7.3 Poverty ratios based on Tendulkar's expert group methodology in India

Year	Head count ratios (%)		
	Rural	*Urban*	*Total*
1993–4	50.1	31.8	45.3
2004–5	41.8	25.7	37.2
2011–12	25.7	13.7	21.9
Annual decline in percentage points between 1993–94 and 2004–05	0.75	0.55	0.74
Annual decline in percentage points between 1993–94 and 2004–05	2.32	1.69	2.17

Source: Planning Commission, GOI (2013)

Overall poverty declined at the rate of 2.2 percentage points per annum during 2004–05 to 2011–12 as compared to 0.74 percentage points per annum during 1993–94 to 2004–05. This is true for both rural and urban poverty. In fact rural poverty declined faster than urban poverty during the period 2004–05 to 2011–12 compared to earlier periods. Both increase in incomes due to growth and public interventions were responsible for this decline.

Performance in nutrition indicators

There are two possible ways to assess the adequacy of food and nutrition and to detect the presence of inadequate intake among individuals and population groups.[1] These are: Nutritional Intake Assessment and Nutritional Status Assessment.

Nutritional Intake Assessment

Hunger has three major dimensions. The first is calorie deprivation. Second, protein hunger is another deprivation, due to inadequate consumption of pulses, milk, eggs, fish and meat. The third is hidden hunger, caused by the deficiency of micronutrients such as iron, iodine, zinc, vitamin A and vitamin B12.

The per capita calorie intake for rural populations declined from 2,240 in 1983 to 2,020 in 2009–10 (Table 7.4). It increased to 2,233 calories in 2011–12 but it was at the same level as 1983. During the same period, the per capita protein consumption declined from 63.5 grams to 55.0 grams per day in rural areas before increasing to 60.7 per capita in 2011–12 (Table 7.4). Only per capita fat consumption has not declined over time. In fact, it increased significantly in 2011–12.

TABLE 7.4 Mean per capita consumption of calories, protein and fats (per day) in India

Year	Calories (kc)		Protein (gms)		Fats (gms)	
	Rural	Urban	Rural	Urban	Rural	Urban
1983	2,240	2,070	63.5	58.1	27.1	37.1
1987–88	2,233	2,095	63.2	58.6	28.3	39.3
1993–94	2,153	2,073	60.3	57.7	31.1	41.9
1999–00	2,148	2,155	59.1	58.4	36.0	49.6
2000–01	2,083	2,027	56.8	55.3	34.6	46.1
2001–02	2,018	1,982	54.8	54.2	33.6	46.1
2002 (2)	2,025	2,014	55.4	54.9	34.7	47.0
2003	2,106	2,020	58.0	55.5	36.4	46.7
2004 (1)	2,087	2,036	56.9	55.9	35.5	46.8
2004–05	2,047	2,021	55.8	55.4	35.4	47.4
2009–10	2,020	1,946	55.0	53.5	38.3	47.9
2011–12	2,233	2,206	60.7	60.3	46.1	58.0

Sources: Deaton and Dreze (2009); NSS (2012)

However, there is a debate on the needed calories in recent years (Patnaik, 2004; Deaton and Dreze, 2009).

Although significant achievements have been made in health indicators, there has not been any decline in the prevalence of anaemia due to iron and folic acid deficiency; the decline in Vitamin A deficiency and iodine deficiency disorders has been very slow. Diet surveys have shown that the intake of Vitamin A is significantly lower than the recommended dietary allowance in young children, dietary adolescent girls and pregnant women. In these vulnerable sub-groups, multiple nutritional problems coexist, including inadequate intake of energy as well as of micronutrients other than Vitamin A (GOI, 2003).

We now examine the performance based on nutrition status or the outcomes using the anthropometric evidence. NFHS (National Family Health Survey) data shows that the proportion of underweight children decreased only marginally from 47% in 1998–99 to 45.9% in 2005–06, although stunting among children declined much more (Table 7.5).

The recent data shows that stunting (height for age) has declined significantly from 48.0% in 2005–06 (NFHS-3) to 38.4% in 2015–16 (NFHS-4) at the all-India level (Table 7.6). There has been significant decline in stunting across states. For example, in Chhattisgarh it declined from 52.9% to 37.6% during the same period.

TABLE 7.5 Trends in child malnutrition (zero to three years of age) in India

Nutritional Parameter	1992–93 NFHS-1	1998–99 NFHS-2	2005–06 NFHS-3
Stunted	52.0	45.5	38.4
Wasted	17.5	15.5	19.1
Underweight	53.4	47.0	45.9

Source: GOI (2009)

TABLE 7.6 Progress in stunting (height for age): 2005–06 and 2015–16 in India

	2005–06	2015–16
Andhra Pradesh	–	31.4
Bihar	55.6	48.3
Chhattisgarh	52.9	37.6
Gujarat	51.7	38.5
Haryana	45.7	34.0
Jharkhand	49.8	45.3
Karnataka	43.7	36.2
Kerala	24.5	19.7

(*Continued*)

TABLE 7.6 (Continued)

	2005–06	*2015–16*
Madhya Pradesh	50.0	42.0
Maharashtra	46.3	34.4
Odisha	45.1	34.1
Punjab	36.7	25.7
Rajasthan	43.7	39.1
Tamil Nadu	30.9	27.1
Telangana	–	28.1
Uttar Pradesh	56.8	46.3
West Bengal	44.6	32.5
All India	48.0	38.4

Source: National Family Health Survey NFHS 3, NFHS 4

In spite of decline, many states have high levels of stunting among children. Bihar showed the highest percentage of malnutrition with 48.3%, followed by 46.3% in Uttar Pradesh, 45.3% in Jharkhand, 42% in Madhya Pradesh and 39.1% in Rajasthan in 2015–16 (Table 7.6). Lowest malnutrition was in Kerala (19.7%), followed by Tamil Nadu (27.1%) and Telangana (28.1%) in 2015–16.

Strategies for improving food security

Availability

Both price and non-price factors are needed for increasing agricultural productivity. The non-price factors are investment, credit, infrastructure, technology, land and water management, market reforms, diversification, institutions, education and skills.

Structure of land holdings

The share of small and marginal farmers in total holdings increased significantly in the last three decades. As shown in Table 7.7, the share of marginal and small farmers increased from 75% in 1980–81 to 85% in 2010–11. Thus the small holding character of Indian agriculture is much more prominent today than even before. It may be noted that 67% of land holdings belong to marginal farmers with less than 1 ha. The average size of marginal holdings is only 0.38 ha. at the all-India level. The average size of small holdings is 1.42 ha.

Small holdings agriculture is important for raising agriculture growth, food security and livelihoods in India. It may be noted that Indian agriculture is the home of small and marginal farmers (85%). Therefore, the future of sustainable

TABLE 7.7 Changes in percentage distribution of operate holdings and operated area in India

Land class	Percentage of no. of holdings		Percentage of operated area	
	1980–81	*2010–11*	*1980–81*	*2010–11*
Marginal	56.39	67.04	12.04	22.24
Small	18.08	17.93	14.14	22.07
Small & Marginal	**74.47**	**84.97**	**26.18**	**44.31**
Semi-medium	14.01	10.05	21.15	23.59
Medium	9.08	4.25	29.64	21.18
Large	2.44	0.73	23.03	10.92
Total	100.0	100.0	100.0	100.0

Source: National Sample Survey (compiled from various rounds), Central Statistical Organization, GOI.

Notes: Marginal 0.01 to 1.00 ha.; Small 1.01 to 2.00 ha; Semi-Medium 2.00 to 4.00 ha; Medium 4.01 to 10.00 ha; Large above 10 ha.

agriculture growth and food security in India depends on the performance of small and marginal farmers. Small holder focus will continue in the future. Government is thinking of market reforms so that they can sell directly to retailers instead of middlemen. There is also a move to form producer organisations of small farmers so that they can cooperate in buying inputs and selling output.

Doubling farm income by 2022

The present government wants to double the incomes of farmers by 2022 through several measures. A panel on doubling farm income set up by the government released a four-volume report, which indicates that the central government's goal is to raise average incomes of agricultural households from Rs.96,703 in 2015–16 to Rs.193,406 in 2022–23 (at 2015–16 prices).[2] The report also says that India will need cumulative private and public investment of Rs.486 trillion (at 2004–05 prices) to achieve this goal.

Recently, the Ministry of Agriculture announced seven strategies to double farm incomes by 2020.[3] These seven points are: (a) increase in production (*Pradhan Mantri Krishi Sanchayi Yojana* on irrigation is the major component); (b) effective use of input cost; (c) reduction of post-harvest losses; (d) value addition (food processing etc.); (e) reforms in agricultural marketing; (f) risk, security and assistance (*Pradhan Mantri Fasal Bhima Yojana*, crop insurance scheme is the major component); (g) allied activities. The last point includes horticulture, integrated farming, white revolution, blue revolution, submission on agro forestry, beekeeping and rural back yard poultry development. The government is rightly focussing on farmers' incomes rather than production.

Food management

Ever since the Bengal famine of 1943, food policy in modern India has had two primary objectives: a large *public distribution system* supplemented by arrangements for moderating prices in the open market and concerted efforts for achieving *self-sufficiency in foodgrains*, coupled with measures for maximising procurement from surplus areas. These objectives have held sway over the past 75 years, with changes in emphasis and varying degrees of rigidity depending on the prevailing situation and assessment at a given time. Currently, the food-security system and the price policy basically consist of three instruments: procurement and minimum support prices (MSP), buffer stocks and the public distribution system (PDS).

Agricultural price policy

Each year, the government fixes the minimum support prices (MSP) for major agricultural products, taking into account the recommendations of the Commission for Agricultural Costs and Prices (CACP). At present, 25 items are covered under the MSP regime, including all important cereals, as well as pulses, oilseeds, cotton, jute and sugarcane.

However, price policy needs to balance the needs of producers against those of consumers. A minimum support policy has long been in favour of cereals like rice and wheat, and corrections have been made in recent years by increasing MSP for protein-rich crops like pulses. As a result, production has increased. Similar incentives must be given for other nutrient-rich foods, such as fruits, vegetables, milk, meat and fish, to increase supply. On the other hand, consumers must have access to these foods at reasonable prices in order to increase consumption.

Buffer stock

The importance of building up a buffer stock of foodgrains, normally rice and wheat, is to provide food security to the country. The argument in favour of buffer stocking is that where variability of foodgrains output is large, either due to weather conditions or due to manmade factors, it would be essential for the state to ensure that food security is maintained for the large mass of the people by building adequate buffer stocks from the surpluses in good production years and/or by arranging to import the requisite foodgrain in times of need. Various committees have suggested the optimal size of buffer stock, which varies from 15 to 25 million tonnes, depending on the season. In July, optimal buffer stock should be around 42 million. The actual buffer stock in July 2017 was 53 million foodgrains. Food subsidy is high at 1.06 lakh crores, which is around 0.7% of GDP.

Food and nutrition programmes

India has direct programmes such as the public distribution system (more on this later) and the Mahatma Gandhi National Rural Employment Guarantee Act (MGNREGA),[4] The Integrated Child Development Services (ICDS) and mid-day meal schemes to improve food and nutrition security. The government is also focussing on the convergence approach of working across sectors and departments to achieve food security.[5] The biggest programme is the recently introduced National Food Security Act (NFSA).

National Food Security Act 2013

The Public Distribution System (PDS) is one of the instruments for improving food security at the household level in India. The PDS ensures availability of essential commodities like rice, wheat, edible oils and kerosene to the consumers through a network of outlets or fair price shops. These are supplied at below market prices to consumers. With a network of more than 462,000 fair price shops (FPS) distributing commodities worth more than Rs.300 billion annually to about 160 million families, the PDS in India is perhaps the largest distribution network of its kind in the world.

Leakages

The main issue in PDS is improvement in the delivery system, as there are still significant leakages in the system. The performance of PDS gives some idea about leakages and also improvement in delivery system in recent years.

There seems to be some revival between 2004–05 and 2009–10 in the working of PDS. NSSO survey 2009–10 shows that 39% of population reported purchasing rice in rural areas compared to 24% in 2004–05 (Table 7.8). Similarly, the percentage share of PDS in total consumption increased from 13% to 24% in rice for rural areas during the same period.

Access to PDS increased from 27.2% in 1993–94 to 44.5% in 2011–12 (Table 7.9). There are significant differences in the access to PDS. Access to Southern states like

TABLE 7.8 Improvement in PDS in India

Commodity	% of hhs reporting consumption from PDS		% of share of PDS in quantity consumed	
	2004–05	2009–10	2004–05	2009–10
Rice rural	24.4	39.0	13.2	23.5
Wheat rural	11.0	27.0	7.3	14.6
Rice urban	13.1	20.5	11.3	18.0
Wheat urban	5.8	17.6	3.8	9.1

Source: NSS reports

TABLE 7.9 Access to PDS by states: population purchasing rice/wheat from PDS in India

States	1993–94	2004–05	2009–10	2011–12
Andhra Pradesh	59.3	58.5	76.8	76.1
Bihar	0.7	0.9	14.1	42.7
Chhattisgarh	12.1	24.2	61.4	57.5
Gujarat	38.4	25.5	27.9	22.7
Haryana	4.8	4.3	16.8	16.2
Jharkhand	13.4	5.5	23.1	29.6
Karnataka	57.1	50.0	60.6	63.1
Kerala	82.1	39.7	61.7	81.9
Madhya Pradesh	12.1	20.8	42.1	36.6
Maharashtra	35.0	22.1	34.6	33.1
Odisha	6.9	18.6	55.0	63.3
Punjab	1.4	0.5	18.9	19.8
Rajasthan	14.5	10.2	17.7	25.4
Tamil Nadu	71.2	72.7	87.4	87.1
Uttar Pradesh	1.8	5.7	23.2	25.4
Uttaranchal	59.4	21.0	35.0	69.0
West Bengal	17.2	13.2	33.7	44.6
All India	27.2	22.4	39.3	44.5

Source: Himanshu and Sen (2013)

TABLE 7.10 Leakages in PDS in India

Years	Leakage (1- (NSS consumption ratio of official off-take))
2004–05	54.0
2009–10	39.9
2011–12	34.6

Source: Himanshu and Sen (2013)

Tamil Nadu, Andhra Pradesh, Kerala and Karnataka is the highest while it is low for Bihar, Rajasthan, and U.P., Punjab and Haryana. On the other hand, Chhattisgarh has improved access significantly over time. Similarly, access improved in states like Bihar, Odish, Madhya Pradesh, West Bengal etc. (Table 7.9). The recent data shows that leakages have declined. Leakages declined from 54% in 2004–05 to 34.6% in 2011–12 (Table 7.10).

In order to make receipt of foodgrains under TPDS a legal right, the Government of India has enacted National Food Security Act, 2013 (NFSA) with effect from July 2013. The NFSA is an important initiative for food security of the people. The Act provides for coverage of up to 75% of the rural population and up to 50% of the urban population for receiving subsidised foodgrains under TPDS at Rs.1/2/3 per kg of coarse grains/wheat/rice respectively at 35 kg per family per month to households covered under Antyodaya Anna Yojana (AAY) and a 5 kg per person per month to priority households. The NFSA is now being implemented in all the states/union territories, covering 80.54 crore persons, against the total targeted coverage of 81.35 crore persons. During the year the 2016–17, the Government of India allocated 51.3 million tonnes under NFSA and 11.5 million tonnes under non-NFSA (Economic Survey, 2016–17).

Nutrition programmes

As mentioned earlier, the recent data shows a reduction in stunting among children from 48% in 2005–06 to 38% in 2015–16. There are programmes like Integrated Child Development Services (ICDS) and National Rural Health Mission (NRHM). It is true that the expansion and increasing efficiency in the delivery systems of these programmes have improved the nutrition status of children. Mid-day meal schemes might have improved nutrition for school going children.

Recent data shows that at the all-India level, the percentage of clean cooking fuel and an improved drinking water source has registered an increase from 25 to 44% and 88 to 90%, respectively, during the period 2005–06 (NFHS-3) to 2015–16. During the NFHS-3, the percentage of households with access to improved sanitation facility was 29%, which has increased to 48% by NFHS-4. At the start of Swachh Bharat Mission-Gramin of the Government of India in 2014, an estimated 55 crore people defecated in the open. With its focus on cleanliness and Open Defecation Free (ODF) India, there has been a significant decline in the number of people who defecate in the open to less than 35 crores (GOI, 2017b). Therefore, improvements in sanitation and drinking water might have also helped in enhancing nutrition.

Agriculture and nutrition

A multi-sectoral approach is needed to tackle the problem of nutrition. However because of several linkages, agriculture is perhaps the single most important sector that influences nutritional levels in India. In order to build a framework for understanding the persistence of malnutrition, Gillespie and Kadiyala (2011) identified seven key pathways between agriculture and nutrition. The first four pathways are: agriculture as a source of food, agriculture as a source of income, interplay between agriculture policy and food prices and allocation of household incomes to food and non-food consumption. The decision-making ability of the women is central to the remaining three pathways: intra household allocation of food and non-food consumption, prioritising health of the children and the nutritional status of women and their dietary intake.

There are three entry points to link agriculture to nutrition. These are: (a) equitable growth in agriculture including diversification; (b) food prices and diversification; and (c) women in agriculture.[6] It is well known that for reducing malnutrition, India requires multisectoral inputs – that is, convergence and inter-sectoral actions involving the fields of nutrition, health, agriculture, livelihoods and women's empowerment (Ved and Menon, 2011).

Nutrition strategies announced by NITI Ayog

NITI Ayog announced in August 2017 a ten-point national nutrition strategy to improve nutrition in districts/states of India.[7] Box 7.1 provides a vision on *Kuposhan Mukt Bharat* (removing malnutrition from India).

In a longer-term perspective, the strategy will also aim to progressively reduce all forms of undernutrition by 2030. The focus of this strategy over the next five years is on preventing and reducing child undernutrition.

The nutrition strategy envisages a framework under which the four proximate determinants of nutrition – uptake of health services, food, drinking water and sanitation and income and livelihoods – work together to accelerate decline of under-nutrition in India. Key nutritional interventions are: (a) infant and young child care and nutrition; (b) infant and young child health; (c) maternal care, health and nutrition; (d) adolescent nutrition; (e) control of micronutrient deficiencies or vitamin and mineral deficiencies; (f) community nutrition. The Nutrition Strategy Framework focusses on the core strategies outlined in Box 7.2.

BOX 7.1 THE VISION – "KUPOSHAN MUKT BHARAT"

Free from malnutrition, across the life cycle.
This is elaborated as:

> *Healthy, optimally nourished children, realizing their growth and develop-ment potential, active learning capacity and adult productivity;*
> *Healthy, optimally nourished women realizing their social and economic development potential; In protective, nurturing, gender sensitive and inclusive community environments – That enhance human and national development in the present – and in the future.*

Source: GOI (2017a)

BOX 7.2 CORE STRATEGIES – "HOW"

- **Governance Reform** – Nutrition Centre Stage and Public Accountability.
- **Leading by Example** – Kuposhan Mukt States, districts and panchayats.

- **Convergence** – of State/District Implementation Plans for ICDS, NHM and Swachh Bharat and others, addressing different determinants of undernutrition together.
- **Prioritise Action** – Reaching the most vulnerable communities in the districts/blocks with the highest levels of child undernutrition.
- **Counselling to Reach the Critical Age Group** – pregnant and lactating mothers, and children under three years, through skilled counsellors, peer counsellors and support groups.
- **Continuum of care** – across the lifecycle that includes preventive, promotive and curative care, linking families, communities, AWCs, health centres and health facilities.
- **Innovative Service Delivery Models** – demonstration and ripple effect, with evidence of impact.
- **Community Based Monitoring** – Making undernutrition visible to families, communities, tracking and informed action.
- **Enabling Actions** – Implementing innovative components of ICDS restructuring; crèches through MGNREGA; extending SABLA and implementing maternity benefits through Pradhan Mantri Matru Vandana Yojana and strengthening nutrition within the Health System.

Source: GOI (2017a)

Regional cooperation on food security

Regional cooperation on food security has to be in tune with Sustainable Development Goals (SDGs). The SDGs are especially relevant for eight countries of South Asia which, despite their economic dynamism and MDG achievements, account for 36% of the world's poor and equal percentage of malnutrition children. SDG goal 2 provides the following targets on hunger and malnutrition.

Target 2.1 – By 2030, end hunger and ensure access by all people, in particular the poor and people in vulnerable situations, including infants, to safe, nutritious and sufficient food all year round. Target 2.2 – By 2030, end all forms of malnutrition, including achieving, by 2025, the internationally agreed targets on stunting and wasting in children under five years of age and address the nutritional needs of adolescent girls, pregnant and lactating women and older persons.

Regional cooperation for achieving SDGs relating to hunger and nutrition has to be in all aspects of food security: availability, stability, access and nutrition. Some measures of regional cooperation such as food banks, seed banks and SAFTA (South Asia Free Trade Area) are already there. There is a need for cooperation in many other activities.

UNESCAP SSWA (UNESCAP South and South-West Asia Office) has prepared a framework of a ten-point strategy for regional cooperation on food security in SSWA region. This is relevant even for achieving SDGs relating to food and nutrition security. These ten points are: (a) climate resilience, sustainable agriculture and agricultural intensification; (b) regional food and seed banks, milk grids, food banks, sharing of information of production and stocks of agricultural commodities; (c) liberalised regional trade for food security including tariffs and NTBs within the SAFTA framework; (d) joint research and development (R&D) to address common problems and technology transfer for productivity enhancements; (e) effective regional knowledge networks for sharing best practices; (f) regional cooperation for greater efficiency in logistics to enable rapid movement and reduce waste and post-harvest losses; (g) coordinated positions in international forums and multilateral negotiations such as the WTO including on agriculture, food security, biodiversity and intellectual property rights; (h) alignment and coherence of regulations and specifications including the food safety regulations and those designed to deal with transboundary transmission of veterinary diseases; (i) natural resources management, including integrated water resource management including through regional and bilateral water treaties and regional cooperation in non-agriculture sectors, including energy sector; and (j) Implementing Integrated Phase Classification (IPC) methodologies for food security.

We have prepared areas where the countries in the region can have regional cooperation. We have quoted some issues and strategies from the South Asian Economic Summit IV (2011). They are still relevant. The discussion on regional cooperation is organised in the UNESCAP SSWA framework in the following way.

Climate resilience, sustainable agriculture and agricultural intensification

This is an important area for cooperation because climate change has cross-sectoral and cross-border impacts. Climate change is likely to have strong adverse effects on food production and the poor in this region. South Asia is one of the least cooperating regions in addressing climate change, although individual countries have national plans for adaptation and mitigation. Many people in the region live in areas of climate sensitive agriculture. First disaster management measures have to be undertaken. South Asia is a disaster-prone area. The countries have developed coping mechanisms with natural disasters. The region will benefit from cooperation in early warning systems. With modern technologies and instruments of surveillance, this would be possible.

There are suggestions to develop a joint project under the SAARC for adaptation to climate change in agriculture (SAES IV, 2011). According to this recommendation, the project should have the following focusses:

- Develop technologies suitable for drought-prone, submerged and saline areas.
- Promote climate resilient crops, e.g., ground nut, chickpeas and other pulses in drought-prone regions instead of highly subsidized irrigation.
- Undertake long-term weather forecasting.
- Disseminate climate impact related information widely through partnerships with regional media.

The climate change policies should not be looked upon from the point of view of disaster management only. The spectrum of the issue is much wider, involving food security, infrastructure, trade, health etc.[8]

Operationalising SAARC Food Bank and SAARC Seed Bank

SAARC Food Bank: It is known that every country having buffer stock is expensive. Therefore, regional cooperation in the form of the SAARC Food Bank would be useful. A decision was taken in the 14th SAARC Summit held in in 2007, to establish the SAARC Food Bank. The Food Bank will supplement national efforts to provide food security to the people of the region. But details are still not clear regarding food stock, replenishment of stocks, procedure for releasing stocks, determination of prices etc. There is a need to have physical reserves for emergency relief and virtual reserves to ward off speculative attacks. Right now, the food bank is not active and needs to be operationalised.

The most important initiative in Asia is the ASEAN emergency food reserves. The relative success of this food reserve is attributed to two important conditions: (a) a growing political cohesion and economic coordination among the member countries; and (b) we have a major food surplus country (Thailand) and a major importing country (Malaysia) in South-East Asia. These conditions find a strong ground for regional cooperation (Vyas, 1990). In the case of South Asia, both of these conditions are absent. Therefore, sustainability of food bank is an issue in South Asia.

SAARC Seed Bank: Based on directives of 16th SAARC Summit in 2010, the Member States agreed to establish a SAARC Seed Bank. The objectives of the Seed Bank are the following:

1   Provide regional support to national seed security efforts; address regional seed shortages through collective actions and foster inter-country partnerships.
2   Promote increase of seed replacement rate (SRR) with appropriate varieties at a faster rate as far as possible so that the use of quality seed for crop production can be ensured.
3   Act as a regional seed security reserve for Member States.

The SAARC Seed Bank is a good step, and it would help South Asian agriculture. Here regulatory framework is important so that beneficiaries do not suffer. It should not harm the farmers' rights on traditional seed varieties and knowledge.

Liberalising Intra-SAARC trade within the framework of SAFTA

The SAFTA Agreement was signed in 2004 during the Twelfth SAARC Summit. Intra-SAARC trade flows under SAFTA are far below the potential. One of the contentious issues is the sensitive list. Most of the countries in the region have reduced the number of items in the sensitive list over time. There are also high agricultural tariffs in the countries of South Asia. The agricultural tariffs are as high as 70% in many of these countries. There is a need for reduction in these tariffs.

Findings of a study using a computable general equilibrium model show that among South Asian countries, Sri Lanka gains the most from the agreement because it initially has relatively low tariffs and faces high tariffs in the region. The study also shows that exempting sensitive products from the agreement limits gains from trade for the lower middle-income members of SAFTA but may be welfare enhancing for the least developed economies (Bouet et al., 2010).

Another issue relates to export bans when global food prices rise. India should avoid banning exports, as it is not good for India as well as other countries in the medium term.

Engaging in joint research and development and promoting technology transfer

The main body formed to address cooperation in agriculture is the Technical Committee on Agriculture and Rural Development (TCARD), which started functioning in 2000. There is also an SAARC agricultural information centre in Dhaka. The activities of the technical committee and centre have to be examined.

There are several opportunities for cooperation in agricultural R&D as follows.

- There is a need to improve productivity of all crops particularly in rice and wheat in the region. Increase in yields in rice and wheat can release the land for other crops.
- Joint agricultural research programmes for development of abiotic stress tolerant improved varieties and hybrids and natural resource management techniques (e.g., minimum tillage).
- Cooperation in new sciences such as GIS, remote sensing, water forecasting and systems modelling.
- Free exchange of technology and information such as germplasm, improved animal breed, improved disease management technologies and practices.
- Capacity building through development of regional training facilities (Hossain, 2011).

Creating effective regional knowledge networks for sharing of good practices

Networking of knowledge networks is important for enhancing food and nutrition security in the region. Networking among academic institutes, universities, civil society, research projects etc., is needed. For example, there are several research projects on agriculture-nutrition linkages in South Asia such as LANSA (Leveraging Agriculture and Nutrition in South Asia, DFID funded), CGIAR's A4NH on agriculture for improved nutrition and health, the World Bank's SAFANSI (South

Asia Food and Nutrition Security Initiative), SPANDAN (System of Promoting Appropriate National Dynamism for Agriculture and Nutrition) project at the Indira Gandhi Institute of Development Research, Mumbai, sponsored by the Gates Foundation, the FOODSECURE project funded by the European Commission, websites on food and nutrition, e.g., POSHAN by IFPRI. There is a need for South-South cooperation CGIAR systems like ICRISAT and other organisations.

Learning from each other on social protection programs

South Asia has several social protection programmes. These programmes improve food and nutritional security, particularly for the poor.

India has programmes such as the MGNREGA (Mahatma Gandhi National Rural Employment Guarantee Act), a public distribution system to be converted into the National Food Security Act, the Integrated Child Development Scheme (ICDS), school mid-day meal schemes and the National Rural Livelihoods Mission. There are many innovative delivery systems in MGNREGA in Andhra Pradesh, PDS in Tamil Nadu, Chhattisgarh, Himachal Pradesh and grain banks by SEWA (Self Employed Women's Association). Bangladesh has 100 days of employment and other programmes, while Pakistan has cash transfers. Similarly, Nepal, Sri Lanka, Afghanistan and Bhutan have social protection programmes. One can learn from each other, particularly in design and delivery systems.

One of the problems in South Asia is poor public delivery systems. There are many good practices in different parts of South Asia. Lessons can be learned on accountability and governance.

Ensuring greater efficiency in logistics and reducing waste and post-harvest losses

Even when the yields are high, producers lose income due to poor post-harvest practices. In India, 30% of the crop production is wasted due to lack of storage, poor handling and lack of processing. Improved post-harvest handling and processing is essential to ensure high quality and value added. Storage is another area needing improvement. Food processing sector needs huge investments in logistics for supporting the value chain from farm to plate. It is largely a private sector activity, but government should provide needed incentives for faster investments.

Here one can learn from each other in South Asia region.

Having coordinated positions in international forums and multilateral negotiations

South Asia should have regional agendas and common positions in forums like WTO. South Asia in general attaches more importance to a rule-based multilateral trading system. It should continue to protect and pursue its regional interests in these negotiations and work together with other WTO members. It is known that agricultural subsidies and domestic support are high in developed countries. The region should continue to press for reduction in subsidies of developed countries and protect the interests of their farmers, particularly small farmers.

Initiatives by G20 (agricultural ministers' meeting in Paris in 2011) commit five main objectives for action as follows (G20, 2011):

- "(i) Improve agricultural production and productivity both in the short and long term in order to respond to a growing agricultural commodities demand
- (ii) increase market information and transparency in order to better anchor expectations from governments and economic operators;
- (iii) strengthen international policy coordination in order to enhance confidence in international markets and to prevent and manage food market crisis more efficiently;
- (iv) improve and develop risk management tools for governments, firms and farmers in order to build capacity to manage and mitigate the risks associated with food price volatility, in particular to the poorest countries;
- (v) improve the functioning of agricultural commodities' derivatives markets through the work of Finance Ministers and Central Bank Governors" (G20, 2011).

G20 has to take initiative on reducing speculative activities and conversion of biofuels. South Asia can cooperate on some of the activities, particularly on productivity and sharing market information and transparency.

Harmonising regulations and specifications

Promotion of livestock and fish are important for food and nutrition security in the South Asia region. In South Asia, livestock contributes more than 25% of agricultural GDP. Livestock provides proteins, calories and micronutrients. It also provides livelihoods for 150 million people, particularly women in South Asia. There is also a lot of synergy between crops and livestock. Animal disease is one important issue, and it spreads to humans. SAARC is already planning to have projects on Transboundary Animal Diseases (TADs) control and Transboundary Aquatic Animal Diseases (TAADs) control. Regional cooperation is needed on animal diseases. Similarly, South Asia has large coastal areas where fishing can be developed further with cooperation.

Collectively managing natural resources, including water and energy resources

Energy and water are crucial for food security in the South Asia region. As far as energy cooperation is concerned, at the national level one observes a mismatch between supply and demand in energy and at the regional level complementarities between energy endowments of subregional countries are visible. This indicates immense scope for intraregional energy trade. There are favourable factors for promoting regional trade, such as change in political mindsets, giving preference to developmental needs, growing importance to private sector in energy, independent regulatory bodies and growing interest in region level discussions. Utilising the potential for hydropower would help to reduce supply-demand gap in the region as well as make progress along sustainable energy pathways.

India is party to and will benefit from the regional level programmes on energy cooperation. SAARC should take measures to move the energy agenda forward by taking concrete steps to realize its various initiatives in this area. These include SAARC initiatives on the Energy Ring Concept (2005), the SAARC Regional Energy Trade Study (SRETS), the SAME Taskforce (2008), the template on technical and commercial aspects of electricity grid inter-connections (2009) and the discussion on efficiency, conservation and development of labelling (2010). The scope of the SAARC Framework Agreement for Energy Cooperation (Electricity) should be expanded to develop a comprehensive SAARC Regional Energy Trade and Cooperation Agreement. Efforts in this direction should be complemented by establishing a reliable energy database accessible to regional stakeholders.

Water has emerged as critical resource in the light of severe localised scarcity experienced in many parts of South Asia. Regional cooperation can be usefully leveraged in several areas of water resource management. Among the most important aspects would be agreements regarding rivers. Some of the examples of cooperation are India-Pakistan Indus Waters Treaty and the agreements between India and Bangladesh on sharing the waters of the Ganges-Brahmaputra river system. Outstanding issues in riverine and marine cooperation are being sought to be resolved chiefly through bilateral negotiations. A regional framework is found lacking in this intervention.

On regional cooperation for water, as regional discourses on this subject validate, a bottom-up approach is perhaps needed, which can promote greater interaction between border provinces with similar agricultural practices and shared dependence on transboundary water resource basins. Regional bodies such as SAARC have an important role to play in hosting discussions along the recommendations of important research results such as that of the *Ganges Strategic Basin Assessment*, which has come up with solid data and evidence with regard to regional water resources. A Joint River Commission established under the India-Bangladesh Treaty of 1972, which contributed to important resolutions on water disputes and subsequent bilateral agreements on river water sharing. Efforts at the regional level under a regionally constituted authority can deliver effective results. Such a regional body can also provide institutional capacity to monitor and provide data and objective analysis regarding water availability and efficient use through a basin-wide approach. Effective regional measures to sustainable resource management requires an integrated approach to infrastructure, technology, institutions, pricing and regulatory measures for both energy and water resources.

Implementing integrated food security phase classification

UNESCAP SSWA advocates that South Asian countries should adopt the Integrated Food Security Phase Classification (IPC). This is a set of standard tools that provides classification on the severity and magnitude of food security. It provides a rigorous analysis of food insecurity for decision makers. This also includes capacity building for designing policies.

Concluding observations

India is self-sufficient in terms of availability of cereals like rice and wheat. However, supply of non-cereals like fruits and vegetables, pulses, oilseeds, milk, fish and wheat have to be increased. Productivity of rice and wheat has to be increased further in order to release land for other crops. India is rightly concentrating on increasing farm income rather than agricultural production. A recent committee has given several recommendations for doubling farm income by 2022. Recently, the Ministry of Agriculture has also announced a seven-point strategy to double farm income in August 2017.

Access to food is one of the problems as many people are poor and lack purchasing power. Problem in India is not from the production side (availability), but it is a distribution problem (higher inequalities). A major problem is malnutrition, as around 38% of children suffer from malnutrition. It is known that levels and changes of malnutrition are determined by several factors such as agriculture, women empowerment, health, sanitation, safe drinking water etc. India has to concentrate on these determinants in order to reduce malnutrition. India recently has unveiled a ten-point action plan on improving nutrition security.

Regarding regional cooperation, there are many areas for cooperation among South Asian countries as discussed earlier. It has to be in tune with SDGs on hunger and malnutrition. Presently there are agreements on food banks, seed banks and SAFTA. However, there is a need to prioritise a few areas for quick-win solutions. We feel that it is important to move forward in three areas. These are trade, climate change, water and energy. We have discussed earlier the details of this cooperation. For example, in trade, there is a need to reduce tariff and non-tariff barriers and improve the working of SAFTA. Similarly, we need cooperation in water and energy. Climate change is an important area for regional cooperation. Another point is that as malnutrition is one of the biggest problems in the regions, learning from each of the determinants of malnutrition is important. For example, one can learn from direct nutrition programmes, gender empowerment, health, sanitation programs etc. Finally, political cooperation is essential for the success of regional cooperation in food and nutrition security. China took a lead in promoting Millennium Development Goals (MDGs). Now India should take a lead in achieving sustainable development goals (SDGs) in the next 15 years.

Notes

1 See Dreze and Sen (1989) for a discussion on intake and outcomes on nutrition.
2 See http://agricoop.nic.in/doubling-farmers for four volumes of Ashok Dalwai Committee on Doubling Farm Income.
3 See http://pib.nic.in/newsite/PrintRelease.aspx?relid=170628 for details of the seven-point strategy to double farm income.
4 See Dev (2011) on MGNREGA and wellbeing of children.
5 See GOI (2012).
6 See Dev and Kadiyala (2011), Dev (2012), Kadiyala et al. (2012) on the entry points for strengthening linkages between agriculture and nutrition.
7 See http://niti.gov.in/writereaddata/files/document_publication/Nutrition_Strategy_Booklet.pdf for the full report on national nutrition strategy.
8 See SAES IV (2011).

References

Bouet, A., S. Mevel and M. Thomas (2010), 'Is SAFTA Trade Creating or Trade Diverting? A Commutable General Equilibrium Assessment With a Focus on Sri Lanka', IFPRI Discussion Paper, No. 00950, International Food Policy Research Institute, Washington, DC.

Deaton, A. and J. Dreze (2009), 'Food and Nutrition in India: Facts and Interpretations', *Economic and Political Weekly*, Vol. 44(7).

Dev, S. M. (2011), 'NREGS and Child Well Being', IGIDR Working Paper, No. 2011-04, Indira Gandhi Institute of Development Research, Mumbai.

Dev, S. M. (2012), 'Agricultural-Nutritional Linkages and Policies in India', IFPRI Discussion Paper, No. 01184, International Food Policy Research Institute, Washington, DC.

Dev, S. M. and S. Kadiyala (2011), 'Pro-Nutrition Agriculture in India: Entry Points and Policy Options', *India Health Beat*, Vol. 5(8).

Dreze, J. and A. Sen (1989), *Hunger and Public Action*, Clarendon Press, Oxford.

G20 (2011), 'Action Plan on Food Price Volatility and Agriculture', Ministerial Declaration, Para. 11, Meeting of G20 Agricultural Ministers, Paris.

Gillespie, S. and S. Kadiyala (2011), 'Exploring the Agriculture – Nutrition Disconnect in India. 2020', Conference Brief, International Food Policy Research Institute.

GOI (2003), 'Economic Survey', Ministry of Finance, Government of India, Government of India.

GOI (2009), 'Eleventh Five Year Plan', Planning Commission, Government of India, New Delhi.

GOI (2012), 'Twelfth Five Year Plan', Planning Commission, Government of India, New Delhi.

GOI (2013), 'The State of Indian Agriculture', Ministry of Agriculture, Government of India.

GOI (2014), 'Economic Survey 2013–14', Ministry of Finance, Government of India.

GOI (2017a), 'Nourishing India: National Nutritional Strategy', NITI Aayog, Government of India.

GOI (2017b), 'Economic Survey 2016–17', Ministry of Finance, Government of India.

Himanshu, and A. Sen. (2013), 'In-kind Food Transfers', *Economic and Political Weekly*, Vol. 48(45–47).

Hossain, M. (2011), 'Food Security in South Asia: Challenges and Required Policy Initiatives', presented at Fourth South Asian Economic Summit, Dhaka, Bangladesh, 22–23 October 2011.

Kadiyala, S., P. K. Joshi, S. M. Dev, T. Nandakumar and V. S. Vyas (2012), 'A Nutrition Secure India, Role of Agriculture', *Economic and Political Weekly*, Vol. 47(8), pp. 21–25.

NSS (2012), 'Nutritional Intake in India, 2011–12: National Sample Survey 68th Round', Ministry of Statistics and Programme Implementation, Government of India.

Patnaik, U. (2004), 'The Republic of Hunger', *Social Scientist*, Vol. September – October 2004.

SAES IV (2011), 'Fourth South Asian Economic Summit', Conference proceedings, Centre for Policy Dialogue, Dhaka, Bangladesh, 22–23 October 2011.

Taneja, N., S. Prakash and P. Kallita (2013), 'India's Role in Facilitating Trade Under SAFTA', ICRIER Working Paper, No. 263, Indian Council for Research on International Economic Relations, New Delhi.

Ved, R. and P. Menon (2011), 'Convergence Framework for Nutrition', Mimeo, International Food Policy Research Institute, New Delhi.

Vyas, V. S. (1990), 'Food Policies and Food Security in Asia, With Particular Reference to South Asia', in *Increasing Access to Food: The Asian Experiences*, D. S. Tyagi and V. S. Vyas (Eds.), Sage Publications, New Delhi.

8

STATE OF FOOD SECURITY IN NEPAL

Addressing concerns of productivity and climate change

Posh Raj Pandey

Background

The Constitution of Nepal has recognised rights related to food as a fundamental human right. It provides 'every citizen the right to be safe from the state of being in danger of life from the scarcity of food' (GoN, 2015). It is part of a larger guarantee of important rights to every citizen, which are relevant to ensure the legal entitlement of food security and dignified living. They include the right to life, right to health, right to employment, right to housing and right to social security, among other rights. In addition, the Rights to Food and Food Sovereignty Related Act 2018, has been recently enacted,[1] and there are many periodic plans, sectoral policies and initiatives that have a strong bearing in the promotion of food security.

Nepal is a member of the South Asian Association for Regional Cooperation (SAARC), which also recognises the importance of regional and subregional collective self-reliance with respect to food security (SAARC, 1987). The Member States signed the Agreement on Establishing South Asia Food Security Reserves in 1997, adopted the SAARC Declaration on Food Security in 2008, and signed the Agreement on Establishing SAARC Seed Bank in 2011. Besides, Nepal is a party to many other international covenants and declarations, including the Universal Declaration on Human Rights and Conventions on Child Rights. These recognise that human beings have rights to be freed from hunger and to have safe and nutritious food. Nepal is also committed to achieve Sustainable Development Goal (SDG) 2, namely to end hunger, achieve food security and improved nutrition and promote sustainable agriculture.

Despite these legal and policy frameworks the state of hunger does not provide an encouraging scenario in Nepal. The percentage of people living below the national poverty line was 21.6% and the proportion below the minimum level of dietary consumption was 22.8% in 2015. This is despite the fact that a large portion of the household budget is spent on food items (NPC, 2017b). The global hunger index (GHI),[2] ranks Nepal at the 72nd position in a list of 119 countries. This indicates a serious situation regarding severity of hunger (IFPRI, 2017).

This chapter assesses the state of food security in Nepal and analyzes the areas of regional cooperation with its South Asian neighbours, which have the potential of supporting the food security initiatives of the government. After assessing the food security situation in Nepal in the second section, the third section briefly reviews the policies related to food security. The fourth section enumerates the challenges for food security. The fifth explores the areas for regional cooperation on food security. The sixth section provides the conclusions.

State of food security

The notion of food security has been constantly shifting and evolving or co-evolving over time, leaving a legacy of alternative viewpoints such as the livelihoods approach, the household perspectives, rights-based approaches, entitlement mapping, food sovereignty and many more (WFP, 2009). Sage estimates that there are approximately 200 definitions and 450 indicators of food security (Sage, 2002). However, for policy purpose, there seems to be consensus on the definition of food security proffered by the Food and Agriculture Organization (FAO) in its Rome Declaration on World Food Security and World Food Summit Plan of Action. It states that 'food security exists when all people, at all times, have access to sufficient, safe, and nutritious food to meet their dietary needs and food preferences for an active and healthy life' (FAO, 1996). It implies that all people, from the individual household level to the level of the world as a whole, should have access to food (in physical and economic terms) at all times. Not only should food be accessible, but it should be sufficient, safe and nutritious and must also cater the dietary needs and preferences of the individual household (Badaru, 2010). Thus the issue of food security is multidimensional. The analytical and policy framework for food security is built around interrelated four dimensions – food availability, food access, stability or vulnerability and food utilisation.

Food availability

Food availability refers to the physical availability of food in sufficient quantities and of appropriate quality within reasonable proximity. At the national level, food can be supplied through various sources – through domestic production and/or imports together with any donation or food aid. Similarly, at the household level, food supply constitutes production supplemented by market purchase and/or food support. This dimension captures the variety and physical availability of food at farms, the state of domestic food markets, as well as infrastructure related to storage and transport of food and food processing technologies. However, the state of food availability is assessed based on five indicators: food production, level of dietary energy supply (DES) and adequacy, protein supply, share of DES from cereals and share of protein of animal origin.

Food production: The average value of food production per capita shows that food production has grown at 2.13% per annum during the 1999–2014 period (Figure 8.1). This was despite a decade long insurgency, political instability and a large-scale outmigration of the youth. There was stagnation in the production of rice between 2001 and 2006 and a decline in recent years. However, Nepal maintained its production levels with significant growth in the production of other food products such as maize, wheat, potato, lentils, soybean and mustard. They registered growth rates of 3.0%, 2.9%, 5.1%, 3.6%, 3.8% and 1.5% respectively between 2001 and 2016 (Figures 8.2 to 8.8). The positive development with regard to food production has been that for all the main three cereals –rice, maize and wheat – there was growth in yield rather than growth in area cultivated (MoAD et al., 2016).

Dietary energy supply (DES) and adequacy: Dietary energy supply (DES) measures the sum total of all food available for human consumption in a country after deducting all other uses such as exports, animal feed, industrial use, seeds and wastage. Here, the adequacy of DES is assessed against average dietary supply adequacy (ADSA), which expresses the DES as a percentage of average dietary energy requirement (ADER), i.e., food requirements associated with normal physical activity. A value of ADSA greater than 100 indicates that, on an average, the total DES available in a country is more than enough to meet the needs of the population for a healthy and active life. The trend in ADSA as a percentage of the average energy requirement shows that dietary energy supply in Nepal was always higher than the

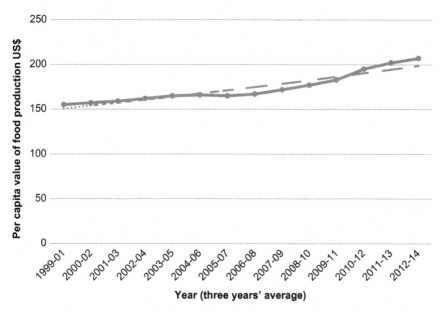

FIGURE 8.1   Average value of food production in Nepal

Source: FAO (2018)

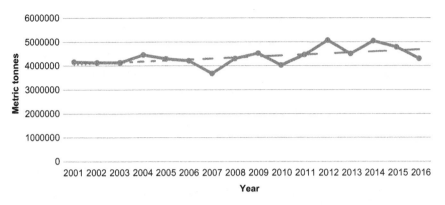

FIGURE 8.2 Rice production in Nepal

Source: FAO (2018)

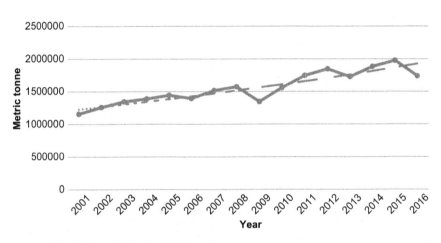

FIGURE 8.3 Wheat production in Nepal

Source: FAO (2018)

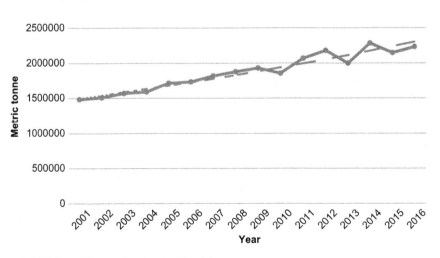

FIGURE 8.4 Maize production in Nepal

Source: FAO (2018)

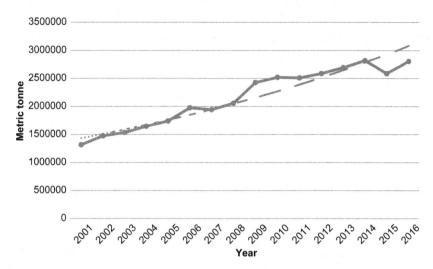

FIGURE 8.5 Potato production in Nepal

Source: FAO (2018)

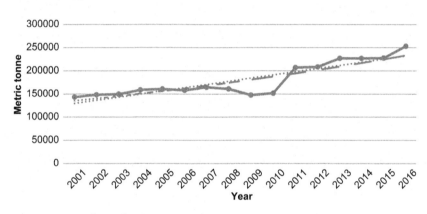

FIGURE 8.6 Lentils production in Nepal

Source: FAO (2018)

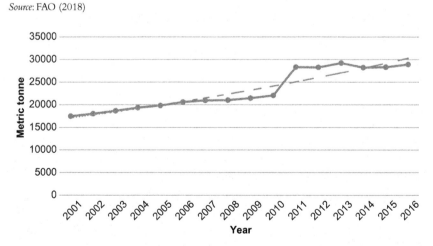

FIGURE 8.7 Soybean production in Nepal

Source: FAO (2018)

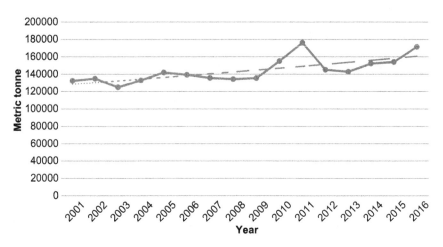

FIGURE 8.8 Mustard production in Nepal

Source: FAO (2018)

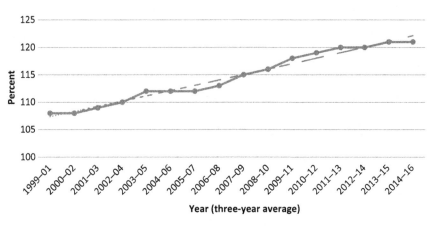

FIGURE 8.9 Average Dietary Energy Supply Adequacy (ADESA) in Nepal

Source: FAO (2018)

required energy during the observation period 1999–2016, with a growth rate of 0.8% per year. The average ADSA during 2014–16 was 21% higher than the average requirement (Figure 8.9).

The sources of energy derived from food shows that the quality of the diet has also improved over the period. The share of cereals has been declining, from 68% in 2008 to 61% in 2013. The share of non-cereals has increased at an annual growth rate of 3.4%. The major non-cereal products with a relatively large contribution include edible oils (with a 4.8% annual growth in DES), potatoes/yam (5.6% annual growth), milk/dairy products (6.1% annual growth) and pulses/beans (9% annual growth). There has been significant growth for sugar (3.3% per annum) and vegetables (4.2% annual growth) (Table 8.1).

Protein supply: The per capita per day supply of protein has increased from 38 grams in 2001 to 53 grams in 2013, an annual average growth rate of 3% (Figure 8.10). Most of the fat is derived from cereals (55%) and meat and milk products contribute about 14%(MoAD et al., 2016). However, there is consistent growth in the share of animal protein with an average annual growth rate of 2.4% (Figure 8.11).

Import dependency: The discussion here shows that there has been improvement not only in food supply but also in the quality of the diet. However, the improvement is associated with increasing dependency on food import. The import dependency ratio[3] was 1.7% in 2001, which increased to 7.6%in 2013 (Figure 8.12).

TABLE 8.1 Trends in the availability of food energy (calories/per capita/per day) in Nepal

Product groups	Food energy: kcal/capita/day						Average share in total energy (%)	Annual growth rate (%)
	2008	2009	2010	2011	2012	2013		
Rice	891	837	818	819	831	846	30	−0.3
Maize	525	535	537	604	608	507	20	1.0
Wheat	386	326	406	340	318	321	12	−3.4
Edible oils/ oilseeds	217	197	242	253	254	259	8	4.8
Potatoes/yam	126	151	156	158	166	176	5	5.6
Milk/dairy products	118	122	147	142	155	158	5	6.1
Pulses/beans	77	79	72	89	84	134	3	9.0
Spices	65	79	87	88	105	86	3	6.4
Other cereals	90	81	81	81	80	89	3	−0.3
Sugar	75	75	84	82	80	92	3	3.3
Vegetables	64	66	69	74	77	77	3	4.2
Meats	60	69	61	59	59	65	2	−0.4
Fruits	55	57	33	34	49	48	2	−3.2
Nuts	7	7	27	17	11	15	0.5	12.2
Alcohol, beverage	10	11	13	13	13	12	0.4	3.9
Fish	3	3	3	3	3	3	0.1	−1.5
Coffee/tea	1	1	1	0	1	1	0.0	6.8
Total	2,772	2,698	2,837	2,855	2,894	2,922	100	1.4
Cereals total	1,892	1,779	1,842	1,844	1,837	1,795	65	−0.5
Non-cereal total	879	919	995	1,012	1,057	1,126	35	4.8

Source: MoAD et al. (2016)

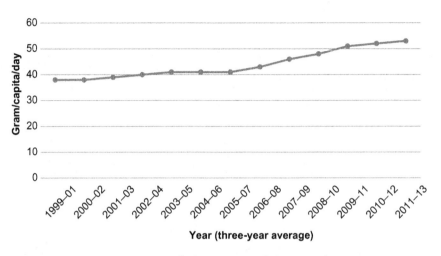

FIGURE 8.10   Average protein supply (gram/capita/day) in Nepal

Source: FAO (2018)

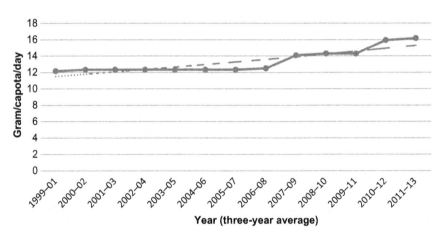

FIGURE 8.11   Share of protein of animal origin in total protein (gram/capita/day) in Nepal

Source: FAO (2018)

Import dependency is higher for energy derived from cereals (6.0% in 2013) than from non-cereals (26.3% in 2013). It is especially high for rice (10.6%), pulses (20.8%) and edible oils (69.7%). All this indicates change in food habits and deficient domestic production with income rise (Table 8.2).

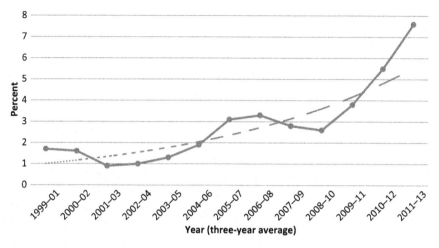

FIGURE 8.12   Cereal import dependency ratio

Source: FAO (2018)

TABLE 8.2 Import dependency rates (%) measured in terms of food energies supplied, 2013, in Nepal

Product groups	Import dependency rate (%)
Rice	10.6
Maize	0.1
Wheat	3.2
Edible oils	69.7
Potatoes/yam	9.0
Milk/dairy products	2.7
Pulses	20.4
Spices	18.6
Sugar	20.8
Vegetables	8.2
Meats	0.2
Fruits	17.2
Nuts	78.6
Alcohol, beverage	45.3
Fish	0.0
Coffee/tea	68.1
Cereals	3.7
Non-cereals	26.3

Source: MoAD et al. (2016)

Access to food

Even if food is physically available in the country or region, it may not be available for people's consumption if they lack purchasing power. The next pillar of food security is the entitlement of appropriate foods for an adequate diet and nutrition. Such an entitlement includes all those measures that are directly under the command of an individual through adequate income, barter and exchange. They can also be indirectly commanded through social arrangements, welfare system, traditional rights, access to common resources or food aid (FAO, 2006). The implication is that access to food refers not only to the ability of an individual to produce or procure sufficient food but also to the functioning of government policy as well as domestic and international food markets. FAO provides nine identified access indicators – percentage of paved road over total roads, road density, rail line density, gross domestic product (GDP) per capita, domestic food price index, prevalence of undernourishment, share of food expenditure of the poor people's income, depth of food deficit and prevalence of food inadequacy (FAO, 2018). Only 4.5% of the roads are black-topped in Nepal and the road density is calculated to be 485 people per kilometre of road. The total length of Nepal's rail line is less than 70 km. Even that is not operational. The per capita GNI grew at an average annual rate of 3.4% during the last decade and is estimated to be US$ 1,012 in 2018. Food inflation was 3.9% – lower than the overall inflation – for the last five years (GoN, 2018).

The three-year average of the prevalence of undernourishment during the 1999–2016 period is presented in Figure 8.13. It measures the population percentage that is at risk of not being able to meet the food requirements for normal physical activity. The figure shows that the proportion of the under-nourished population has been declining steadily at an annual rate of 7.5%. It was 8.1% in the 2014–16 period. The indicator of the depth of food deficit – the amount of calories needed to lift the undernourished from their status – also corroborates the improvement in access to food (Figure 8.14). Food deficit declined by 7.8% per annum between 1999 and 2015. Thus, Nepal's overall food security situation, based on the indicators of food supply, shows significant improvement. However, the national level data hides regional disparities as well as disparity based on the levels of income. For instance, people residing in the mountains, the mid- and far-western hills and *Tarai*, have lower food consumption scores, a higher percentage of inadequate consumption and higher rates of food poverty than the rest of the population. Similarly, the poorest people have expressed extremely high levels of consumption inadequacy (34%) compared to the top richest (3.9%) (Table 8.3). The inequality in food consumption is reflected in various other measures of food insecurity. For instance, the prevalence of severe stunting is almost three times higher among children from the poorest households compared with those from the richest households. The prevalence of stunting (both moderate and severe), is found to be higher in the mountains and mid- and far-western regions compared to other regions of Nepal (NPC, 2013).

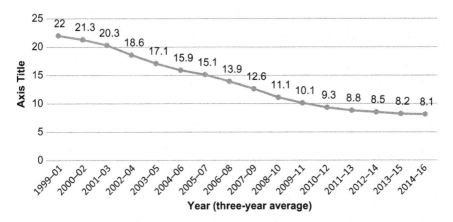

FIGURE 8.13 Prevalence of undernourishment in Nepal

Source: FAO (2018)

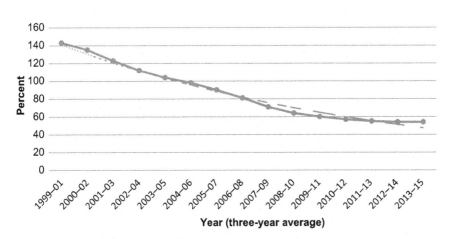

FIGURE 8.14 Depth of food deficit in Nepal

Source: FAO (2018)

Utilisation of food

The rationale for the utilisation dimension of food security is that people may have access to adequate food, but they may not be able to properly utilise the food due to factors personal to the consuming individual, such as illness and infection, prolonged inadequacy of food intake, repeated episodes of infection or undernutrition; or due to the environment under which food is consumed. The environment may be unsanitised or eating practices may be unhealthy; or the condition and quantity of the food product may be unsafe, or consumption may be inadequate or the food

TABLE 8.3 Distribution of food consumption by degree of adequacy (%) in Nepal

Development region	Less than adequate	Just adequate	More than adequate
Eastern	11.2	88.1	0.7
Central	10.8	87.0	2.2
Western	20.1	75.0	4.9
Mid West	24.8	73.4	1.9
Far West	25.4	73.2	1.4
Ecological region			
Mountains	29.8	69.3	0.9
Hills	15.9	81.4	2.7
Terai	13.4	84.6	2.0
Consumption quintile			
Poorest	34.8	64.4	0.7
Second	23.1	75.8	1.1
Third	15.1	83.2	1.7
Fourth	10.7	86.6	2.8
Richest	3.9	92.0	4.1

Source: CBS (2012)

itself may be inaccessible. The utilization dimension of food security is interpreted as ensuring efficient and maximum use of food- to its fullest potential. In other words, it directly refers to people's ability to absorb the nutrients from the food they eat (Gibson, 2012).

FAO has identified ten indicators related to utilisation. They include improved water sources and sanitation facilities; prevalence rates for wasting among under-five children, their stunting and underweight bodies; prevalence of underweight adults; prevalence of anaemia among women and under-five children; and deficiencies in vitamin A and iodine. However, here, we use the outcome indicators of utilisation, namely prevalence of wasting, stunting and underweight bodies among children under five years. Trends of children's nutritional status in Nepal for the 1996 to 2016 period indicate significant improvements (Figure 8.15). The absolute percentage of stunted children, wasted children and underweight children has declined by 21%, 5% and 15%, respectively, during the period. This decline has been in line with the Millennium Development Goals (MDGs) target. However, there is still a long way to go to meet the Sustainable Development Goals (SDGs) target.

Stability

To be food-secure means to have access to adequate food at 'all times'. Thus, the issue of stability, or vulnerability, regarding all dimensions of food security should be addressed, i.e. availability, access and utilisation. Stability addresses the inherent, impending or conditional risks that impact negatively on the availability, access or

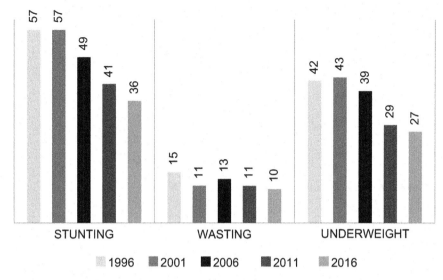

FIGURE 8.15   Trends in nutritional status of children (in %) in Nepal

Source: MoH et al. (2017)

utilisation of food (Gibson, 2012). The risk may be not only sudden shocks but also an inability to manage the risk.

In principle, the indicators of stability should include all the key drivers of availability, access and utilisation, but FAO in its suite of food security indicators has identified seven indicators, two related to production shocks (percentage of irrigated land and per capita food production variability), two related to food imports (cereal food import dependency ratio and value of food imports over total merchandise exports), domestic food price stability, per capita food supply variability and political stability.

With regard to production stability, the share of irrigated land shows improvement (Figure 8.16), whereas per capita food production remains highly fluctuating and volatile, worsening in the recent past (Figure 8.17). Trade indicators – cereals import dependency and proportion of food imports in total exports – are worsening. Food import dependency has increased from 1.7% in the 1999–2001 period to 7.6% in 2011–13, with an annual growth of 14%. Even the capacity to import food has deteriorated, with the surging ratio of food imports to merchandise exports, from 23% in 2000–02 to 69% in 2011–13 (Figure 8.18). This was an annual growth rate of 7.3% (Figure 8.16). Despite highly volatile food production, there seems to be improvement in the per capita food supply (Figure 8.19). This is attributed to increased food imports, largely financed by remittance flows. Thus it could be argued that while trade indicators in themselves appeared negative, they could have contributed to the positive outcome on overall food supply (MoAD et al., 2016).

An analysis of the state of food security in Nepal shows that there has been good progress on food availability and cereal production, as well as dietary energy supply

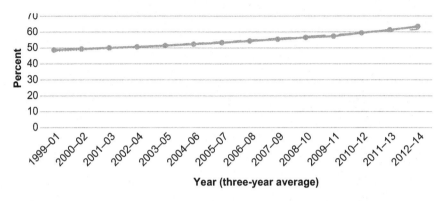

FIGURE 8.16 Arable land equipped for irrigation in Nepal

Source: FAO (2018)

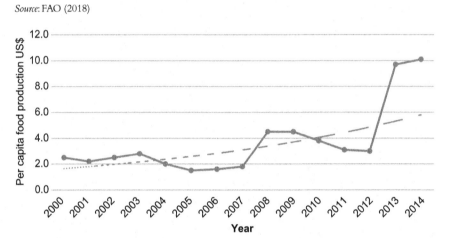

FIGURE 8.17 Per capita food production variability in Nepal

Source: FAO (2018)

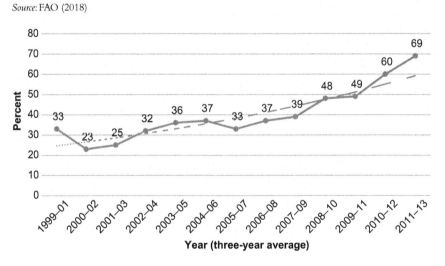

FIGURE 8.18 Value of food imports over total merchandise exports in Nepal

Source: FAO (2018)

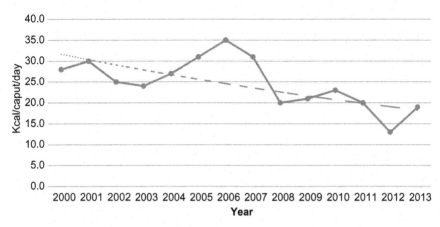

FIGURE 8.19 Per capita food supply variability in Nepal

Source: FAO (2018)

and its composition. Production growth is largely due to growth in yield rather than growth through cultivable area expansion. However, import dependency has been increasing over the period. Nepal attained impressive rates of reduction in stunting, wasting and underweight children, despite the fact that they are still quite high, compared to the values in countries at a similar level of development.

Policy initiatives

Long before the enshrinement of the food rights and food security provision in the Constitution of Nepal, many plans, policies and strategies had already incorporated the issues following the universal declaration on human rights, conventions on child rights and other international documents. The periodic plan documents, Multi-Sector Nutrition Plan 2013–17, National Agriculture Policy 2005, Climate Change Policy 2011, and Agriculture Development Strategy 2015, are the relevant policy instruments that address the issue of food security. The Three-Year Interim Plan (2007/08–2009/10) introduced the issue of food security with a separate section in the document. The subsequent plan documents have also provided goals and targets on food security. In congruence with Nepal's commitments to the Sustainable Development Goals (SDGs), the Fourteenth Development Plan (2016/17–2018/19) has devoted a separate chapter on food security. The Plan's long-term vision is to ensure adequate, hygienic and nutritious food to all the people all the time. It aims to increase basic food products through increased production of agriculture and livestock, to improve the access of quality food products to vulnerable regions and groups and to establish a fair and equitable food distribution system (NPC, 2016).

Based on the recommendations of the Nutrition Assessment and Gap analysis, the government developed and implemented Multi-Sector Nutrition Plans (MSNP). The second MSNP (2018/19–2023/24) recognises that the early period of human life is critical for cognitive, mental and physical development. Poor nutrition during the first two years of life may cause irreversible damage and lifelong burdens. The long-term policy of the MSNP is to improve maternal and child nutrition as it focusses on the critical period – from conception through pregnancy, infancy and early childhood or the first two years – of a child's life. It has identified essential nutrition specific, as well as nutrition sensitive, interventions. The former is to be delivered largely through the health sector and the later mostly by other sectors including education, agriculture, water and sanitation (NPC, 2017a).

The National Agriculture Policy (NAP) 2004, a comprehensive policy document for agriculture development, aims to contribute to ensuring food security and poverty alleviation and achieving high and sustainable economic growth by increasing agriculture production and productivity, developing the base of commercial and competitive farming and conservation, promotion and proper utilisation of natural resources and biodiversity. It also contains provisions of free inputs, technical support, leasehold land and irrigation facilities for the landless and farmers with less than half a hectare of land. It also makes provisions for special facilities such as provisioning of foodstuffs, transportation subsidies and concessional credits for regions and groups facing food security risks (MoAD, 2004).

The government also implemented its Agriculture Development Strategy (ADS) in 2015, with the vision of a self-reliant, sustainable, competitive and inclusive agricultural sector that drives economic growth and contributes to improved livelihoods and food and nutrition security. The focus of ADS is not only on the growth of the agriculture sector but also on the availability, access and utilisation of more nutritious food, particularly for those who are currently food insecure. The food and nutrition security dimension runs through all components and many of the activities of ADS. ADS is also aligned with Multi-Sectoral Nutritional Plans and the Food and Nutrition Plan of Action. It also addresses the food and nutrition security needs of the most disadvantaged rural population, including lactating and pregnant women, Janjatis, Dalits and groups in disadvantaged regions, such as Karnali. ADS has set a target of food poverty reduction, reducing the number of children under five who are stunted, underweight and wasted and lowering the number of reproductive age of women with chronic energy deficiency (MoAD, 2015).

Climate Change Policy 2011, is another document adopted with one of its goals related to food security. The policy targets improving rural livelihoods by mitigating and adapting to the adverse impacts of climate change on agriculture production and productivity as well as on the food security situation. It has identified policies to enhance the adaptive capacity of farming systems, ecosystems and health systems.

The Rights to Food Security and Food Sovereignty Related Act 2018 (Federal Parliament of Nepal, 2018), was enacted to implement the constitutional rights of the citizen to food, food security and food sovereignty. It defines food security as physical and economic access to food for an active and healthy life by guaranteeing every citizen the rights to food security. It has enumerated rights to food security as: (a) regular access to adequate, nutritious and quality food without discrimination; (b) freedom from hunger; (c) security from life threatening risks from lack of food;

(d) sustained access to food and nutrition support to individuals or households who are at risk of food insecurity or famine; and (e) consumption of culturally acceptable food. The law obligates federal, provincial and local governments to respect, protect and discharge the citizen's rights to food in a coordinated manner. It includes prevention and control of famine, identification of target households and issuance of food aid identity cards, provisioning of free or subsidised food, maintenance of food reserves and declaration of food crisis areas, among others. The different tiers of government – federal, provincial and local – are required to publish their food reserve situation, quantity of reserved food, price of food, food distribution systems and types of food. The federal government is required to prepare a National Food Plan along with its monitoring mechanism and indicators in coordination with provincial and local level governments. In addition, there are provisions with regard to protection and promotion of food sovereignty and mitigation of the adverse impact of climate change on food security.

The constitutional provision and enactment of the law is an assertion for a rights-based approach to food security; thus, the primary responsibility to ensure food security rests with the state. However, the focus is primarily on the access and distribution pillars of food security rather than a holistic approach to food security. It is silent on health-related complimentary policies. In addition, the legislation is de-linked from other social security programmes, such as employment guarantee schemes, income generating programmes, pension facilities for single women and the like. Thus the challenge is to create micro-level synergies and complementarities with other programmes and initiatives.

The implementation by-laws and modalities of the law are yet to be formulated, prompting many grey areas to crop up. What would be the criterion to identify the households entitled to food aid and how many people will be entitled? How can the quality of diets, not just the quantity of food, be improved and the dietary diversity enhanced? How would the food reserves be maintained and what would be the procurement mechanism? What would be the economic costs of implementing the legislation, including procurement, storage and distribution? How would the food distribution system be created and operationalised? How would the vulnerable section of the population be able to access the food? What would be the role of the private sector in ensuring food security and how will market distortions be addressed in the case of bulk purchases of food for food reserves? How would the rights to food and food sovereignty be synchronised with Nepal's multilateral WTO obligations and regional obligations under the South Asia Free Trade Agreement (SAFTA)? These are some of the issues that need to be seriously considered in the formulation of by-laws, regulations and operational modalities.

At the institutional level, the government's High Level National Nutrition and Food Security Steering Committee (HL NNFSSC) under the National Planning Commission (NPC) is chaired by the Prime Minister and in his absence by the Vice Chairperson. It has the responsibility to coordinate policy and implement food and nutrition activities across different ministries. There is also a Nutrition and Food Security Coordination Committee (NFSCC) chaired by a NPC Member.

This committee meets more frequently than HL NNFSSC and includes officers of five key ministries – Health and Population (MoHP), Education (MOE), Agriculture Development (MoAD), Federal Affairs and Local Development (MOFA) and Ministry of Local Development (MOLD) – in addition to development partners and other experts. The Right to Food and Food Sovereignty Related Act establishes National Food Council and Province Food Council under the chairmanship of the agriculture minister at the national and provincial level, respectively, to coordinate the activities related to rights to food, food security and food sovereignty. Similarly, the Local Food Coordination Committee, under the chairmanship of the Mayor of Municipality, or Chairman of Village Committee, is established at the local level. It has the added responsibility of facilitating food supply and the food distribution system.

Food security challenges

Despite a surplus in the food balance sheet (NPC, 2016), improvement in the state of poverty, hunger and nutrition and adoption of various programmes and policies, food and nutrition security remains a challenge for Nepal. There are myriad factors that have contributed to food insecurity at the individual, household and community levels. They are the state of poverty and unemployment, low agriculture production and productivity, environmental degradation and climate change, poor health facilities, unstable food markets, social strictures and insufficient awareness and weak and uncoordinated policies and institutions, among others. However, the increased purchasing power of people, improved awareness regarding food and nutrition security, changes in food habit, increased commercialisation of agriculture, improvements in agriculture infrastructure and rural roads, policy priority forced by commitments to SDGs and constitutional provisions on right to food and food security have provided ample opportunities to address those challenges.

Low agriculture production and productivity

The major challenge for food security is finding ways to increase food production and agriculture productivity. Nepal's agriculture growth rate – 2.9% per annum during the last decade – (GoN, 2018) is among the lowest in South Asia. In addition, Nepal's cereal yield of 2,650 kg per hectare of land in 2016 remained significantly lower compared to other South Asian countries such as Bangladesh (4,639 kg), Bhutan (3,410kg) and India (2,993 kg) (World Bank, 2018). The productivity of labour in agriculture is about one-quarter the productivity of labour in Nepal's non-agricultural sector. There is a significant productivity gap in production of all agricultural commodities, and all the commodities are performing significantly below their production potential – rice with 22% of the potential, fish with 36% of the potential and vegetables with 75%of the potential (MoAD, 2015).

The farm size of a majority of farmers is small. The average size of agricultural land holding is 0.7 hectares. The size of cultivable land per capita is on the decline

(CBS, 2013). Of the total 26 lakh 41 thousand hectares of cultivable land, only 45.2% is irrigated (GoN, 2018). Government investment in agriculture, as well as in irrigation, measured by the share in capital expenditure, has been declining (Pant, 2014). The degradation of natural resources, such as land, water and biodiversity, particularly in the mountain region is chronic. Feminisation of agriculture is on the rise, as 57% of the agriculture labour force is women (CBS, 2009). Outmigration of male members of the households in search of jobs has further increased the risks of deepening the feminisation of agriculture. Most of the farming systems are traditional and the use of high yielding varieties of seeds, chemical fertilisers and modern equipment is low.

A holistic approach is required for the development of the agriculture sector. It should focus on infrastructure, land and water management, research and extension, inputs including credit marketing and price policy and diversification and development of the rural non-farm sector. Public investment in agriculture including in irrigation and watershed development, rural roads needs to be upscaled and private investment incentivised. A 'crop-neutral' agriculture policy – a policy which creates a level playing field and allows farmers to respond to market signals – would promote diversification towards more nutritious crops and livestock products. At the moment there appears to be a policy bias towards a particular set of crops.

Climate change

The anticipated change in global climate in the form of rising temperatures, increased amount of carbon-dioxide in the atmosphere, greater frequency of extreme weather events (e.g., floods and droughts) and greater incidence of pests and diseases are likely to make things more complicated for agriculture production in the future. The evidences of a changing climate have been well documented. There is general warming, snowlines are receding and drought and unpredictable rainfall patterns are prolonged (MoEnv, 2010). There is general agreement that (a) the average temperature in Nepal, between 1977 and 2004, increased at the rate of 0.06 °C per year; (b) the rise in temperatures was greater at higher altitudes – i.e. 0.04 °C increase in Tarai and 0.08 °C increase in Himalaya; and (c) the increase in temperatures was more pronounced during the cooler months (0.06–0.08 °C per year from October–February, for all of Nepal) than for the warmer months (0.02–0.05 °C per year form March–September) (Shrestha et al., 1999 and Shrestha and Aryal, 2010; MoEnv, 2010). Various studies have projected further changes in temperatures and precipitation in the future. An OECD study on General Circulation Models (GCM), run with the SRES B2 scenario, shows that the mean annual temperature is likely to increase by an average of 1.2 °C by 2030, 1.7 °C by 2050 and 3 °C by 2100, compared to a pre-2000 baseline. Similarly, a NCVST (2009) study that used GCM and Regional Circulation Models projected the mean annual temperature to increase by 1.4 °C by 2030, 2.8 °C by 2060 and 4.7 °C by 2090.

Unlike temperature trends, precipitation data for Nepal does not reveal any significant trends (Practical Action, 2009). The annual variation in rainfall, particularly between two monsoons, is so large that observed trends are not very conclusive and the changes could be a part of the natural cycle (MoEnv, 2010). However, estimates based on General Circulation Model (GCM) portray an overall increase of precipitation in Nepal (Maharjan and Joshi, 2013). Seasonal breakdown of estimated precipitation shows that monsoon rain is going to be more intense, where the dry season will be drier. The increased intensity of summer monsoon can be translated into an increase in intensity of water-borne disasters like floods, landslides and sedimentation. Consequently, there will be an enormous loss of settlement, infrastructure and fertile topsoil, leading to a lowering of agriculture productivity.

Such climate variability and change could affect food security and nutrition through a combination of reduced food production, high food prices and lower food utilisation due to increased infections and more intense and frequent climate-related disasters. It is estimated that around 30,845 hectares of land owned by almost 5%of households will become uncultivable due to climate related hazards in a decade (CBS, 2004). Available studies project that rice yields – the main staple – will decline by 1.5% relative to current levels by 2030, 4.2% by 2060 and 9.8% by 2090 (Karn, 2014). In addition, yields of other food crops such as wheat, barley, maize and millet are also projected to decline (Maharjan and Joshi, 2013). Decline in food production due to climate change could have detrimental impacts on the income of households dependent on farm and agriculture labour. In addition, food prices would increase due to reduced agriculture production.

Post-harvest food losses

Post-harvest loss is a qualitative and quantitative food loss along the supply chain. The chain starts at the time of harvest until it reaches consumption or other end uses (Hodges et al., 2011). Loss can occur either due to food waste or due to inadvertent losses along the supply chain. Thus a reduction of post-harvest food losses could be a critical component in improving food security as food availability and accessibility can be increased through it.

The Department of Agriculture's Post-Harvest Management Directorate has estimated that there is a post-harvest loss of 25% in vegetables, 20% in fruits and 32% in potatoes and its seeds. However, there is no information on the quantity of cereal products lost. The underlying causes for high post-harvest losses are traditional and subsistence farming, lack of market orientation, limited use of post-harvest technology, pest infestation and disease, poor or inadequate storage infrastructure, poor or inadequate packaging, lack of dedicated transport systems for food to move from producers to consumers, limited knowledge base of stakeholders and weak institutional support to the post-harvest system.

At the national level, it is imperative that reliable data on post-harvest losses are collected and awareness increased about reducing food waste and losses among all stakeholders – farmers, farmers' organisations, producers, processors/manufacturers, wholesalers/retailers, consumers, policy makers, academia and civil society organisations. In addition, it is crucial to promote and adopt internationally established good agriculture and manufacturing practices and food safety standards; provision appropriate technology and infrastructure, including storage facilities and other support services; coordinate the actions of all actors from producers to market chain participants in a harmonious manner; and promote responsible and sustainable consumption. A sustained public-private partnership should be established by ensuring effective participation of business chambers and consumers associations.

Food price volatility

Between 2004 and 2008, real food prices in international markets rose by 55%. They began to drop back late in 2008, only to rise steeply again at the end of 2011, along with the prices of energy raw materials, and again in the latter half of 2012. (Anderson et al., 2013) Nepal's exposure to fluctuations in international markets is high because of its high food import dependency. It was manifested in 2008 with food prices increasing by 16% (NRB, 2018). In addition, seasonal/annual ups and downs in local food prices due to crop failures and supply disruptions also have a great impact. An innovative mechanism of marketing such as self-help groups, small producer cooperatives and contract farming could protect the farmer from national and international price volatility.

Converting food availability to nutrition security

Nepal's development strategy has internalised modernisation of agriculture systems in the policy agenda as a pathway for income growth and structural transformation. However, it has been shown that green revolution-led agriculture development that promotes staple crop productivity inadvertently results in the crowding out of traditional micronutrient-rich food crops, such as coarse grains, millets and pulses, from areas in which they were historically grown (Pingali, Mittra and Rahman, 2017). It also holds true for Nepal (GoN, 2018). Nepal's food policy focusses on calorie availability and has been slow to respond to the problem of micronutrient malnutrition. This means inability to address child stunting among the poor households and obesity and overweight among the middle-class households. It has been found that regions with an overall food surplus have the highest malnourishment indicators (MoAD, 2014). The Multi-Sector Nutrition Plans (MSNP) look beyond calories and adopt a life cycle approach to nutrition, but there is still a disconnect with the agriculture system and related food policies.

Regional cooperation for food security

The state is primarily responsible for protecting the citizen's rights to food and food security. The government has adopted various policies to intervene in the demand for and supply of foodgrains. The interventions largely include policies that affect prices or costs and policies that affect production and productivity. As the nation progressively becomes integrated in regional and global groupings, the regional, and in many cases global, initiatives acquire an added importance in national efforts. Regional cooperation can complement national strategies to address short run and long run food security challenges by ramping up greater international linkages in food production systems and value chains and for policies to ensure resilience and management of volatile economic and other shocks to food supply and prices (UNESCAP SSWA, 2012) It is in this perspective that regional cooperation in the following areas can help Nepal in taking forward the rights to food security.

Cooperation on climate resilient agriculture systems

Climate change is real and if nothing is done to reduce its impact agriculture production and productivity will drop, thus exacerbating the problem of food security. It is imperative that appropriate adaptation policies are formulated, investments are made and institutions are strengthened. In this context, there is a need to integrate food security and climate change policies. This means that provisions for better climate information through a better forecasting and early warning system, research and development of climate resilient crop varieties, use of moisture-conserving tillage, improving irrigation efficiency and enhanced participation of stakeholders in decision making would go a long way.

Building on the SAARC Declaration on Climate Change, a regional initiative could support national initiatives on climate change by collaborative work on an early warning system for climate disaster management; policy coherence and collaborative activities on agriculture research, including transboundary diseases and development of drought and heat resistant crop varieties; cooperation in conservation and utilization of natural resources, including river water utilisation; knowledge sharing and facilitating transfer of agriculture technology and similar measures.

Strengthening SAARC Seed Bank

With more than half the farmers working on less than 0.5 hectare of land, the farming system in Nepal is traditional and is a means of their livelihood. Farmers rely significantly on informal farmer-to-farmer exchange of seeds. Thus, the challenge for the policy maker is not only to increase the seed replacement rate but also to identify effective strategies to conserve seeds *in ex situ* (gene banks) and *in situ* (farm fields) conditions. The challenge is coupled with the need for promoting exchange of seeds for breeding of plant varieties that are important for food security and climate change adaptation.

Cooperation at the regional level would help address these challenges simultaneously. However, the SAARC member countries, recognising the importance of seed in ensuring food security, agreed to establish the SAARC Seed Bank in 2011 (SAARC, 2011) and also signed an operationalising agreement on material transfer to help farmers get quality seeds in the case of seed shortage due to natural and man-made calamities. It mandates members to maintain at least 1% of seed stock of the common varieties of rice, wheat, maize, pulses and oilseeds. However, there has not been any incident of use of the regional seed bank and material transfer, despite the fact that the system could be an instrument in ensuring seed and food security, preserving traditional seed systems as well as promoting the conservation and sustainable use of local genetic resources. For this, the SAARC agreement should go beyond increasing seed replacement rates (SRR) of improved or modern varieties and come up with a plan of action to promote the conservation of local varieties and local seed systems. In addition, a balanced approach to safeguard the interest of farmers, vis-à-vis intellectual property rights of the breeders, needs to be devised. In this context, the Framework for Material Transfer Agreement, which has been conceptualised in accordance with International Treaty on Plant Genetic Resources for Food and Agriculture (ITPGRFA), also requires one to adopt the equity principles of the Convention on Biological Diversity (CBD), mainly in terms of the provisions for the protection of traditional knowledge and access to genetic resources and benefit sharing.

Revitalising the SAARC Food Bank

The Rights to Food and Food Sovereignty Related Act 2018, has mandated the national and provincial governments to establish food reserves to provide free or subsidised food to targeted households. The mandate also ensures food and nutrition security in emergency situations such as earthquakes, flooding, landslides, fires etc., not to mention food crisis areas. Under the existing food reserve system, only Nepal Food Corporation (NFC) maintains a national buffer stock of 25,000 metric tons of rice to meet emergency requirements. The food reserve system for the provinces has not yet been devised. The SAARC Food Bank (SAARC, 2007), a regional food security reserve for SAARC Member States, was set up to address normal and emergency food shortages as well as to provide regional support to national food security efforts, foster inter-country partnerships and regional integration. By collectively resolving regional food shortages, the bank could support the government in discharging its responsibilities of ensuring food security in times of emergency and crisis. The food bank was initiated with the total reserves of 242,800 metric tons of foodgrains. The reserves were doubled to 485,600 metric tons by the third meeting of the SAARC Food Bank Board in 2009. The reserve is an asset of respective members and is under the control of the SAARC Food Bank Board.

The SAARC Food Bank is yet to be operationalised. Not a single member so far has been able to access food from the bank due to institutional and infrastructural bottlenecks, such as lack of a regional network for transporting foodgrains, lack of institutional arrangements for making periodic estimates of food demand and lack of price advantages in drawing from the reserves, (Pant, 2014; IPS, 2008). In addition, there are inherent weaknesses in the agreement related to the eligible criterion, the procedure for drawing from the reserves and the price mechanism to be followed. Thus, to revitalise the SAARC Food Bank, it should come into operation through a transparent procedure of withdrawal, a replenishment system and a price setting mechanism. This should be coupled with initiatives to increase the reserve levels on the regional front. At the national level, Nepal needs to strengthen its public distribution system and establish its links with the SARRC Food Bank, expand its storage capacity, improve quality standards, fortify local and regional connectivity and improve trade facilitation and border measures.

SAARC Milk Grid

The dairy sector directly contributes to food security for a significant portion of the population of Nepal. A part of the milk production is consumed within the farm households (availability and access to food), it provides a steady stream of food and revenues for households and livestock can be used as collateral for credit or sold in case of emergency cash needs (stability) and its micronutrients improve immunity (utilisation). However, consumption of milk and milk products is low. In the Nepalese diet, animal protein sourced food (APSF) is only about 13% (of which 7% is from milk, 6% from meat and 1% from eggs) compared to the requirement of about 30% of APSF for optimal nutrition (MoAD, 2014). From the supply side, about 125,000 farm families, 1,500 primary cooperatives produced 1.7 million metric tons in 2014 – buffaloes contributed 69% and cows 31%. The import of milk products is minuscule (MoAD, 2014). There is seasonal fluctuation in milk production and collection, which affects the supply of pasteurised milk in the market (flush season- August-September to January-February; lean season-rest of the months).

The ratio of lean-to flush season production is about 1:3. The seasonal fluctuations, together with the fragmented market and inadequate distribution system, means some of the farmers are forced to observe milk holidays. On the other hand, it is projected that the supply of milk and milk products should be increased by 17% per annum to meet the demand. The 'SAARC Quadrangle Milk Grid' under consideration of the SAARC Technical Committee on Agriculture and Rural Development (TCARD), could contribute to meeting the deficient supply of milk, address seasonal fluctuation of supply and manage milk distribution. However, the necessary conditions for effective use of the grid is speedy operationalisation of BBIN Motor Vehicle Agreement, exclusion of milk from the SAFTA sensitive list and diary related technology transfer at the regional level.

Regional trade liberalisation

The South Asian Free Trade Agreement (SAFTA), signed in 2004, has been in operation since mid-2006. The primary objectives of SAFTA are eliminating barriers to trade and facilitation of cross border movement of goods among the contracting states. The major instruments of SAFTA are its trade liberalisation programme, including sensitive lists, rules of origin and safeguard measures. The agreement does not include any provision for food security *per se*, but regional trade could be a means to achieve food security as it eases the impact of deficiency of and instability in domestic agriculture production. (Panagariya, 2002). A detailed examination of surpluses and deficits of food in the region reveals that South Asia has large surpluses of rice, sugar and meat and small surpluses of eggs and vegetables at the current levels of consumption (UN and ADB, 2015).

Nepal is a net food importing country. Its agriculture imports comprise 4.2% of gross domestic consumption and more than 80% of agriculture imports are sourced within the SAARC region. In addition, agriculture exports constitute 4.5% of agriculture GDP. Thus regional trade in agriculture products could be an important policy instrument for food security in Nepal.

It was expected that SAFTA would establish binding schedules for trade liberalisation and provide a predictable and transparent trade regime that would contribute to regional trade expansion, including trade in agriculture products. However, trade liberalisation has been slow. There is a large number of agriculture products on the sensitive lists – list of products exempted from the trade liberalisation programme. The number of agriculture products on the sensitive lists ranges from 26 for Maldives to 542 for Sri Lanka. Nepal has 125 agriculture products on its sensitive list. India has reduced its list to 25 products for least developed countries (LDCs) and does not include any agriculture products. In addition, sanitary and phytosanitary and technical standards are increasingly taking the form of non-tariff barriers. Trade facilitation measures, including simplification and harmonisation of customs procedures and transit facilities, have not received the desired prominence in the trade cooperation agenda. Member States have also resorted to export bans or minimum export prices during times of high price volatility (Rahaman and Iqbal, 2012).

To ensure that regional trade remains an instrument of food security, it is essential that the sensitive lists, particularly of food items, be reduced drastically. The work of the South Asian Regional Standard Organisation (SARSO) needs to be expedited to remove Technical Barriers to Trade (TBT) and Sanitary and Phytosanitary Standards (SPS) related barriers. The coverage of common products for harmonization of standard must be expanded to include more agriculture products. SAFTA also needs to take a decision to prohibit export bans on food items. In addition, initiatives should be taken to reduce transaction costs through better connectivity, trade facilitation measures and a regional transit treaty.

Conclusions

This chapter assesses the state of food security in Nepal and finds that there has been good progress on food availability, food access and utilisation of food. However, around one-sixth of the population is food hungry and prevalence of stunting, wasting and underweight children is still high. Nepal's food import dependency has been increasing with time. The enshrinement of rights to food and food security in the Constitution as fundamental rights and the enactment of laws related to food rights and food sovereignty would be a game changer in ensuring food security. The implementation of the law should ensure that needy households have access to adequate and nutritious food even within their fiscal constraints. But, there are challenges of low agriculture productivity and acquiring the means of addressing the threats from climate change and risks of price volatility. Above all, there is a need to deal with ways of translating food availability into nutrition security. To address these challenges, there is a need for a paradigm shift from short-term fixes to long-term plans and strategies, from the fragmented approach to a holistic one, from symptomatic treatment to tackling the root causes and from inherent vulnerability to inherent stability. Regional cooperation in the areas of climate change and agriculture technology, food and seed banks, a milk grid and trade in agriculture products would go a long way to support national initiatives towards food security.

Notes

1 The Act came into force on 17 September 2018.
2 Global Hunger Index (GHI) is developed by the International Food Policy Research Institute (IFPRI), which is an aggregation of the average of three dimensions of hunger; the proportion of the population undernourished, the proportion of children under-five underweight and the under-five mortality rate.
3 The cereal imports dependency ratio tells how much of the available domestic food supply of cereals has been imported and how much comes from the country's own production. It is computed as (cereal imports − cereal exports)/(cereal production + cereal imports − cereal exports) * 100. Given this formula the indicator assumes only values <= 100. Negative values indicate that the country is a net exporter of cereals.

References

Anderson, K., S. Jha, S. Nelgen and A. Strutt (2013), 'Re-Examining Policies for Food Security in Asia', *Food Security*, Vol. 5, pp. 195–215.

Badaru, O. (2010), 'Food Security in Africa', in *Protecting Human Security in Africa*, A. Ademola (Ed.), Oxford University Press, Oxford.

CBS (2004), 'Nepal Living Standards Survey 2003/2004', Central Bureau of Statistics (CBS), Government of Nepal, Kathmandu.

CBS (2009), 'Nepal Labour Survey 2008', Central Bureau of Statistics (CBS), Government of Nepal, Kathmandu.

CBS (2012), 'Nepal Living Standards Survey 2010/11', Central Bureau of Statistics (CBS), Government of Nepal, Kathmandu.

CBS (2013), 'National Sample Census of Agriculture 2011/12', Central Bureau of Statistics (CBS), Government of Nepal, Kathmandu.

FAO (1996), 'Rome Declaration on World Food Security and World Food Summit Plan of Action', World Food Summit 13–17, Food and Agriculture Organization, Rome.

FAO (2006), 'Policy Brief: Food Security', Food and Agriculture Organization, Rome.

FAO (2018), 'FAO Statistics'. Available at: www.fao.org/faostat/en/.

Federal Parliament of Nepal (2018), 'Rights to Food Security and Food Sovereignty Related Act 2018', Government of Nepal, Kathmandu.

Gibson, M. (2012), 'The Feeding of Nations: Redefining Food Security for the 21st Century', CRS Group.

Government of Nepal (2015), 'The Constitution of Nepal', Ministry of Law, Justice and Parliamentary Affairs, Government of Nepal, Kathmandu.

Government of Nepal (2018), 'Economic Survey 2017–18', Ministry of Finance, Government of Nepal, Kathmandu.

Hodges, R. J., J. C. Buzby and B. Bennett (2011), 'Postharvest Losses and Waste in Developed and Less Developed Countries: Opportunities to Improve Resource Use', *Journal of Agricultural Science*, Vol. 149, pp. 37–45.

IFPRI (2017), 'Global Hunger Index 2017', International Food Policy Research Institute, Washington, DC.

IPS (2008), 'Strengthening Economic and Social Integration in South Asia: Summary of Proceedings of Regional Conference', Institute of Policy Studies, Colombo, May 30–31.

Karn, P. K. (2014), 'The Impact of Climate Change on Rice Production in Nepal', SANDEE Working Paper, No. 845–15.

Maharjan, K. L. and N. P. Joshi (2013), *Climate Change, Agriculture and Rural Livelihoods in Developing Countries*, Springer, Tokyo.

Ministry of Agriculture Development (MoAD) (2004), 'National Agriculture Policy, 2004', Government of Nepal, Kathmandu.

Ministry of Agriculture Development (MoAD) (2014), 'Statistical Information of Nepalese Agriculture 2013/14', Government of Nepal, Kathmandu.

Ministry of Agriculture Development (MoAD) (2015), 'Agriculture Development Strategy', Government of Nepal, Kathmandu.

Ministry of Agriculture Development (MoAD), Central Bureau of Statistics (CBS) and Food and Agriculture Organization (FAO) (2016), 'Food and Nutrition Security in Nepal: A Status Report', Government of Nepal, Kathmandu.

Ministry of Environment (MoEnv) (2010), 'National Adaptation Programme of Action (NAPA)', Government of Nepal, Kathmandu.

Ministry of Environment (MoEnv) (2011), 'Climate Change Policy, 2011', Government of Nepal, Kathmandu.

Ministry of Health (MoH) (2016), 'New Era and the DHS Program 2017: Nepal Demographic and Health Survey 2016: Key Indicators Report 2016', Government of Nepal, Kathmandu.

Ministry of Health (MoH), New ERA, and ICF International (2017), 'Nepal Demographic and Health Survey 2016: Key Indicators', Government of Nepal, Kathmandu.

National Planning Commission (NPC) (2013), 'Nepal Thematic Report on Food Security and Nutrition', Government of Nepal, Kathmandu.

National Planning Commission (NPC) (2016), 'Fourteenth Plan (Fiscal Year 2016/17–2018/19)', Government of Nepal, Kathmandu.

National Planning Commission (NPC) (2017a), 'Second Multi-Sector Nutrition Plan', Government of Nepal, Kathmandu.

National Planning Commission (NPC) (2017b), 'National Review of Sustainable Development Goals', Government of Nepal, Kathmandu.

Nepal Climate Vulnerability Team (NCVST) (2009), 'Vulnerability Through the Eyes of Vulnerable: Climate Change Induced Uncertainties and Nepal's Development Predicament', Government of Nepal, Kathmandu.

Nepal Rastra Bank (NRB) (2018), 'Quarterly Economic Bulletin', Vol. 52(3).

Panagariya, A. (2002), 'Trade and Food Security: Conceptualizing the Linkages', Paper presented to the Conference on Trade, Agriculture, Development and Food Security: The Impact of Recent Economic and Trade Policy Reforms, FAO, Rome, 11–12 July 2002.

Pant, K. P. (2014), 'The SAARC Food Bank for Food Security in South Asia', South Asia Watch on Trade Economics and Environment (SAWTEE), Kathmandu.

Pingali, P., B. Mittra and A. Rahman (2017), 'The bumpy road from food to nutrition security – Slow evolution of India's food policy', *Global Food Security*, Vol. 15, pp. 77–84, Elsevier.

Pingali, P. and T. Rao (2017), 'Understanding the Multidimensional Nature of the Malnutrition Problem in India', in *Agriculture and Rural Development in a Globalized World*, P. Pingali and G. Feder (Eds.), Routledge Press, New York.

Practical Action (2009), 'Temporal and Spatial Variability of Climate Change Over Nepal (1976–2005)', Practical Action, Kathmandu.

Rahaman, M. and A. Iqbal (2012), 'An Analysis of Bangladesh Food Security Concerns: Nature of the Problem and Potentials', Regional Trade Agreement and Food Security in Asia, Food and Agriculture Organization.

SAARC (1987), 'Agreement on Establishing the SAARC Food Security Reserves', South Asian Association for Regional Cooperation, SAARC Secretariat, Kathmandu.

SAARC (2007), 'Agreement on Establishing the SAARC Food Bank', South Asian Association for Regional Cooperation, SAARC Secretariat, Kathmandu.

SAARC (2011) 'Agreement on Establishing the SAARC Seed Bank', South Asian Association for Regional Cooperation, SAARC Secretariat, Kathmandu.

Sage, C. (2002), 'Food Security', in *Human Security and the Environment: International Comparisons*, E. A. Page and M. Redclift (Eds.), Edward Elgar, Cheltenham.

Shrestha, A. B. and Aryal R. (2010), 'Climate change in Nepal and its impact on Himalayan glaciers', *Regional Environmental Change*, Vol. 11(1), pp. 65–77, Springer.

Shrestha, A. B., N. D. Acharya, N. B. Shrestha, H. Adhikari, T. Bhatta and S. K. Shrestha (2010), 'An Assessment of Drought in Ramechhap District, Manthali', District Development Committee, Nepal.

Shrestha, A. B., C. P. Wake, P. A. Mayewski and J. E. Dibb (1999), 'Maximum Temperature Trends in the Himalaya and Its Vicinity: An Analysis Based on Temperature Records From Nepal for the Period of 1971–94', *Journal of Climate*, Vol. 12, pp. 2775–2786.

UNESCAP SSWA (2012), 'Regional Cooperation for Inclusive and Sustainable Development', United Nations Economic and Social Commission for Asia and the Pacific, Subregional Office for South and South-West Asia, New Delhi.

United Nations (UN) and ADB (2015), 'Food Security in South Asia: Developing Regional Supply Chains for the Food Processing Industry', Asian Development Bank.

WFP (2009), 'Emergency Food Security Assessment Handbook', World Food Programme.

World Bank (2018), World Development Indicators. Available at: https://data.worldbank.org/indicator.

9

NATIONAL FOOD SECURITY CHALLENGES AND STRATEGIES IN PAKISTAN

Cooperation for technology and trade

Abid Qaiyum Suleri and Mehreen Iqbal

State of food security in Pakistan

The Islamic Republic of Pakistan, under its constitution, implicitly recognises access to safe and nutritious food as a basic right of citizens of the country. The current Federal Government administration has also committed to ensure a food secure and well-nourished population. Food security is among the greatest challenges for Pakistan. Four out of ten children under the age of 5 in Pakistan are stunted, while one in six suffer from wasting, and almost one in three children are underweight. Over one-third of the country's households are found to be food insecure, with 18.3% of the households suffering from severe food insecurity (Figure 9.1) (GOP and UNICEF, 2019). FAO (2017) stated that Prevalence of Undernourishment (PoU) has decreased from 23.3% in 2004–06 to 19.9% in 2014–2016 of total population, which is still slightly above the regional average of 14.9% in South Asia. Although the PoU has reduced compared to 23.3% in 2004–06, the number of undernourished people has increased from 35.7 million in 2004–06 (28.7 million in 1990) to 37.6 million in 2014–16. The high PoU, particularly among women and children, gave Pakistan the 26th highest under-five mortality rate in the world. Further, according to latest Global Hunger Index (GHI) report published by IFPRI in 2018, Pakistan is ranked at 106 with a score of 32.6; only above Zimbabwe, Liberia, North Korea, Timor-Leste, Afghanistan, Sudan, Haiti, Sierra Leon, Zambia, Madagascar, Yemen, Chad and Central African Republic.[1] This situation is even more critical considering the country faces great volatility from natural and man-made causes. Pakistan has a history of severe floods, and the Long-Term Climate Risk Index ranks Pakistan as the 7th most affected country from 1996 to 2015 (Kreft et al., 2016).

Food insecurity in the country has exhibited a rising trend during the last two decades. The findings of the first report on food security in 2003 showed that 37.6% of the population was food insecure (SDPI and WFP, 2004). According to

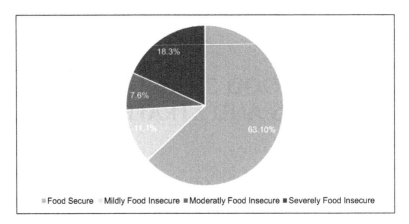

FIGURE 9.1 Household food insecurity in Pakistan

Source: Government of Pakistan (2016)

Note: Reference period for data collection: 14 to 30 days between November 2015 and March 2016.

the 2009 report, about 48% of the population was food insecure (SDPI et al., 2010). The 2016 Food Security Assessment Survey (FSA) states that almost 18% of the population in Pakistan is severely undernourished and almost 44% of households have below 2350 kcal per adult equivalent daily intake. Based on Multi-Dimensional Poverty Index (MPI), a world food programme conducted an integrated context analysis (ICA) study to find out the vulnerability to food security at the district level in Pakistan. According to the analysis, Balochistan and some parts of Sindh have high chances of recurrence of vulnerability to food insecurity.

Food availability

Three elements primarily determine food availability: production, stocks and net trade of food items. Based on these three indicators it can be argued that food availability in Pakistan at the national level is fairly good. However, there is unequal regional distribution. For example, production of staple foods has shown a positive trend in recent years but there are regional inconsistencies. Production of cereal or crop-based food is heavily concentrated in Punjab and Sindh, while Balochistan lags in production of crop-based food. However, animal-based food production has increased in Balochistan. KPK is dependent on the production in Punjab, Sindh or imports to meet its demand for food.

Pakistan has made remarkable progress in the production of prime cereals, particularly wheat – it has turned from being a net-importer to having regular surplus production. In the case of rice, the country has been a net-exporter for decades. As far as the production of other food groups like pulses and edible oilseeds is concerned, the quantities and import bills of pulses have been regularly rising since decades. For instance, during July 2018 to March 2019, the country has spent nearly USD 1.45 billion on the import of edible oils (2.420 million tons).[2]

Government of Pakistan (2016) presents the historic trends of wheat production and consumption in Pakistan since 1960. Yields have grown from around one tonne to three tonnes per hectare. However, despite the fact that Pakistan is currently the 9th largest producer of wheat, it's per unit wheat yields are 12% less than the world average.[3] Thus there is considerable potential for increasing production with adequate investment in research and innovation. There is a significant geographic variability in wheat production. For example, in 2014–15, more than three quarters (77%) of the national wheat production was produced in Punjab followed by Sindh (15%), while the production in KP-NMD, Balochistan, and GB was very little. Similarly, for the 2015–16 harvest, about 80% of production is estimated to be produced in Punjab alone.[4] Total national wheat production for 2018–19 is estimated at 25.19 million MT, negligibly higher than the 2017–18 level of 25.07 million MT.[5]

The production of rice, the second main staple crop of Pakistan, is estimated at 7.20 million MT (milled basis), 3.3% lesser than the previous year's production of 7.45 million MT. Cultivated area under rice was decreased in 2018–19 by 3.2% as compared to 2017–18 which was mainly attributed to decline in domestic prices of rice which reduced the area under the crop and growers shifted to sugarcane and maize crop.[6] Globally, large carryover stocks depressed prices nationally due to less exports. On average, Pakistan exports 3–4 million MT annually and the rest is consumed domestically.[7]

Food accessibility

Ensuring an adequate supply of food is necessary, but not sufficient, to achieve food security when households do not have adequate resources to obtain appropriate foods for a nutritious diet.[8] The second dimension of food security deals with the economic and physical dimensions of food accessibility, which are examined in detail in this section. Food accessibility is heavily dependent on the purchasing power of the consumers by considering their income vis-à-vis food prices and other indicators like debt, livelihood, social protection coverage and level of education.

Food access is a major concern for Pakistan. Poverty, which has been on the rise, is the leading contributor to limiting access to food. According to multidimensional poverty index (MPI), poverty in Pakistan is as high as 39%, which points to a large vulnerable and potentially food-insecure population.[9] Another estimate by the Ministry of Planning indicates that almost 29.5% of people live below the income poverty line, which means roughly 60 million people are surviving beneath the poverty line. Incidence of poverty has increased in Pakistan due to a variety of reasons, which include periodic floods, energy crises, political instability, stagnant industrial growth and war on terror etc.

Poverty has also limited the kinds of food people can access, a consequence of which is unbalanced nutrition. In Pakistan, food diversification is very narrow, especially for people in the lower socio-economic strata. As noted earlier, despite the fact that yields are failing to meet their full potential, national availability of food is sufficient to feed the entire population of Pakistan. However, for a range of interdependent factors, many households cannot access the food available in the country. This is because many communities, households and individuals do not have the economic and physical resources that would allow them to purchase sufficient quantity and quality of food for a nutritious diet. In spite of overall national availability, if domestically produced food is not accessible and/or affordable outside of certain socio-economic parameters, then it will not ensure a population's food security.

While talking about access to food, the Ministry of Planning, Development and Reforms conducted a study on Cost of Diet, which tells us that almost 68% of households in Pakistan cannot afford to spend on staple adjusted nutritious diet, which on the contrary means two out of three households are not able to afford the minimum diet with their current household expenditures.[10] Generally the trend shows that urban areas have higher affordability than the rural areas but at the provincial level, both urban and rural areas could not afford a nutritious staple diet. Among the provinces/regions covered by the analysis, it was found that Balochistan has the highest prevalence of households not able to afford a staple adjusted nutritious diet, with 83% of households in this category. This prevalence for Sindh, KP and Punjab was 71%, 67% and 66% respectively, while it was 32% in Islamabad. As explained, poor households – and those who spend a higher proportion of their monthly expenditure on food – are particularly vulnerable to food price inflation, which is the prime shock experienced by many households.

A well-functioning marketing and distribution system is also one of the important prerequisites to improve physical and economic accessibility of food. At present, losses in the distribution system are high in Pakistan. It is estimated that out of the total production of fruits and vegetables, about 35–40% goes to waste, which includes 10–12% loss during transportation.[11]

Generally, households in Pakistan are highly dependent on markets for purchasing food and non-food items, agricultural inputs, labour and sale of farm outputs. Input-output prices not only determine the level of use of agricultural inputs in farming, but they also to a certain extent determine the prices of produce for net consumers. Households enjoy better food security when markets are well functioning (abundant supplies at stable prices) and prices are within affordable limits. The FSA 2016 report[12] stated that, on average, Pakistani households spend 49% of their monthly cash on food, illustrating the important role of markets in food security. Overall, Pakistani households are market dependent for 79% of their cereals, 92% of vegetables, 50% of milk and 70% of meat intake. There has been some downward trend noticed towards the end of 2011 and through 2012, which was averted in early 2013 with a steady increase continued until 2014. Prices to some extent stabilised in the year 2015, with some decline noted in wheat prices (for example, in May 2016, the average retail price of wheat was lower by 2% compared to a year ago). For the year 2017, the price of wheat and wheat flour negligibly increased by 0.1% and 0.5%, respectively.[13] Negligible decrease was noticed for pulses (non-cereal commodities) for the year 2017. Fuel prices can also indirectly impact overall prices of food commodities, as increased fuel price would increase both the production cost as well as the transportation cost of food. There has been an increase in fuel prices in international markets during the last two years. This would definitely affect the food prices in domestic markets.

Livestock product prices have also increased significantly because production has not kept pace with the increasing demand from the growing population. Between January 2010 and May 2016, the prices of all livestock products have almost doubled. In May 2016, compared to January 2014, the prices of Mutton and Milk have registered an increase of 15% each, and beef has registered a price increase of about 12% over this period.[14]

Utilisation of food

Utilisation or food absorption is the way the body makes the most of various nutrients in the food. Sufficient energy and nutrient intake by individuals is the combined result of good care and feeding practices, availability of water, sanitation and hygiene, food preparation, diversity of the diet, intra-household distribution of food and basic education about nutritional importance of food. Combined with good biological utilization of food consumed, this determines the nutritional status of individuals. Since this dimension of food security is dependent on the biological ability of the individual to make use of the nutrients consumed, issues such as access to safe drinking water and sanitation coupled with health status and literacy rates implicate food utilisation ability.

In Pakistan, most of the population (87%) has access to piped drinking water but the access to safe and treated drinking water is almost scarce, which challenges the utilisation of food. A study suggests that only 20% of the population has access to safe drinking water, while 80% population is forced to drink unhealthy and untreated water contaminated with industrial waste, sewage, rusted pipes and agricultural waste. Moreover, waterborne diseases constitute 80% of all diseases and cause 33% of deaths in Pakistan.[15] This turns 13% of households in Pakistan who don't have the access to piped water and still depend on rivers, ponds, unprotected wells/springs, canals, tankers and water bearers for drinking purposes, into extremely vulnerable persons on the food absorption index. If we analyze the provincial status, the situation is poorest in FATA with only one-third (33%) of households with access to drinking water sources, followed by AJK (37%) and Balochistan (70%). On the other hand, the situation is better in Punjab (96%), Sindh (88%) and Islamabad (87%).[16] Similarly, a recent study conducted by the Pakistan Council of Research in Water Resources (PCRWR) showed that out of the 72% of water supply schemes in the country that are functional, 84% supply water that is not fit for consumption. In addition, 14% of water supply sources in Punjab and Sindh were heavily contaminated with arsenic.

Utilisation of food not only depends on access to safe drinking water but hygiene and sanitary practices and facilities are vital components of proper absorption of food. In Pakistan, 46% of the population did not have a handwashing facility at home with soap and water in 2015.[17] Moreover, great disparities among wealth quintiles are also evident, where 80% of the richest and only 13% of the poorest have access to improved sanitation.[18] Among schools, toilets, boundary walls, electricity and drinking water are the basic infrastructure facilities and only 48% of the schools in Pakistan are equipped with these facilities.[19]

Despite the access to water there is a severe lack of access to safe drinking water and sanitation facilities, as well as poor hygiene practices, which not only is a major contributor to comorbidities like diarrhoea and pneumonia, which adversely impact a child's nutritional status but also has negative implications for school attendance.

Food sustainability

In order to ensure food security of a population, it is essential to ensure access to adequate quantity and quality of food at any given time. Periodic disruptions in food access deteriorate the nutritional status and thus hamper food security of a population. Food stability entails efforts at both demand and supply side aspects and encompasses all three dimensions (availability, access and utilisation) of food security. Another factor to consider is rapidly increasing population, which requires a country to increase the food production of a country to ensure stable food access and economic stability of a country. Pressure exerted by growing population on farmland has been steadily increasing in the provinces of Pakistan (Figure 9.2).

A strategic review by IFPRI conducted in 2017 displays the estimates of yield growth and associated per capita production, which gives the overview of food availability in Pakistan. According to the strategic review, during the last 25 years the population on each acre of land increased by 85%, and the food production needed to support that growing population has grown consistently without any obvious change. The population to be supported on each acre is expected to

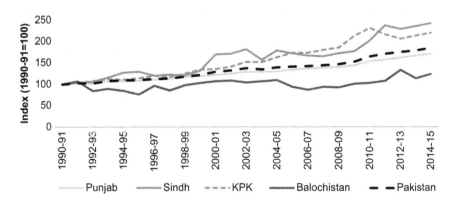

FIGURE 9.2   Population pressure on cultivated land, 1990–2015

Source: Agriculture Statistics of Pakistan (various issues) and Population Estimates from Population Census, 1998

further increase by 28% from 2015 to 2030. The pressure of food vs population more than doubled in Sindh and KP. For sustainable food availability, it is important that output per unit of land should keep up with population growth, and if we observe the data from 1981–2014, it can be seen that growth in crop yields in general, and especially in wheat (1.6%), did not keep up with population growth (2.4%).

Emergency situations created by floods, droughts and earthquakes, exacerbated by climate change, are major elements of Pakistan's natural environment that challenge the sustainability of agriculture and associated livelihoods and thus food security. Pakistan continuously ranks among the most affected countries in various climate risk indices. In the Long-Term Climate Risk Index, Pakistan ranked 8th highest in 1995–2014 and 7th highest for 1996–2015.[20] The frequent disasters, attributed to climate change (except the earthquake), have a huge impact on the food security and livelihoods of the population, and their impact is worsened by mismanagement of natural resources and poor maintenance of rural infrastructure, which results in low food production and increased risk to lives and livelihoods.

Various coping strategies are used by people for confrontation with natural disasters or man-made disasters such as violence and conflict, which often lead the population to food insecurity. These strategies are usually limiting food intake, eating less nutritious/less desirable food, borrowing money/taking on debt and in the most severe cases, selling productive assets to be able to feed their families, thereby further decreasing resilience to future shocks. The FSA survey[21] reported that 57% population of Sindh, followed by KP (48%) and FATA (47%), Balochistan (22%) and Islamabad (2%) had opted for negative coping strategies to feed their families, hence making them more vulnerable to future shocks.

The earlier indicates that unless strategically tackled with action-oriented policy focus, persistent food insecurity may threaten the social fabric of a nation by inciting conflict and unrest contingent upon the extent and scale of hunger and poverty.

Institutional framework for food security in Pakistan

Historically, food security and nutrition have had a low political visibility, but this situation appears to have changed since 2010. In a historic decision by the Parliament of Pakistan in April 2010, an amendment (18th) was introduced in the Constitution of Pakistan. Along with many other changes the amendment stopped the Federal Government to legislate on 47 subjects, which were part of the concurrent list and were being concurrently looked after by the federal and provincial governments. Most areas of social sector development including agriculture, livestock and fisheries etc., were part of the concurrent list. Through the 18th amendment legislation on these subjects was mandated to the provinces.

As a result of the 18th amendment, the functions of the Federal Ministry of Food, Agriculture, and Livestock (MINFAL) were also devolved to provinces. Article 38-d of the Constitution of Pakistan (1973) obliges the State as a whole to

> provide basic necessities of life, such as food, clothing, housing, education and medical relief, for all such citizens, irrespective of sex, caste, creed or race, as are permanently or temporarily unable to earn their livelihood on account of infirmity, sickness or unemployment.

To fulfil its constitutional obligations, the Federal Government established a National Ministry of Food Security and Research (MNFSR) in October 2011. The ministry had three major goals, (a) establish a National Zero Hunger Program, (b) formulate food security policy and (c) rearrange the institutional framework for food security.

In the context of food security, the major burden lies on provinces now, as the

1 Availability of food is a function of agriculture, irrigation, livestock and agro-marketing departments which are all under the provincial domain now.
2 Socio-economic access which requires livelihood generation opportunities, social safety nets and poverty reduction strategies is again a provincial domain.
3 Utilization and stability of food for which health, sanitation, hygiene, safe drinking water and education are prerequisites, are also under provinces.

The challenge is not only to have coordinated efforts and seamless institutional arrangement for ensuring food security between federal government and provincial governments but also to have intra-provincial coordination; for example, to ensure food availability, agriculture, irrigation and livestock departments in a province will have to work in coordination.

MNFSR is not mandated to take care of social protection programmes which are vital to ensure access to food. Pakistan's largest social safety net scheme, the Benazir Income Support Program (BISP), a federally administered cash-transfer programme benefiting about 5.8 million families living below poverty line, is outside the domain of MNFSR.

The current government has created the Ministry of Poverty Alleviation and Social Safety (MPASS) in 2019 to address the currently fragmented social protection initiatives. Around nine social protection schemes including BSIP would work under this ministry by developing a social-window operation for social protection programmes.

As illustrated in Figure 9.3, the four pillars of food security stand alone with most of the powers, with provinces and lacking a formal coordination mechanism between the Federal and Provincial Governments.

MNFSR has taken a number of policy level initiatives in collaboration with its national and international partners for the betterment of the food security situation in Pakistan. A major milestone that was recently achieved by MNFSR is drafting a

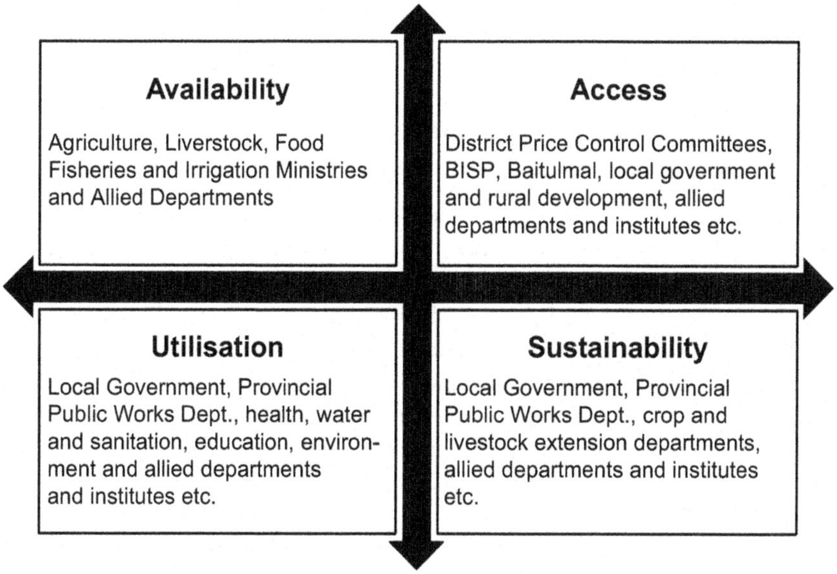

Availability	Access
Agriculture, Liverstock, Food Fisheries and Irrigation Ministries and Allied Departments	District Price Control Committees, BISP, Baitulmal, local government and rural development, allied departments and institutes etc.
Utilisation	Sustainability
Local Government, Provincial Public Works Dept., health, water and sanitation, education, environment and allied departments and institutes etc.	Local Government, Provincial Public Works Dept., crop and livestock extension departments, allied departments and institutes etc.

FIGURE 9.3   Provincial institutional framework of food security in Pakistan

Source: Authors' compilation

National Food Security Policy, which aims at achieving SDG 1 and SDG 2. Similarly, several initiatives under the umbrella of Food Secure Pakistan were initiated by MNFSR, which mainly were the National Zero Hunger Program; the National Agriculture, Food Security Action Plan; various livestock related interventions; Seed Certification and Registration systems; and strengthening and up-gradation of agriculture research in Pakistan.

National Food Security Policy

Achieving food and nutritional security for its population has remained one of the core underlying objectives of all the policies, programmes and strategies of Pakistan since its independence. Over the past several years, federal and provincial governments also have put forward a number of policies related to food security and nutrition, with particular acceleration after 2011. Furthermore, a draft National Agriculture and Food Security Policy has been prepared by the MNFSR to improve agriculture production and food availability in Pakistan. The policy is yet to be approved by the Government. The policy is aimed to ensure modern and efficient food production and a distribution system that can best contribute towards food security and nutrition, in terms of availability, access, utilisation and stability. The policy leads to a number of important initiatives, which include concept development of the National Zero Hunger Programme, food security assessment survey, the recent commitment of the Government for Sustainable Development Goals, particularly to the SDG-1 and 2 about poverty and Zero Hunger Challenges.

National Zero Hunger Programme

Soon after its establishment in 2011, MNFSR organized a National Food Security Conference in March 2012. Acknowledging that food insecurity is a serious issue in Pakistan requiring immediate and coordinated action, a National Zero Hunger Programme was announced at the conclusion of the conference. Following the announcement, in-depth consultations were carried out with national and international experts, civil society organisations and provincial representatives. The recommendations of these consultations were compiled in a list of 15 suggested interventions aimed at enhancing access to food and improving nutrition. The programme was later renamed as National Zero Hunger and Family Farming Programme and a zero hunger cell was established at the MNFSR with support from World Food Programme (WFP).

The important components of the zero hunger programme were: (a) home grown school feeding; (b) family farmers support programme; (c) income generation support programme; and (d) nutrition support programme. Despite its promising announcement and establishment of the zero hunger cell, the programme never took off due to funding allocations.

Scaling-Up Nutrition (SUN)

In efforts to improve the nutrition situation of Pakistan's population, the government has taken initiatives to reduce different forms of undernourishment with especial focus on the most vulnerable groups: pregnant and lactating women and children under five prioritising the first 1,000 days – from conception to two years of age. The Scaling-Up Nutrition (SUN) Movement is a renewed global effort to eliminate all forms of malnutrition based on the principle that everyone has a right to food and good nutrition. Pakistan became part of the SUN movement in December 2013, to join hands with partner countries and relevant stakeholders for improving nutritional status and thus alleviating malnutrition globally. The Government of Pakistan has been working in partnership with WFP, UNICEF, FAO, WHO, GAIN and other nutrition development partners including donors to facilitate mainstreaming of this initiative through the provision of technical support and assistance to national authorities at federal and provincial levels.

In 2016–17, provincial steering committees and SUN Focal Points were nominated. A high-level task force on early childhood development was also established at the National Planning Commission. National and Provincial Fortification Alliances have been established, which makes another multi-sectoral platform (MSP) for nutrition.[22] The World Bank created a Multi Donor Trust Fund (MTDF) for Sindh and Punjab provinces with the aim to reduce stunting.

In 2016–17, the SUN Civil Society Alliance (CSA) membership was expanded to include 129 civil society organisations. More than 45 universities have joined the SUN Academia and Research Network. In 2016, the province of Khyber Pakhtunkhwa established rules on the protection of breastfeeding and child nutrition, while pieces of legislation are currently under development in other provinces. Resolutions on universal salt iodization have also been approved by the provincial assemblies of Khyber Pakhtunkhwa, Balochistan and Punjab. United Nations agencies are supporting the revision of the food fortification standards. Pakistan's Multi-Sectoral Nutrition Strategy for 2018–2025 is being finalised. A health and nutrition dashboard has been created by the Ministry of Health Services, Regulation and Coordination; integrating programme data from the provinces. Provincial multi-sectoral plans have been costed. A thematic working group was established to initiate the implementation of the Pakistan Business Engagement Strategy.

Regional cooperation in ensuring food security for Pakistan: possibilities and constraints

According to The World Bank Annual Report (2017), South Asia remains the fastest-growing region, with economic growth projected to rise from 6.7% in 2016 to 6.8% in 2017 and 7.1% in 2018. Inflation in the region decelerated, mainly because of lower food and commodity prices. Strong growth has translated into declining poverty and impressive improvements in human development. Yet the proportion of people living on less than $1.90 a day was estimated at 10.7% of the total population as of 2017. Hundreds of millions more live slightly above the poverty line, more than 200 million live in slums and about 500 million go without electricity. Many countries in the region suffer from extreme forms of social exclusion and significant infrastructure gaps, and the larger countries are experiencing increases in inequality.[23]

It was expected that SAARC would spur the cooperation among the nations and will boost the regional economic growth. Notwithstanding the huge growth in the areas of cooperation, it can be clearly seen that even after approximately 33 years of its inception, SAARC has been unable to build a strong regional cooperation. Nor it has been able to deliver social and economic benefits to the people of region. The geo-politics is a major setback which never let the SAARC build regional cooperation. But there lies a hope that, SAARC might come up with a regional solution towards the betterment in regional food security. There are several regional initiatives by SAARC related to agriculture and food security. Some of those are described here within the context of Pakistan.

Given the political realities in the South Asian region it may be important to distinguish between what may be desirable and what may be feasible for ensuring food security through regional collaboration both bilaterally and under SAARC and similar mechanisms.

Climate change and agricultural resilience

By 2050, South and South East Asia will be among areas where millions of people are likely to face food insecurity as a result of changing climate.[24] In the light of analytical evidences and predicted impacts, climate change will affect food security through its four dimensions. In the future, south Asian region will be the worst effected not only because of climate change but also overwhelming vulnerable populations depending on the agriculture. The region heavily relies on rain-fed agriculture and, with erratic rainfall patterns, agriculture has been severely affected in recent years. Financial and material resources available to these countries are primarily allocated to priority sectors such as education, poverty alleviation and public health. Progress in research and development (R&D) of technologies and implementation of measures to minimise the impact of climate change on the economy falls short of actual requirement. Agriculture was among the five key areas of cooperation identified by the South Asian nations under SAARC. Sharing of technologies, plant and seed varieties and collaborative research with scientists from across the borders have been carried out in the past.

The path to future food security in the region would require higher productivity in crops and livestock sub-sectors as well as conservation of water and land resources. With their limited resources all the countries of the region can address the new challenges through cooperation in agricultural research efforts, sharing research-based technologies and exchanging the experiences related to agricultural support services. The promising areas of cooperation include sharing of genetic materials and experiences in biotechnology, tissue culture, plant genetics and hybrid seed technology. Every country has some specialisation in relevant climate smart strategies, and all countries of the region can benefit through exchange of information and collaboration on climate change and its impact on food security of the region.

Price and market integration in food and agriculture

Price and market integration in food is very important for enhancing the food security in region as well as Pakistan. A prerequisite for this is to have integrated markets across the region as well as within the countries. In theory, spatial price determination models suggest that, if two markets are linked by trade in a free market regime, excess demand or supply shocks in one market will have an equal impact on price in both markets. The implementation of import tariffs, in general, will allow international price changes to be fully transmitted to domestic markets in relative terms. A study by ADB concluded that commodity markets within each country in South Asia are not adequately integrated and in particular, the integration of domestic wheat and rice markets is of concern.[25] South Asian markets are integrated in the long run but only partially integrated in the short run with each other.

Interventions of the respective governments in the food markets of South Asia appear to be one of the causes of low degrees of integration in the short run of wheat and rice markets of South Asia with each other and with their respective international prices. Although these policies are implemented with intentions to stabilise prices and ensure food security, by protecting their producers through support price policy and consumers through subsidising wheat flour. But actually, these policies are impediments to the efficient market functioning.

To enhance and ensure food security in longer run, the interventions of the Pakistan government should be reduced, the private sector should be encouraged to actively participate in the efficient functioning of markets. Pakistan's Government should encourage and facilitate trade within South Asia. This will not only reduce the fiscal burden of Pakistan's economy and trade with neighbouring countries at lower cost rather than with more distant countries at higher costs. Integration and right interventions by Pakistan will not only stabilise the prices in the country but will also be helpful in ensuring food security in the South Asian Region.

Sharing food production technology

Wide yield gaps in the case of wheat, rice and pulses exist from the top yields realised elsewhere in the world as well as within the South Asian countries. The presence of such yield gaps are indicative of existence of unrealized potential through improving yields of foodgrains by sharing production technologies. This also implies that merely entering into technology sharing network for these crops can bring a considerable boost in production of these valuable foodgrains for attaining and sustaining broader food security in the region.

Paradigm shift

At present all South Asian countries are following the policy of self-sufficiency with little consideration to self-reliance. The key feature of self-sufficiency policy is that food consumed is produced within the borders of a country. It considers the diets that are simple and natural should be produced domestically. While under the self-reliance policy, food is bought wherever it is cheapest from the international market to supplement domestic food supplies. In other words, there is a need to promote regional trade in food commodities. The advocates of self-reliance argue that trade could contribute to the promotion of food in a number of ways like augmenting domestic supplies to meet consumption needs, reduce supply variability, lowering price instability and fostering economic growth using global resources more efficiently by allowing production in the areas having due comparative production advantages. In summary, an agreement among South Asian countries may be signed for exporting surpluses of foodgrains (wheat, rice, pulses) out of the region only after ensuing that no member country is interested in buying it. Food insecurity at the individual level can threaten regional, global and national securities. It is about time that all the SAARC countries start working together to enhance collective political will directed towards improving regional food security. The multiple dimensions of regional food and nutrition security are influenced by and equally impact national food security, hence it's the issue of food security that must be taken as a regional threat.

Liberalisation of regional trade

The intraregional trade among South Asian countries is comparatively very low and South Asia is the often characterised as the least integrated region in the world. Several studies point out that cross-country conflicts are the most important reason for very low levels of integration in the subregion.[26] There are however sharp differences in the patterns of intraregional trade among South Asian countries. Unfortunately, South Asian Free Trade Area (SAFTA) has not been able to boost intraregional trade, including of food products, due to several reasons. For example, a large number of items having prospects of trade within the region are placed in the sensitive lists of member countries, which are excluded from tariff reduction commitments. There are also a host of non-tariff barriers, mainly related to sanitary and phytosanitary measures, affecting intraregional trade of agriculture and food products. Moreover, during times of crises countries have resorted to banning exports of some products, thereby making food items unavailable in importing member countries. Therefore a substantial development of agricultural trade in the region cannot be envisaged without any change in the sensitive or negative lists of the member countries.

While if we have a look on trade and specifically agricultural trade, despite conflicts between Pakistan and India, it can be seen that the overall agricultural trade has increased compared to the 1990s. In 1998–99, the total agricultural trade between Pakistan and India was US$ 163.1 million while it escalated to US$ 1005.4 million in year 2012–13.[27] Trade flows also depict that India's export to Pakistan remained far above Pakistan's export to India. Although agricultural trade between the two countries is somehow satisfying, the share of bilateral trade in the total trade with the world remained quite low for both the countries.

Increased regional agricultural trade in food for Pakistan can have a direct impact on food security by augmenting domestic food supplies and thereby increasing the availability of food. This will push food prices down and reduce food supply variability. In order to balance the deficits in one country with surpluses in another country, free movement of food items across countries is necessary. Enhanced intraregional trade of agriculture and food products is essential to ensure overall food security in all countries of South Asia and for Pakistan as well.

Revisiting the SAARC Food and Seed Banking mechanism

Operationalisation of the SAARC Food and Seed Banks has been riddled with a number of problems. Member countries have frequently failed to meet their commitments for foodgrain reserves, and the vague definition of 'emergency' has made it near impossible for members to access food from the bank. There seem to be several issues and concerns related to operationalisation of the seed and food banks of SAARC. In order to qualify for drawing food from the bank, the necessary condition is that the member country shall face a shortfall in the production by 8%, lower than the average of last three years. However, it is not clear how the storage shortfall shall be measured. The SAARC Food Bank Board has to make a final decision about releasing food from the bank. Second, there is no clearly specified provision for a food transport mechanism, border formalities and institutional mechanisms for swift delivery of the food. The mechanism of price determination of this food is also lengthy, as it involved negotiating prices, terms and conditions of payments for each request, despite that a broad guideline is present that the charged price must be lower for the member countries than the international/market prices.

The member countries need to increase the transfer and share of technology to promote economic growth as well as regional cooperation in terms of food security. The countries must work together, realising SAARC initiatives to better serve the affected member countries in times of food crisis. The governments of SAARC must work towards liberalising the agricultural trade. This will enable the region to increase resilience and improve the regional food security.

Notes

1 The GHI score is based on four indicators: prevalence of undernourishment, wasting and stunting among children under 5 and under 5 mortality rates. See IFPRI (2015).
2 Government of Pakistan (2019).
3 Government of Pakistan (2016).
4 Pakistan Space and Upper Atmosphere Research Commission (SUPARCO) Crop Monitoring Cell.
5 Government of Pakistan (2017), as stated by Economic Wing of Ministry of National Food Security & Research, June 2017.
6 Government of Pakistan (2019).
7 United States Department of Agriculture world rice export estimates for 2016.
8 Capore et al. (2014).
9 Multidimensional Poverty in Pakistan. Islamabad: Ministry of Planning, Development and Reforms.
10 Government of Pakistan and WFP (2016).
11 IFPRI and Aga Khan University (2017).
12 See Government of Pakistan (2016).
13 WFP (2018).
14 Government of Pakistan (2016).
15 Daud et al. (2017).
16 Government of Pakistan (2016).
17 WHO and UNICEF (2015).
18 Government of Pakistan (2015).
19 Alif Ailaan (2016).
20 See Long-Term Climate Risk Index by GermanWatch Available at: https://germanwatch.org/en/cri.
21 Government of Pakistan (2016).
22 SUN, Pakistan. http://scalingupnutrition.org/sun-countries/pakistan/.
23 World Bank (2017).
24 FAO (2017).
25 UNCTAD and ADB (2015).
26 Ghani and Ahmed (2009).
27 Chand and Saxena (2017).

References

Alif Ailaan (2016), 'Pakistan District Education Rankings 2016', Alif Ailaan, Islamabad.

Capone, R., H. El Bilali, P. Debs, G. Cardone and N. Driouech (2014), 'Food Economic Accessibility and Affordability in the Mediterranean Region: An Exploratory Assessment at Micro and Macro Levels', *Journal of Food Security*, Vol. 2(1), pp. 1–12.

Chand, R. and R. Saxena (2017), 'Agricultural Trade Between India and Pakistan: Status and Potential', in *India-Pakistan Trade Normalisation: The Unfinished Economic Agenda*, N. Taneja and I. Dayal (Eds.), pp. 15–59, Springer, Singapore.

Daud, M. K., M. Nafees, S. Ali, M. Rizwan, R. A. Bajwa, M. B. Shakoor, M. U. Arshad, S. A. Chatha, F. Deeba, W. Murad and I. Malook (2017), 'Drinking Water Quality Status and Contamination in Pakistan', *BioMed Research International*, Vol. 2017.

FAO (2017), 'The State of Food Security and Nutrition in the World: Building Resilience for Peace and Food Security', Food and Agriculture Organization, Rome.

FATA Secretariat and FAO (2015), 'Agriculture Based Livelihoods Assessment of Returnee Households in Bara Tehsil Khyber Agency', Rehabilitation and Reconstruction Unit of the FATA Secretariat and the Food and Agriculture Organization.

Ghani, E. and S. Ahmed (Eds.) (2009), *Accelerating Growth and Job Creation in South Asia*, Oxford University Press, Oxford.

GoP and UNICEF (2019), 'National Nutrition Survey 2018', Ministry of National Health Services, Regulations and Coordination, Government of Pakistan, Islamabad.

Government of Pakistan (2015), 'Pakistan Social and Living Standards Measurement Survey (PSLM) 2014–15', Pakistan Bureau of Statistics, Islamabad.

Government of Pakistan (2016), 'Food Security Assessment Survey (FSA 2016)', Ministry of National Food Security and Research, Islamabad.

Government of Pakistan (2017), 'National Food Security Policy', Ministry of National Food Security and Research, Islamabad.

Government of Pakistan (2019), 'Pakistan Economic Survey 2018–19', Ministry of Finance, Islamabad.

Government of Pakistan and WFP (2016), 'Minimum Cost of the Diet: Pakistan', Ministry of Planning, Development and Reforms (GoP) and World Food Programme.

IFPRI (2015), 'Global Hunger Index: Armed Conflict and the Challenge of Hunger', International Food Policy Research Institute, Washington, DC, and Concern Worldwide.

IFPRI and Aga Khan University (2017), 'A Strategic Review of Food Security and Nutrition in Pakistan', International Food Policy Research Institute.

Kreft, S., D. Eckstein and I. Melchior (2016), 'Global Climate Risk Index 2017: Who Suffers Most From Extreme Weather Events?', Briefing Paper – November 2016, Germanwatch, Bonn.

SDPI and WFP (2004), 'Food Insecurity in Rural Pakistan 2003', Sustainable Development Policy Institute and World Food Programme.

SDPI, WFP and SDC (2010), 'Food Insecurity in Pakistan Report', Sustainable Development Policy Institute, World Food Programme, and Swiss Development Cooperation.

UNCTAD and ADB (2015), 'Food Security in South Asia: Developing Regional Supply Chains for the Food Processing Industry', United Nations Conference on Trade and Development and Asian Development Bank.

WFP (2018), 'Pakistan Market Price Bulletin', January 2018 Issue, World Food Programme.

WHO and UNICEF (2015), '25 Years of Progress on Sanitation and Drinking Water – 2015 Update and MDG Assessment', Joint Monitoring Program for Water Supply and Sanitation, World Health Organization and United Nations Children's Fund.

World Bank (2017), 'Annual Report 2017', The World Bank, Washington, DC.

10

FOOD SECURITY POLICY FRAMEWORK IN SRI LANKA

Market reforms, diversification and safety nets

Saman Kelegama and Dilani Hirimuthugodage

Food security scenario in Sri Lanka

Food security indicators for Sri Lanka shows a comparatively better position among South Asian countries. Sri Lanka was ranked the highest in South Asia in the Global Food Security Index 2018.[1] Among various sub-indices, better than average global scores for agricultural infrastructure, farmers' access to credit and containment of food loss were found as Sri Lanka's core strengths, besides achievements in terms of poverty reduction and enhanced access to food. However, food security remains an unfinished policy agenda, as incidence of hunger continues to be unacceptably high in the country. Incidence of undernourishment is currently found to be about 10.9% of the population.[2] High levels of malnutrition and micronutrient deficiencies prevalent among the lowest income strata has been a persistent policy challenge in Sri Lanka.

Though child and maternal nutrition has improved over time due to better availability, access and utilisation of food, along with improvements in health services, availability of clean water and Sanitation, regional disparities in nutritional intake is evident. High levels of acute malnutrition were found in several districts by the national nutrition and micronutrient survey conducted in 2012 by the Medical Research Institute (MRI).[3] The survey results showed an increase in acute malnutrition from 11.7% in 2009 to 19.6% in 2012, indicating that nutritional deficiency is widespread and poses much more policy challenges than abject food deprivation in Sri Lanka.[4] Further indication of chronic undernourishment in the country is the high prevalence of wasting. At 21.4% in 2015, Sri Lanka had the third highest prevalence of wasting in a global ranking of 130 countries.[5]

Despite significant achievements made in terms of the overall food security scenario, persistent issues of malnutrition point towards gaps in the national food security policy framework. Efforts in the past have not effectively addressed dietary diversity and targeting of lower income strata. Requirement of a multi-sectoral and integrated approach to tackle issues of the agrarian sectors, including stagnation in productivity and investment deficits in infrastructure and agricultural R&D as well as cross cutting issues of inequality, insufficiency in health and sanitation services, climate change etc., is highly relevant in the case of Sri Lanka. This chapter examines the features of national policy frameworks in Sri Lanka with respect to development of the agriculture sector and food market reforms to identify challenges and remedies for achieving food and nutrition security.

Agricultural reforms: self-sufficiency and the challenges of diversification

Agriculture is the main source of livelihood for Sri Lanka's rural population. Despite a gradual transformation from a predominantly agricultural economy to a service-based economy, agriculture still employs nearly a third of the population, and a vast majority are indirectly dependent on agriculture. Growth of the agricultural economy has had a significant bearing on improvements in access to food markers and thus constitute an important aspect of food security. At the same time, transformations in the agriculture sector, particularly the relative balance in growth of production of food crops and cash crops and the impact of domestic production by way of changing dynamics of trade in food products, have had their role in dictating overall food availability and stability of food markets. Historical changes in the agricultural systems have therefore had substantial influence on food security through their influence on both demand and supply sides.

The traditional farming system of Sri Lanka may be described as a subsistent and self-sufficient system based on wetland paddy farming, rain-fed highland chena and home gardens.[6] The advent of the colonial era in the early 16th century brought significant structural changes to the composition of domestic agriculture, driven by the trade competition for commodities such as spice crops, tea, rubber and coconut. This led to the development of export-oriented agriculture based on large-scale estate plantations, which gradually became the backbone of the national economy as the cost of food crops, especially paddy farming, created severe deficits in supply of food.[7]

Adverse impacts of the aggressive pursuit of plantation systems by way of waning subsistence farming of food crops and unsustainable growth of import dependency for essential food commodities were felt during the colonial era. To overcome the rising expenditure on the import of food items, food scarcities experienced during war periods and growing problem of landless peasantry, the government embarked on an ambitious programme of land settlement and irrigation rehabilitation aiming at self-sufficiency in major food products such as paddy.[8] Irrigated resettlements for food crops subsequently became the mainstem focus of national agricultural policy, also reflected in the Accelerated Mahaweli Development Programme of 1980s.[9] The introduction of green revolution technologies also assisted this reformation in a major way.

Sri Lanka's agriculture sector today is broadly composed of the plantation and non-plantation sectors. About 750,000 hectares of lands in wet and intermediate zones are under plantation crops such as tea, rubber and coconut, which predominantly contributes to export earnings. Close to one million hectares, roughly one-sixth of land cover, mainly falling in the dry zone plains of the country, belongs to the non-plantation sectors, which together provides supply of food items. About 70% of the dry zone comes under irrigated settlements and predominantly produces rice besides other food crops such as chilli, onion, vegetables, pulses, tuber crops, maize and other cereals cultivated in smaller extents of up to about 15% of aggregate non-plantation farm lands.

Refocus on the food sector and facilitative policies have helped to achieve self-sufficiency in rice, the primary staple in the national diet, substantially reducing dependency on rice imports and thereby saving a significant share of foreign exchange earnings that were spent on rice imports. However, the excessive attention given to paddy came at the cost of secondary food crops grown locally as supplements. The import dependency on food items except rice continues to be significant, as food commodities such as wheat, milk products, sugar, lentils and oil and fats together constitute a major share of imports of consumer goods.[10] The skewed domestic food production patterns have had adverse nutritional impacts due to lack of sufficient dietary diversity. As a result, though the overall food security situation has improved over time, food security at the household level remains a concern. Widespread undernourishment in the country is indicative of the poor status of food utilisation and nutrition, which appears to be low even by the South Asian standards. Roughly one in five remain undernourished and 26.3% of children below age five do not have the recommended weight for age.[11]

Though the urgent need for diversification of food crops has been well recognised in Sri Lanka, efforts in this regard have met with several challenges. Diversification requires significant areas of land to provide the critical volume to ensure continuous supply. A major factor working against diversification strategies has been the built-in bias in favour of paddy cultivation in the agricultural incentive regime. Land utilisation policies over the years have been evolved for consolidation and promotion of rice production. For instance, under the Agricultural Development Authority Act of 2000, approval was made mandatory for converting paddy land for cultivation of any other crop. The inability of paddy farmers operating on low profit margins to bear the risks of changing cropping patterns is cited as another major reason. Some of the other major factors which hindered diversification are:[12]

- The seed policies pursued by successive governments have not taken into account the requirements of diversification of crops, to the extent that even certain seed and planting materials are banned from import to the detriment of new crops. This is a major problem because as permit requirement to import agricultural raw material is a time-consuming exercise. Restrictive quarantine regulations have indirectly imposed constrains by way of inability of farmers to access improved varieties of seeds.[13]

- Limitations with respect to R&D in agriculture for higher-value-added crops and lack of adequate marketing support have been constraining factors. Attempts have not been made to setup a national private company with private traders and farmers' organisations as stakeholders to undertake the purchasing and marketing of agricultural items.
- Post-harvest losses of certain non-rice food items have been noted to be very high, especially of fruits and vegetables, due to improper packing. handling and transfer. Besides such inefficiencies, high duties imposed on agricultural raw material increase the costs of Sri Lanka's agro-industrial goods and render many of these products uncompetitive in the domestic markets, limiting the scope of new crops.

These constraints have significantly affected the supply potential of the agricultural sector and, consequently, diversification of the nonplantation sector away from the focus on rice to other foods has not been accelerated. A plethora of domestic impediments, including lack of facilitative farm support programmes, are responsible for this state of affairs. Further reforms in the domestic agricultural sector, on which the Sri Lankan government has embarked, are required to ensure that domestic production, along with trade liberalisation interventions, caters to the needs of food availability.

Trade and market reforms

Besides domestic production and conditions in the domestic agricultural sector, policies related to agricultural trade has had a decisive impact on the food security situation in Sri Lanka. As mentioned in the previous section, though the import dependency on rice has come down, Sri Lanka relies on imports for many of the other major food items. The country has relied heavily on the export earnings from the plantation sector for footing its import bills. Stagnation in the plantation sector had a significant influence on the way food trade and allied market reforms have shaped up in Sri Lanka.

The Sri Lankan plantation sector exports are highly dependent on world market conditions. For instance, several external factors such as the sharp drop in oil prices and drop in demand in key export markets have contributed to a fall in exports of commodities such as tea and rubber. While these external shocks causes short- to medium-term losses in the plantation export sector, there are more long-standing structural issues that retard the growth potential of the plantation sector, particularly with regard to high cost of production, low productivity and low profitability in comparison with other producing countries. For instance, international comparison indicates that the cost of production (COP) of tea is the highest in Sri Lanka relative to the other competing tea producers such as India, Kenya, Bangladesh and Vietnam.[14]

Inadequate replanting, price fluctuation, labour shortage and high wages, land degradation and low living/working conditions of the labour force are often highlighted as the reasons for stagnation in the plantation sector. The declining soil fertility due to the continuous practice of mono cropping for a long period of time is another factor that contributes to the downfall of plantation crops, making crop production less profitable. While these factors have affected the access to food of the workforce dependent on the plantation sectors,[15] because of the close interaction of markets for plantation and non-plantation (food) products access to food has also been impacted due to relative price changes and the way trade policies were used to tackle food prices.

Sri Lanka pursued a relatively more liberal trade regime in agriculture compared to other South Asian countries, albeit with certain exceptions. Although general tariffs were lowered from the late 1970s onwards, and those for certain agricultural commodities were high. Quantitative restrictions (QRs) were applied for some domestic food crops, such as potatoes, chilis, onions, wheat flour and rice, in order to promote domestic production with less competition. A number of state-owned enterprises involved in purchasing and distribution of agricultural products operated actively until about the mid-1990s. However, Sri Lanka's policies adhered to the WTO commitments from very early on, as all agricultural export taxes were abolished and domestic production subsidies were brought under AoA limits.

Though QRs were retained on selected agricultural products after the AoA came into operation with a justification on balance of payment grounds,[16] they were mostly removed by July 1996, causing losses to the producers of potatoes, onions and chilis, as the price advantage enjoyed by local farmers in the protected market eroded. The situation compelled the policy makers to implement a seasonal tariff policy for the affected sectors, in which imports were liberalised when there was a shortage of domestic production and normal agricultural tariffs were imposed when there was a glut in domestic production. The seasonal tariffs had a number of problems associated with them: timing, hoarding and unscrupulous traders making maximum use of the loopholes to gain profits. Various lobbies also influenced the seasonal tariffs, and thus ad hoc manipulations resulted.

Against the slow response of the domestic agricultural sector to tariff protection afforded for production and self-sustenance, the government was forced to roll-back certain tariffs to maintain short-term price stability for food items of critical importance. Accordingly, agricultural import duties were periodically waived for essential food items. The periodic application and revocation of import duties gave confusing signals to producers and it added to the uncertainties faced by the farmers.[17] Roughly between the mid-1990s to early 2000s the government resorted to an ad hoc tariff policy regime, trying to balance conflicting interests of producers' lobbying for tariff protection and consumer interest groups for price reduction and stability.

One of the policy oversights was lack of productivity enhancing policies to complement trade reforms. It has been pointed out that trade interventions for tariff protection to rice producers has been initially at the cost of the consumers. Though this strategy gave the expected boost to rice farming, it was not followed-up with preparatory measures for the eventual withdrawal of protection for making the rice sector internationally price competitive to the benefit of the consumers. As adequate attention was not given in the meanwhile to productivity growth and gaining cost competitiveness, reversal of tariff protection was observed to have resulted in producer welfare losses in the rice sector.[18]

Using trade policy to drive agricultural development and domestic market stability has not been by and large successful in Sri Lanka because of the frequent changes in policy stance. Starting in the mid-2000s, the administration partially withdrew from aggressive agricultural trade reforms, allowing the agricultural sector to develop according to its comparative advantage. One of the main concerns for Sri Lanka's agrarian reforms is to bring in the right mix of market stability strategy that balances trade concerns and the aspirations of achieving agriculture stability.

Another critical area of improvement is the role of state-owned enterprises such as the Cooperative Wholesale Establishment (CWE) and the State Trading Corporation (STC) etc., the institutional weaknesses of which were brought to the fore by market uncertainties arising out of inconsistent tariff policies. For instance, the market intervention role for public procurement of rice entrusted with the erstwhile Paddy Marketing Board (PMB) could not be carried out effectively, leading to the closure of the Board in 1997. In addition to strengthening the state-owned enterprises, the government also has the responsibility of implementing effective market instruments aimed at stability and predictability such as the forward sales contract mechanism, which may redefine the role of state-owned enterprises as effective forward contracts could replace the public procurement system. Some studies have shown the effectiveness of forward contracts in certain respects in the context of sectors such as maize farming in Sri Lanka and has recommended pursuit of a well-regulated and structured approach to forward contracts for correcting food market distortions.[19]

National food security policies and strategies

Sri Lanka has a long history of social protection policies, including welfare programmes and food subsidy programmes. The Sri Lankan government's food and nutrition policies generally reflect a high degree of concern for poor and vulnerable households. The food subsidy has been one of the major elements of the welfare-oriented strategies in Sri Lanka. Food security, in the immediate post-political independence period was considered a macro-level concern regarding targets for availability of food to ensure sufficient food for the entire population.[20] Food accessibility, considered a more micro aspect, was driven by a key policy of universal ration scheme for rice which was introduced in 1942 with the intention of assisting the difficulties in consuming basis food items during the Second World War.[21] The food ration system was continued until 1979 with some changes to the initial programme. The food ration system was mainly conducted via a cross subsidisation of selected food items, i.e., some food items were given at a lower rate of their market price and some were at a higher price. By the year 1952, the total cost of food subsidy was increased up to one-third of total government expenditure. After 1973 selection criteria was introduced to food ration scheme where taxpayers were excluded from the subsidy system. Later in 1979 the food ration scheme was banned by the then appointed government, who introduced a food stamp scheme.

The food stamp programme was initiated by the government in 1979 to protect the nutritionally vulnerable, the segment of the population. It provided a fixed amount to the families with an annual income less than Rs. 3,600.00 in January 1978. The programme is essentially an income transfer scheme enabling those eligible (annual income less than Rs. 3,600.00) to receive free stamps cashable against a basket of food.[22] Recipients were able to redeem these food stamps from government owned cooperative shops.

The Janasaviya Programme was introduced in 1989 after abolishing the food stamp scheme. Janasaviya was the reappointed new government's primary poverty reduction programme. The original purpose of this programme was to provide income transfers to about half the population until 1991. However, due to high cost it was trimmed and phased over fewer rounds and areas. Monthly cash grants of Rs. 2,500.00 were given to households who earned less than Rs. 700.00 per month. There was a mandatory savings of Rs. 1,042.00 per month and the amount was transferred to each families account at the National Savings Bank of Sri Lanka. In total nearly 2.3 million people received this during the programme period. Further, it was compulsory for Janasaviya recipients to provide 24 days per month of labour for social activity or it was a must for them to engage in some productive activity chosen and approved by the Assistant Government Agent of the area. The Janasaviya was discontinued in 1995 after only five rounds. It was replaced by the Samurdhi Programme, which then became the government's main vehicle for poverty reduction.

Samurdhi combined the functions of the Janasaviya Programme and the Trust Fund, which were disbanded in 1998. It was established to alleviate poverty and create opportunities for youth and the disadvantaged groups. The programme has three components. The first provided direct income support in the form of food coupons, and the second was aimed at promoting savings and credit programmes carried out via Samurdhi Banks for poor. And the third component is to provide labour for area development programmes. For an example; a household receiving Rs. 500 is expected to contribute four to five man-days for community development projects.

Successive governments have diversified the portfolio of food security programmes and projects, catering to the specific requirements of various sections of the population. Annex I provides an overview of some of the main public policy interventions addressing food security issues in various forms. Sri Lanka's food security-related policies focus heavily on promoting subsistence farming and aim to increase locally produced grains, cereals and fresh milk, promote new technology for livestock products, introduce new technology and innovations into agriculture and promote research and development in the sector. The National Nutrition Council (NNC) anchors the implementation of various food security projects and programmes in Sri Lanka (Box 10.1).

The Janasaviya poverty alleviation programme was renamed as National Development Trust Fund (NDTF) in 1995. The beneficiaries of the programme were identified from the households originally entitled to receive food stamps. Four key programs were implemented under NDTF; the Human Resources and Institution Development (HRID) programme, the Credit programme, the Community Projects programme, and the Nutrition programme. The HRID programme develops human resources of the poor by increasing awareness within poor households, promoting group action and facilitating self reliance through the provision of technical and financial assistance to partner organisations. The partner organisations in turn train the beneficiaries in income-generating skills. The Community Projects programme addresses the 'poverty pockets' by creating wage employment through short-term labour-intensive rural works. The Credit programme supplies credit at the market rate to socially mobilised poor groups through partner organisations such as local financial institutions and NGOs. The poor are given credit to initiate self-employment activities and microenterprises. The nutrition programme includes a set of activities with specific nutritional goals.

In spite of a lack of rigorous evaluation on the impact of the NDTF programme, there is a consensus that the programme has not been effective in reducing poverty among the participating households.[23] Several reasons are attributed to this poor performance. First, the poverty alleviation objective of the programme has been sidelined by the emphasis given to transferring resources to the participating households. Second, the targeting mechanism has not been effective in keeping the nonpoor out and ensuring the inclusion of the ultra poor. Third, the poor choice of partner organisations, mostly NGOs, and their strained relationships with government officials have reduced the cooperation of these organisations in implementing the programs. Fourth, the lack of interdivisional collaboration and coordination among the four programs has resulted in poor follow-up. Finally, the lack of a rigorous monitoring and evaluation system has resulted in poor feedback on the impact of the programme on the beneficiaries and has reduced the opportunity to improve the programme design and implementation.

Successive programmes such as the Samurdhi have also suffered from design and implementation weaknesses that have reduced their effectiveness in terms of allocative efficiency.[24] From the perspective of agricultural development of poverty alleviation and food security, commentators and evaluators have argued that the effectiveness of safety nets must be enhanced through better targeting and increasing the volume of support to the needy.[25]

BOX 10.1 MAIN ACTORS IN THE FOOD SECURITY POLICY FRAMEWORK IN SRI LANKA

The National Nutrition Council (NNC) is the main body responsible for food security in the country and its functions come under the direct purview of the President of Sri Lanka, which facilitates for better coordination of nutrition related activities of all relevant ministries. The NNC is chaired by the President of Sri Lanka and consists of relevant Ministers, Chief Ministers of the nine provinces and selected Members of Parliament (See Figure 10.1). NNC has prepared the Multi Sector Action Plan for Nutrition (MsAPN) for 2013–16, which has covered most of the criteria identified in the Zero Hunger Challenge.

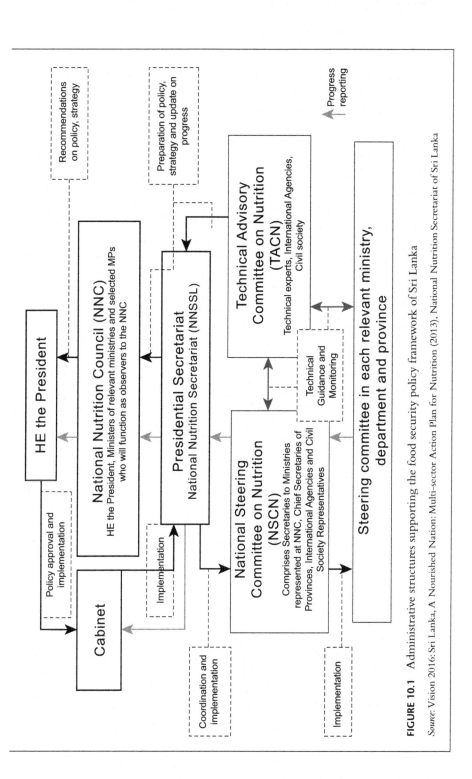

FIGURE 10.1 Administrative structures supporting the food security policy framework of Sri Lanka

Source: Vision 2016: Sri Lanka, A Nourished Nation: Multi-sector Action Plan for Nutrition (2013), National Nutrition Secretariat of Sri Lanka

Regional dimensions of food security and policy concerns for Sri Lanka

The fight against food insecurity is at a critical juncture today in Sri Lanka. In the past, the country has attempted to achieve food security through policy interventions in the realm of food production, correction of food market distortions and a variety of safety net programmes. As elaborated in the previous sections, each of these three dimensions of interventions has delivered significant results but have left some untended shortcomings of their own. It has been particularly observed in the case of Sri Lanka's attempts to achieve food self-sufficiency that agricultural production and markets interact very closely, and it requires careful planning and implementation to fulfil the diverse interest of producers and consumers. Safety net programmes have often been found to have issues of targeting in the context of Sri Lanka. In addition to improvements required in traditional approaches to food security, Sri Lanka also needs to prepare for facing the new issues that are on the rise. In this regard, the nation may have to broaden its outlook and be willing to cooperate with neighbouring countries to address commonly faced policy questions.

Being a complex system, the agriculture sector currently faces several simultaneous and interlinked challenges that may have short-to long-term repercussions. The problems of the agriculture sector in Sri Lanka are multifaceted and they rest upon many factors such as agricultural technology, trade, food production and distribution, natural resource and environmental problems, food consumption patterns and national planning and government policies. None of these factors are static and hence, any policy or strategy to solve them also must be dynamic in nature. The foremost important set of challenges are associated with the task of meeting the food security needs of the growing population. Measures are required to recover the growth potential of both the food sector and the export agriculture sub-sector. Closely related to the revival of the agriculture sector is the need for renovation and sustained management of the fragile natural resources base, including through greater resilience against the imminent threat of climate change.

It is a matter of great concern that a steady decrease has occurred in the profitability of the basket of domestically produced food staples. These trends have not been compensated by adequate productivity improvements or favourable trends in input prices. When considered together with the level of protection these trends confirm that Sri Lanka is a high-cost producer of rice and of many subsidiary food crops. The degradation of the natural resource base that supports all sub-sectors of agriculture has become a major challenge. Rapid deforestation initiated in wet and intermediate zones by plantation agriculture has spread into the dry zone areas with major colonisation schemes and expansion of chena cultivation with population growth. Despite the positive contribution made by the green revolution to increase agricultural productivity, it is now being identified as a major source of environmental degradation and ecosystems damage. Continuation of and increase in further production, unless brought about by productivity improvements, will be at a very high cost to the economy, undermining the efforts for achieving zero hunger targets.

Agricultural diversification has also been slow to emerge. A number of restrictions in the land market created a bias towards rice production and posed other obstacles to diversification. The environment has not been conducive to commercialised agriculture. Institutional constraints and tariff policy on agricultural inputs also acted as impediments to agricultural diversification. Due to the high cost of production, low productivity and low profitability, agriculture growth rates slowed down in Sri Lanka. While slowdowns in the plantation sector severely affected agricultural income and affordability of masses dependent on the plantation subsector, poor performance of the non-plantation sector led to food imports.

One of the pitfalls of the policy approaches of the past has been that many agricultural policies pursued a piecemeal approach rather than taking the entire value chains into consideration. The agriculture sector is organized as a network of value chains, some having links connected to global and regional markets that extend beyond the boundaries of the country. Very often, the problems in agriculture are interconnected along the value chains, creating impacts across various layers. Sri Lanka will do well by recognising the linkages of its domestic value chains with countries in the immediate neighbourhood. South Asian markets can have significant complementary effects on Sri Lanka's domestic value chains, particularly in terms of sourcing of agricultural inputs including seeds and fertilisers at affordable prices. Market integration is the foremost important aspect of regional cooperation in South Asia that Sri Lanka can benefit from, in terms of the agricultural and food security reforms. As other chapters in this volume have pointed out, there exists significant complementarities in terms of the scope for agricultural trade within South Asia. Regional integration will also help to guard against transmission of volatility in the global markets to domestic food markets.

However, the depth and scope of regional cooperation are beyond market integration. Cooperation in the areas of agricultural research and technology is vital for Sri Lanka. As the country is likely to enter into a phase of heightened structural changes in the agricultural sector and greater market volatility, regional linkages are essential to impart stability. Regional knowledge networks are important for the next phase of reforms expected in Sri Lanka, including efforts to improve the safety net programmes. Perhaps the greatest contribution of regional cooperation would be in terms of developing resilience against threats raised by climate change which are common to all South Asian countries.

The National Adaptation Plan for Climate Change Impacts in Sri Lanka: 2016–2025, developed through an exhaustive expert consultation process that covered several economic sectors, is a good starting point to initiate the climate action plans at the national level. It identified nine areas that need special attention in adaptation against climate change. Out of these nine areas, two (food security and export agriculture) represent core sub-sectors of agriculture and two others (water and biodiversity and ecosystems) are closely related areas. The plan also identified impacts and actions on agro-based industries and biomass energy under the respective areas. In all, it indicates agriculture is the major sector of the national economy which is most vulnerable to the impacts of climate change than industry or services sectors.

Successful implementation of the Plan would also depend on the regional alliances that Sri Lanka is able to form with neighbouring countries, given the transboundary nature of climate change impacts.

The South Asian region thus far has not proactively worked on the farmer's traditional knowledge and seeds which are very important in terms of achieving food security within the region. Furthermore, a proper management of regional 'commons' is also very important. As an example; managing genetic resources, biodiversity, seeds and technology transfers in the region are very essential in terms of achieving food security and facing challenges of climate change. Hence, development of new technology deserves acknowledgement. It is important to see 'what can deliver the best', while ensuring environmental and social sustainability. Agricultural productivity improvements have been closely linked to investments in agricultural research and extension (R&E). Technology and material transfers between South Asian countries will significantly increase the productivity in the sector.

The South Asian region has not been able to pursue their common goals through relevant international channels such as the World Trade Organization (WTO). This is mainly attributable to the fact that South Asian countries have generally acted individually at the world's forums and not collectively. It is important to have a collective vision as a region to achieve common goals. Food insecurity and malnutrition are complex problems that cannot be solved by one sector or stakeholder alone but need to be tackled in a coordinated way, with the necessary political commitment and integrated leadership. Developing a regional platform for collaborative research on food production and adaptive agriculture practices is an immediate step that South Asia needs to foster in order to achieve food security in a socially inclusive manner.

ANNEX

Main Food security policies and programmes of Sri Lanka

Food production national programme (2016–2018): presidential task force on national food production

This was initiated in 2015 by the newly appointed government for a three-year period to achieve self-sufficiency in traditional local foods, ensure availability of high-quality food items, maintain food stocks, implement a crop production programme based on agro-ecological zones, increase productivity of food crops, maintain proper coordination amongst institutions, provide high-quality inputs for food production etc. Several institutions are involved in this programme including Presidential Secretariat, Ministry of National Policy and Economic Affairs, Ministry of Finance, Ministry of Agriculture, Ministry of Fisheries and Aquatic Resources, Ministry of Irrigation, Several Departments, All Provincial Councils etc.

Mahinda Chinthana – vision for the future 2010

'Mahinda Chinthana – 2010' was a statement of the government's vision on food security in 2010. It stated that 'Food security will be achieved through adoption of technically feasible, socially acceptable, economically viable and environmentally sustainable agricultural production technology and marketing'. Most of the policies and programmes adopted by ministries and institutes during that period were compatible with the "Mahinda Chinthana- 2010" statement.

National Agriculture Policy 2007

The National Agriculture Policy has a goal to meet the basic needs of farming communities in terms of food and nutrition security, enhanced employment opportunities and incomes, through the adoption of technically feasible, socially acceptable, economically viable and environmentally friendly agricultural production technologies, marketing and related strategies.

The policy has seven objectives:

1   Increase domestic agricultural production to ensure food and nutrition security of the nation.
2   Enhance agricultural productivity and ensure sustainable growth.
3   Maximise benefits and minimise adverse effects of globalisation on domestic and export agriculture.
4   Adopt a productive farming system and improved agro-technologies with a view to reduce the unit cost of production and increase profits.
5   Adaptation of technologies in farming that are environmentally friendly and harmless to health.
6   Promote agro-based industries and increase employment opportunities.
7   Enhance the income and the living standards of the farming community.

This document presents policy statements for agricultural research, export agriculture, post- harvesting, agriculture marketing[26] etc. Presently the Ministry of Agriculture is in the process of updating the Agriculture Policy for Sri Lanka.

National Livestock Development Policy 2011

The main objective is to achieve self-sufficiency in milk, 40% self-sufficiency in swine products and meet demand and required quality in chicken, mutton and eggs. It also aims enhance local production through value addition, breeding programmes and animal health management.[27] Apart from livestock development policy, the Master Plan (2010–2015) of Livestock Ministry consists of 'Five Year Dairy Sector Development Plan', 'Five Year Poultry Sector Development Plan', 'Five Year Swine Sector Development Plan', 'Five Year Goat Sector Development Plan' and 'Plan for Potential Livestock Animal Species with Future Promising Economic Value'. All food security programmes conducted by the ministry are in line with the Master Plan.

National Nutrition Policy of Sri Lanka 2010

This policy was introduced by the Ministry of Healthcare and Nutrition. It provides a platform for inter-sectoral coordination in order to accelerate efforts to achieve optimum nutrition for every Sri Lankan. The main objectives of this policy are to ensure optimal nutrition throughout the life cycle, enhance capacity to deliver effective and appropriate interventions, to ensure effective management of adequate nutrition to vulnerable population, to ensure food and nutrition security for all citizens, to strengthen advocacy, partnerships and networking and to strengthen research, monitoring and evaluation. The main institutes which are involved in achieving these objectives are the National Nutrition Steering Committee, National Nutrition Coordination Committee, Nutrition Coordinating Committee at Provincial level and Nutrition Coordination Unit.

National Fisheries and Aquatic Resources Development Policy 2007–2016

It envisages policy measures, strategies and activities to accelerate the growth of the fisheries sector with the target of increasing fish production to achieve per capita availability of 22kg of fish and fish products per year. Whereas in 2009 per capita consumption of fish was 20.9kgs.

Multi-sectoral Action Plan for Nutrition (2014–2016)

This was prepared by the National Nutrition Council of Sri Lanka with the consultation of professionals, technical experts, international agencies, ministry officials, non-governmental organisations etc. The objective of this plan is to enhance nutrition through a multi-sectoral approach. The process to develop a multi-sector action plan for nutrition in Sri Lanka involves facilitating consensus on the planning work frame and activities in the next three years to reduce child and maternal nutrition. Presently, there are several ministries (Ministry of Health, Ministry of Education, Ministry of Economic Development etc.) conducting different food security interventions. Thus, the establishments of the action plan will target and coordinate all nutrition related activities by the different ministries as one comprehensive programme.

Divi Neguma (Samurdhi Assistance) Programme (2011)

This programme mainly focusses on strengthening people's economic status and minimising their dependence on the market for food requirements (Ministry of Economic Development, 2012). There are three phrases in the programme covering agriculture, small-scale industries, fisheries and livestock sectors. To date, all three phases have been implemented across the country. The programme is implemented at district, provincial and national levels. The prime objective of the Divi Neguma programme is to strengthen the people economically and minimise their dependence on the market for food requirements. Several programmes have been identified under each phase. The households were given the option of deciding a particular phase that they wish to be engaged in.

- Agriculture sector – Mainly focusses on home gardening
- Livestock sector – Mainly focusses on fishery, poultry and dairy sectors
- Small-scale industry sector – Focussing cottage industries and handicraft sectors

The Divi Neguma Programme could be identified as the main food security programme that presently exists in Sri Lanka, where it was implemented according to the previous government's plan on 'Mahinda Chinthana and Mahinda Chinthana-Vision for the Future'. Further, the objectives of the Divi Neguma programme are closely related with the Zero Hunger Challenge concept as it covers most of the criteria, such as 100% access to adequate food all year round, making all food systems sustainable, 100% growth in stallholder productivity and income etc. explained in the Zero Hunger Challenge.

Presently, the programme is conducted by the Department of Divi Neguma with the support of the Ministry of Agriculture, Ministry of Livestock, Ministry of Fisheries, Local Governments etc. In 2015, the total value of benefits provided to 1,453,078 of beneficiaries and the department has spent Rs.40,210 million in carrying-out these activities.

Divi Neguma (Samurdhi) Programme

The largest welfare programme in the country since 1995, the Samurdhi Programme comprises multiple components, including the household subsidy programme, social security programme and the nutrition programme. Currently, the Samurdhi subsidy is received by around 1.5 million families and the programme has spent Rs.40 billion in 2015.[28] 'Samurdhi' is the National Programme introduced by the government in 1994 to alleviate poverty. The objective of this programme was to find solutions to eradicate poverty. The Samurdhi Programme priority has been given to activities such as development of rural infrastructure facilities, improving health and nutritional conditions among the rural community and creating opportunities for rural entrepreneurship.

Api Wawamu Rata Negamu Programme (2007–2010)

This was initiated by the Ministry of Agriculture with the presidential task force. Some of the main objectives of the programme were to:

- Increase the production of essential food crops.
- Ensure food and nutrition security of the people.
- Improve consumption pattern of the people.
- Increase youth involvement in agriculture.
- Promote environment-friendly and local/traditional agricultural methods.

Agriculture Development Division of the Ministry of Agriculture is responsible for operation, supervision and coordination of agricultural development activities.

Thriposha Programme

The Thriposha Programme was initiated in 1973 by the Ministry of Health, with the assistance of the Cooperative for Assistance and Relief Everywhere (CARE) Sri Lanka, to combat the high incidence of child malnutrition, low birth weight and iron deficiency anaemia in Sri Lanka. Expenditure on the programme is currently about US$ 6.5 million a year. Thriposha is a food supplement comprising cereals, pulses and micronutrients, provided free of charge to mothers of low-income groups with infants less than one year of age. In spite of its clear contribution to general food security, the Thriposha Programme is based on health considerations relating to children and lactating mothers. Further, it is administered by the Department of Health on a targeted group. The Nutrition Coordination Division of the Ministry of Health conducts this programme with the support of CARE International and the Food Promotion Board.

Mid-day Meal Programme (2006)

The importance of school feeding is emphasized in Sri Lanka's national development strategy (Mahinda Chinthana – Vision for the Future) as one of the main support systems for addressing nutritional deficiency among school children. The National Nutrition Policy (Ministry of Healthcare and Nutrition) includes the policy of school feeding in its stated objective of "creating a good nutrition enabling environment in schools". For fulfilling this objective, the programme on mid-day meals was implemented in schools which have less than 100 students, and this provides for children from Grade 1–5.

At present the programme covers nearly 160,000 school children. The World Food Programme (WEF) is also providing support to conduct this programme. WFP provides a food basket consisting of 75 grams of rice, 35 grams of pulses, 15 grams of oil and 30 grams of canned fish. Pulses and canned fish are provided on a rotational basis for a child per day. And the Ministry of Education provides funding to purchase vegetables from farmers. Targeted schools are assisted with the construction of school kitchens and stoves, and provision of kitchen utensils. Previously CARE International, UNICEF and the Ministry of Education provided Rs.22.50 per week per child (i.e. for meals with two eggs per week).

Parents and Samudhi beneficiaries in that village organise and carry out this programme amongst selected schools. The menu is prepared by the School Health and Nutrition Unit of the Ministry of Education in consultation with the staff of the Family Health Bureau (FHB) of the Ministry of Health. Currently, it covers nearly 85% of the schools and 35% of the total students.

The main objectives of this programme are:

- Improve the nutritional status of children from low income families.
- Promote active participation in education.
- Reduce the high level of malnutrition among school children.
- Improve the daily school attendance of children in difficult area schools.
- Promote a balanced diet.
- Popularise good health habits.

Fresh Grass of Milk Programme for School Children (2012), circular no: 2012/18

This programme aims at improving the nutritional levels in schoolchildren by providing them with a glass of milk and at the same time to support increase in income levels amongst dairy farmers, by purchasing liquid milk from small holders. Currently, this programme is being conducted in 1143 schools and targeting 150 ml liquid milk per day per student. Ministry of Education provides Rs.9.00 per student per day. This programme has been implemented through the Early Childhood Development Centres/Preschools since 2011 and coordinated by Early Childhood Development Officers at Divisional Secretariat Division. It has been proposed to provide a nutritious breakfast instead of this programme from 2017 for the divisions with the highest levels of nutrition deficiency.

School Canteen Management Programme (2007)

The first circular with regards to a school canteen programme was issued in 2007 by the Ministry of Education (circular 2007/02) The Ministry of Education has issued a new circular in 2011 (2011/03) to all schools in the country with a set of guidelines to be followed by school canteens. These include assurance that all schools have proper facilities for students to obtain food, making sure the canteen and all equipment used are clean, hygienic and meet the standards of the Food Act of 1980.[29] Accordingly, the canteens are encouraged to provide food items that include pulses, food made of Kurakkan and rice as well as fruit and vegetable items, food rich in protein and beverages such as milk, fruit juice, kolakanda (Herbal porridge), king coconut and water. At the same time, this programme intends to discourage high sugar, high oil and high fat food items.

Poshana Malla Programme (2010)

This programme is carried out by the Food Promotion Board – Ministry of Agriculture. This programme targets pregnant and lactating mothers whose body mass index (BMI) is below average. This provides a bag which contains 1Kg of rice flour, 2 packs (200g) of Suwa posha and 1Kg of Maw posha, which is worth Rs.500 per month. This nutritional pack is formulated and identified by the Industrial Technology Institute (ITI) and produced by the Food Promotion Board. This is distributed via Samurdhi Banks in divisions.

Fertilizer Subsidy Programme

Sri Lanka introduced a price subsidy for fertiliser in 1962. Presently, this scheme is restricted only for paddy farmers and the government provides fertilizer subsidy allowance of Rs.25,000.00 to farmers. The National Fertiliser Secretariat under the Ministry of Agriculture assures and recommends fertiliser to paddy and other crops. This programme supports increasing the food availability in the country. The fertiliser subsidy has accounted for 2–2.5% of total government expenditure in the recent past (Annual Report, Central Bank of Sri Lanka).

Other programmes related to food security also exist but they target limited areas or selected groups of people. Furthermore, there are some other programmes (School Water Sanitation and Hygiene WASH Programme, Ten Year Development Framework (2006–2016)) which do not give any direct impact to increase food security, but they help indirectly.

Projects relating to address Zero Hunger Challenge

Promotion of packaging methods and transportation for the reduction of post-harvest losses in fruits and vegetables: In order to prevent the serious losses occurring in fruits and vegetables during post-operations from farmer to consumer, amounting to 30–35% of the annual production (Institute of Post-Harvest Technology), a project funded by the Treasury under the guidance of the Ministry of Agriculture Development and Agrarian Services has been implemented since 2006 to introduce plastic crates to farmers, collectors and wholesale traders at subsidised rates for transportation of fruits and vegetables.

Under this project the Institute of Post-Harvest Technology (IPHT) has purchased 64,360 plastic crates consisting of five types, which can be used for tomatoes, other vegetables and fruits such as papaw, pine-apple for distribution among farmers, traders and collectors at 50% subsidy. In this regard, 54,017 plastic crates have been provided to farmers and collectors of fruits and vegetables in some of the districts. In addition, 4200 farmers and collectors were trained to create awareness among them on the benefits of using improved packages for handling and transportation of fruits and vegetables.

Initiation of agro-processing enterprises (grain and spice) at the rural level: The objective of the project is to introduce identified appropriate agro-processing industries to the small/medium entrepreneurs, farmers and unemployed youth in the project area in order to increase their income levels through value addition to their produce.

Projects cover the area including the grain growing areas and spice processing. Project activities will include the following.

- Identification of prospective small/medium entrepreneurs.
- Training of identified entrepreneurs in grain/spice processing technologies, production management and marketing.
- Assisting in preparation of feasibility reports.
- Provision of 50% of the investment for initiation of agro industries to the entrepreneurs by the project as a non-recoverable incentive and providing assistance to the entrepreneurs in machinery selection, installation and commissioning.

Notes

1 The Global Food Security Index considers the core issues of affordability, availability and quality across a set of 113 countries. See Global Food Security Index 2018, the Economic Intelligence Unit, *The Economist*.
2 Three year moving average for the period 2015–17. See Food Security Indicators, FAO, 2018.

3 See WFP (2017).

4 Ibid.

5 IFPRI (2016).

6 See Kelegama (2016).

7 Ibid. Creation of plantations were pursued also by taking control of land by colonial powers through laws such as the Crown Land Encroachment Ordinance of 1840 and forced migration of labourers to work in plantations.

8 Ibid. Large-scale land colonisation programmes were launched to resettle landless peasantry from the wet zone upcountry to the dry zone low country areas, facilitated by the recommendations of the Land Commission Report in 1927 that led to the establishment of the Land Commissioner's Department.

9 The Mahaweli Development Programme, initiated in 1961, is often referred to as the largest multipurpose national development programme in the history of Sri Lanka aimed at large-scale transformation of farming and power generation along the Mahaweli River Basin.

10 In 2015, Sri Lanka has imported over Rs.270 billion worth of food including wheat and maize imports as intermediate goods. See Kelegama (2016). Agricultural goods accounted for about 12% of Sri Lanka's total imports in 2015, mainly comprising of foods needed for domestic consumption purposes. See WTO (2017).

11 Fifteen percent of children under five are acutely malnourished, rates of which have remained stagnant over the last ten years. See WFP (2018).

12 For a detailed discussion of limits to diversification, see Kelegama and Babu (2005).

13 Gunawardana and Somaratne (2000) observes that malfunctioning of factor input markets creates negative economic performance in non-plantation agriculture.

14 For instance, the current average tea productivity in Sri Lanka (1,620kg/ha) is lower than that of Kenya (2,480 kg/ha) and India (1,640 kg/ha). These issues are common to rubber as well. See Kelegama (2016).

15 Ibid. According to a labour force survey, worker population is drastically declining from 39% of total estate population in 1992 to 20% in 2012.

16 See Athukorala and Kelegama (1998).

17 See Kelegama and Babu (2005).

18 See Rafeek and Samaratunga (2000).

19 Noting the success of contract farming in certain subsectors, Wijesooriya and Champika (2015) shows that the sustainability of forward contracts depends on practicing the whole concept of contract farming through vertically integrated value chain rather than limiting only for forward sales buying agreement. Effective coordination among concerned parties and stakeholders through awareness programmes is vital for sustainability.

20 Weerahewa et al. (2018) observes that political objectives of the governing parties largely shaped the design of the food policies in the early phases of development of the economy, while subsequent policies have become more targeted to the food and nutritional security of marginalised segments.

21 Sandaratne and De Alwis (2014), National and Household Food Security in Sri Lanka, Centre for Poverty Analysis, Colombo.

22 Hersi, D,T.Abeysekera and W. Wickremanayake (1989), Food Consumption Behaviour of Urban Food Stamp Recipients in Sri Lanka, *Ceylon J. Med. Set.* 32. pp. 101–116.

23 See Hewavitharana (1999).

24 See World Bank (2000).

25 See De Silva et al. (1999) and Kelegama and Babu (2005).

26 National Agricultural Policy (2007), Ministry of Agriculture and Agrarian Services.

27 Livestock Master Plan: A Strategy for Livestock Development for Self- Sufficiency (2011), Ministry of Livestock and Rural Community Development.

28 Performance Report (2015), Department of Divi Neguma Development

29 Circular No: 2011/03, Ministry of Education.

References

Athukorala, P. and S. Kelegama (1998), 'The Political Economy of Agricultural Trade Policy: Sri Lanka in the Uruguay Round', *Contemporary South Asia*, Vol. 7(1), pp. 7–26.

De Silva, K. T., S. B. de Silva and S. Kodituwakku (1999), 'No Future for Farming?: The Potential Impact of Non-Plantation Agriculture on Rural Poverty in Sri Lanka', Centre for Intersectoral Community Health Studies, Kandy, Sri Lanka.

Gunawardana, P. J. and W. G. Somaratne (2000), 'Non-Plantation Agricultural Economy of Sri Lanka: Trends, Issues and Prospects', *Sri Lankan Journal of Agricultural Economics*, Vol. 3(1), pp. 15–45.

Hersi, D., T. Abeysekera and W. Wickremanayake (1989), 'Food Consumption Behavior of Urban Food Stamp Recipients in Sri Lanka', *Ceylon Journal of Medical Science*, Vol. 32, pp. 101–116.

Hewavitharana, B. (1999), 'The Two Leading Meso Policy Interventions for Rural Poverty Alleviation-Sri Lanka: A Case Study: Rural Poverty Alleviation in Asia and the Pacific', Asian Productivity Organization, Tokyo.

IFPRI (2016), 'Global Nutrition Report: From Promise to Impact – Ending Malnutrition by 2030', International Food Policy Research Institute, Washington, DC.

Kelegama, S. (2016), 'Policy Challenges in Agriculture Sector and Way Forward', Keynote address delivered at the 10th Annual Research Forum of the Sri Lanka Agricultural Economics Association.

Kelegama, S. and S. C. Babu (2005), 'Market Reform, Diversification, and Food Security in Sri Lanka', in *Economic Reforms and Food Security in South Asia: The Impact of Trade and Technology*, S. C. Babu and A. Gulati (Eds.), pp. 311–327, The Haworth Press, New York.

Rafeek, M. I. M. and P. A. Samaratunga (2000), 'Trade Liberalisation and Its Impact on the Rice Sector of Sri Lanka', *Sri Lankan Journal of Agricultural Economics*, Vol. 3(1), pp. 143–154.

Sandaratne, N. and S. De Alwis (2014), 'National and Household Food Security in Sri Lanka', Centre for Poverty Analysis, Colombo.

Weerahewa, J., C. S. Wijetunga, S. C. Babu and N. Atapattu (2018), 'Food Policies and Nutrition Transition in Sri Lanka Historical Trends, Political Regimes, and Options for Interventions', IFPRI Discussion Paper, No. 01727, International Food Policy Research Institute.

WFP (2017), 'National Strategic Review of Food Security and Nutrition: Towards Zero Hunger', Independent Review Commissioned by the World Food Programme.

WFP (2018), 'Sri Lanka Country Brief, October 2018', World Food Programme.

Wijesooriya, N. and J. Champika (2015), 'Agricultural Forward Contracts as Pre-Harvest Commodity Marketing: Problems and Prospects', Research Report No. 180, Hector Kobbekaduwa Agrarian Research and Training Institute, Colombo.

World Bank (2000), 'Sri Lanka: Recapturing Missed Opportunities', World Bank Country Report. Washington, DC: The World Bank.

WTO (2017), 'Trade Policy Review: Sri Lanka', Trade Policy Review Report by the Secretariat, WT/TPR/S/347/Rev.1, World Trade Organization, Geneva.

INDEX